Cartographic Poetry

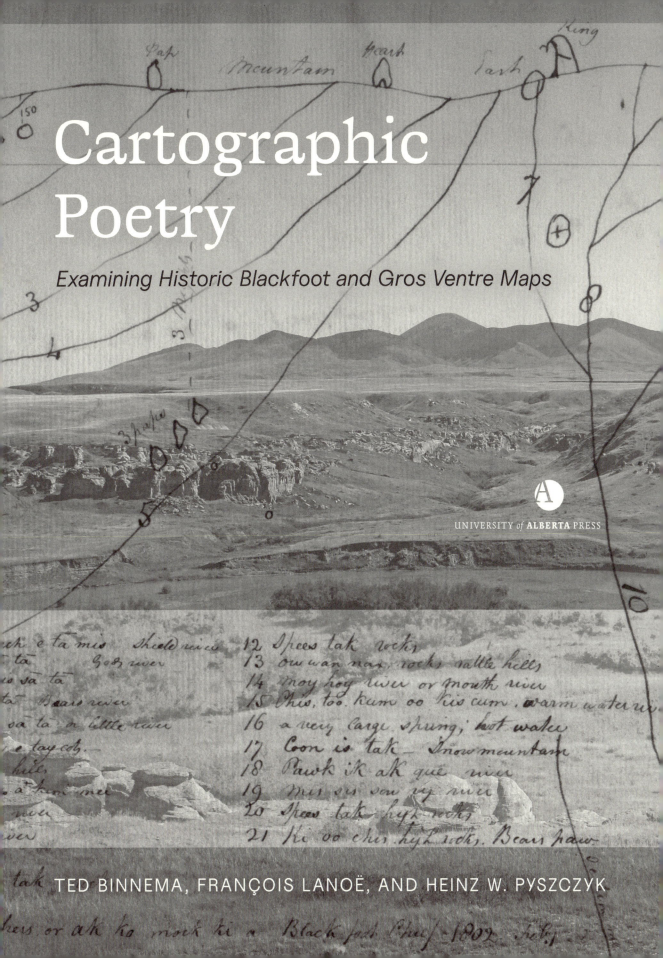

Published by

University of Alberta Press
1-16 Rutherford Library South
11204 89 Avenue NW
Edmonton, Alberta, Canada T6G 2J4
amiskwacîwâskahikan | Treaty 6 | Métis Territory
ualbertapress.ca | uapress@ualberta.ca

Copyright © 2025 Ted Binnema, François B. Lanoë, and Heinz W. Pyszczyk.

LIBRARY AND ARCHIVES CANADA CATALOGUING IN PUBLICATION

Title: Cartographic poetry : examining historic Blackfoot and Gros Ventre maps / Ted Binnema, François B. Lanoë, and Heinz W. Pyszczyk.
Names: Binnema, Ted, 1963– author | Lanoë, François B., author. | Pyszczyk, Heinz W., author
Description: Includes bibliographical references and index.
Identifiers: Canadiana (print) 20240480600 | Canadiana (ebook) 20240480716 | ISBN 9781772127997 (softcover) | ISBN 9781772128178 (PDF) | ISBN 9781772128161 (EPUB)
Subjects: LCSH: Great Plains—Historical geography—Maps. | LCSH: Names, Geographical—Great Plains—Maps. | LCSH: Ethnohistory—Great Plains. | LCSH: Great Plains—History—19th century—Maps. | CSH: Blackfoot—History—19th century—Maps. | CSH: Aaniiih—History—19th century—Maps.
Classification: LCC E78.G73 B56 2025 | DDC 978.004/97—dc23

First edition, first printing, 2025.
First printed and bound in Canada by Friesens, Altona, Manitoba.
Copyediting and proofreading by Joanne Muzak.
Indexing by Stephen Ullstrom.

All rights reserved. No part of this publication may be reproduced, stored in a retrieval system, or transmitted in any form or by any means (electronic, mechanical, photocopying, recording, generative artificial intelligence [AI] training, or otherwise) without prior written consent. Contact University of Alberta Press for further details.

University of Alberta Press supports copyright. Copyright fuels creativity, encourages diverse voices, promotes free speech, and creates a vibrant culture. Thank you for buying an authorized edition of this book and for complying with the copyright laws by not reproducing, scanning, or distributing any part of it in any form without permission. You are supporting writers and allowing University of Alberta Press to continue to publish books for every reader.

GPSR: Easy Access System Europe | Mustamäe tee 50, 10621 Tallinn, Estonia | gpsr.requests@easproject.com

This book has been published with the help of a grant from the Federation for the Humanities and Social Sciences, through the Awards to Scholarly Publications Program, using funds provided by the Social Sciences and Humanities Research Council of Canada.

University of Alberta Press gratefully acknowledges the support received for its publishing program from the Government of Canada, the Canada Council for the Arts, and the Government of Alberta through the Alberta Media Fund.

University of Alberta Press gratefully acknowledges the support from the University of Northern British Columbia's Office of Research and the Provost's Author Support Fund at the University of Arizona.

Contents

VII   *Foreword*
      JERRY POTTS JR.

IX   *A Note on Indigenous Names*

XIII   *A Note on Orthography*

XV   *Preface*

XIX   *Acknowledgements*

1   **Maps and Photographs**

45   **1 | Learning from Early Nineteenth-Century Blackfoot Maps**

65   **2 | The Ac ko mok ki Map of 1801**

77   **3 | Three Indigenous Maps Drawn in 1802**

99   **4 | The Ki oo cus Map of 1802**

119   **5 | Tours and Trips on the Ac ko mok ki and Ki oo cus Maps**

129   **6 | Exploring the "Different Tribes" of Ac ko mok ki's Map and the Gros Ventre Map**
      TED BINNEMA, ANDREW COWELL, FRANÇOIS LANOË, AND
      HEINZ W. PYSZCZYK

145   **7 | Contributions of Indigenous Cartography to Western Cartography**
      TED BINNEMA

161   Notes

187   Bibliography

197   Index

Foreword

BLACKFOOT HISTORY IS NOT WRITTEN DOWN but is told by our Elders, and so it has long been neglected by white historians. We Piikani conduct our own research on our places. Recently, Elder Allan Pard and I worked on some of the old campsites and historic sites near the Piikani Reserve, and I continued this work after Allan passed in 2016. We have many sites there and elsewhere in our territory that we never had access to, and for the most part our Elders took knowledge about the places with them when they passed. To aid in this research we have been collecting and mapping records of Blackfoot places and sites. María N. Zedeño and François Lanoë of the University of Arizona have helped with this project since 2018 and have been great support to the Blackfoot for their effort to bring understanding to our territory through the eyes of archaeology.

In this book, Ted Binnema, François Lanoë, and Heinz Pyszczyk complement our place name project by focusing on maps made by our people two hundred years ago. Like our general mapping project, the book shows the deep understanding that we've always had of our land and allows us to understand the scope of the Blackfoot presence throughout our territory. Alongside efforts to preserve our language and our culture, we are able to give meaning to many of these places and how they relate to our stories of creation.

JERRY POTTS JR.
Piikani Ceremonial Elder
Blackfoot Ceremonial Pipe Maker
Southern Piikani (Blackfoot Confederacy: North and South Piikani, Blood Tribe, Siksika Nation)

November 21, 2022
Brocket, Piikani Reserve, Alberta

A Note on Indigenous Names

THERE ARE MULTIPLE WAYS by which Indigenous people are referred to, including *Indigenous, Native, First Nations, Aboriginal, Indian,* or *Amerindian*. We use the term *Indigenous*, acknowledging that acceptance and use of each of those terms varies across regions and communities. We use *Indian* only when quoting historical documents.

European explorers did not record the names of Indigenous individuals and place names in a consistent manner; nor did they always correctly transcribe the intricacies of Indigenous languages. We provide known name variants and sources on first occurrence, as well the standardized modern words, when known. In the case of Blackfoot names, we refer to the most authoritative Blackfoot dictionaries.[1] After first occurrence, we use the Indigenous names in their most common known spelling.

We favour the official or most used and familiar names of Indigenous communities. Many are exonyms (names given by outsiders) not used within those communities, although some communities prefer that outsiders (including governments) use exonyms, rather than endonyms (names used by people to refer to themselves in their own language), to refer to them. Because many communities do not consider it disrespectful for outsiders to use exonyms (indeed, might consider it presumptuous for them to use endonyms), we provide in the table below the official names (appearing on treaties and historical documents over many years) and corresponding endonyms as found in the *Handbook of North American Indians*. The table also provides names that, though unofficial today, have and may remain commonly used. Names of Blackfoot tribes need an additional explanation. *Piikani* refers to the Piikani tribe that includes both the Piikani Nation (Alberta) and the Blackfeet Nation (Montana). We use *Siksika* (from *sik* meaning 'black,' and *siika* meaning 'feet') for the Siksika Nation ("Blackfoot proper"). We reserve the term *Blackfoot* to refer collectively to the three tribes that today form the Blackfoot Confederacy (Piikani, Kainai, and Siksika) as well as their shared language.

Table 0.1 Names of Indigenous Peoples Mentioned in This Volume

Official Name	Endonym	Common Anglicizations	Other Commonly Used Names
Arapaho	hinóno'éí	Hinono'ei	
Arikara	sáhniš	Sahnish	
Assiniboine	nak^{h}óta	Nakota	
Bannock	nɨmɨ	Numu	
Bitterroot Salish	séliš	Salish	Flathead
Blackfoot	saokítapiksi or niitsitapi or siksikaitsitapi		
Cheyenne	tsétsėhéstȧhese	Tsistsistas	
Chipewyan	dëne sųłįné	Denesuline	
Comanche	nɨmɨ	Numu	
Cree	nehiyaw		
Crow	apsâroke	Absaroka	
Dakota	dak^{h}óta	Dakota	Yankton, Sioux
Dane-zaa	dane zaa	Dane-zaa	Beaver
Gros Ventre	'ɔ'ɔ́ɔ́niiih	Aaniiih	
Hidatsa	hiráca	Hidatsa	
Inuit	inuit	Inuit	Eskimo
Iroquois	hotinǫhsyǫ́ni?	Haudenosaunee	
Kainai	káínai	Kainai	Blood
Kalispel	qlispél	Kalispel	Pend d'Oreille
Kiowa	kɔ́ygú	Kiowa	
Kootenai	ktunaxa	Ktunaxa	Kutenai
Lakota	lak^{h}óta	Lakota	Teton, Sioux
Mandan	rų́ʔeta	Nueta	
Mi'kmaq	mikəmaq	Mi'kmaq	
Nez Perce	nimípu	Nimipu	
Northern Paiute	nɨmɨ	Numa	
Ojibwe	aniššinape	Anishinaabe	Chippewa
Omaha	umą́hą	Omaha	
Pawnee	cahiksícahiks	Chaticks-si-chaticks	
Pend d'Oreille	qlispél	Kalispel	
Piikani	piikani	Peigan	Blackfeet
Plains Apache	nąʔišą́ dená	Na-i-sha Dena	Kiowa Apache

Official Name	Endonym	Common Anglicizations	Other Commonly Used Names
Ponca	ppą́kka	Ponca	
Sekani	tθhéek'ehneh	Tse'khene	
Shoshone	nɨwɨ	Newe	
Shuswap	sexʷépemx	Secwépemc	
Siksika	siksiká	Siksika	Blackfoot
Skiri	ckíri	Skiri	Wolf Pawnee
Stoney	nakʰóta	Nakoda	
Tsimshian	ćmsyan	Tsimshian	
Tsuut'ina	cúùt́ínà	Tsuut'ina	Sarcee
Ute	núčiu	Nuchu	

A Note on Orthography

IN A BOOK SUCH AS THIS, aimed at the public and several scholarly audiences (historians, anthropologists, archaeologists, linguists, geographers, and cartographers, among others), we made difficult decisions regarding presentation. Conforming to practices in linguistics, when a word is rendered in an Indigenous language using the standard orthography of that language, and can be considered linguistically accurate and official, we use *italics*. Other attempted transcriptions of Indigenous-language words (such as by Peter Fidler, J.C. Nelson, James Willard Schultz, Jean L'Heureux, George Mercer Dawson, or A.L. Kroeber) are enclosed in {curly brackets}. With English-language glosses of Indigenous words, we use 'single quotes,' to distinguish from "double quotation marks," which signify quoted words.

Preface

ON 10 JANUARY 1801, Peter Fidler (1769–1822), Hudson's Bay Company (HBC) trader and surveyor, noted in his journal that "All the Blackfoots returned from war, fortunately they found nobody."[1] Fidler was referring to a Siksika war party that had left Chesterfield House on 22 November 1800, hoping to find and raid some Shoshone in the area around the Three Forks of the Missouri. On 7 February, Fidler asked Ac ko mok ki (Old Swan) (*Akaimiihkayii* in modern Blackfoot), one of the most prominent leaders of the Siksika, to draw him a map (Map 1A) focused on the region south of Chesterfield House—an empty space on European maps at the time and a region of great interest to Europeans, particularly to North West Company (NWC) and HBC traders. Fidler had spent the winter of 1792–93 living and travelling with the Piikani far enough southwest to have seen Chief Mountain, in present-day Montana, from a distance. So he knew that there was no practical transportation route across the Rocky Mountains between Chief Mountain and the North Saskatchewan River. NWC trader and surveyor David Thompson had previously established that neither the North Saskatchewan nor Athabasca Rivers were practical transportation corridors, and Alexander Mackenzie's travels along the Mackenzie River and Peace River showed that no such route existed north of that. The NWC and HBC (and the New North West Company, normally called the XY Company) established Chesterfield House in large part to explore the possibility that they could learn of a convenient transcontinental route south of the Oldman River. That context is crucial for understanding why Fidler wanted a map of the region southwest of Chesterfield House. Fortunately for Fidler, Ac ko mok ki obliged.

When he drew his map, Ac ko mok ki did what all mapmakers do. He interpreted the landscape he wanted to depict by selecting the most important features of those landscapes and presenting them in a way that he expected his audience would understand. He used cartographic conventions and symbols devised to facilitate communication between cartographer and reader. No part of this enterprise is objective. Each step is shaped by the context in which the cartographer lives. Cartographers cannot help but embed in their maps important evidence about themselves and their societies. That is as true of maps drawn by professional cartographers today and by the famous British cartographer Aaron Arrowsmith as it is of Indigenous mapmakers around the world. But in the case of Ac ko mok ki's map of 1801 and four other maps drawn a year later by Ac ko mok ki and two of his Siksika compatriots, Ak ko wee ak, and Ki oo cus (Little Bear, Bear's Child) (*Kiááyoko'si* in modern Blackfoot),[2] and by one or more Gros Ventre people, these are the oldest surviving written documents produced by these Indigenous communities. Indeed, maps are the oldest surviving written documents of other Indigenous Peoples too. The non-Indigenous authors of this book agree that the Blackfoot maps collected by Peter Fidler are priceless treasures that deserve to be well-known, studied, and admired, not only by scholars but by members of the public, whether they are Indigenous or not. This book represents an attempt on our part to give these maps their due.

While we share a fascination with these maps, our interest originates from different disciplines. When the opportunity arose for us to collaborate to produce a work that would permit each of us to contribute our own perspectives, we jumped at it. From archaeological, linguistic, and historical perspectives, we examine how these maps shed light about places on the landscape, and about historic Blackfoot people's views of their territories on the Northern Great Plains and Parkland of North America. The maps examined here may have been intended primarily to convey information needed to navigate an immense area of western North America, but the landforms and locations included on these maps also had significance for the Blackfoot-speaking people well beyond wayfinding. Their significance ranged from the mundane (resource procurement) to the spiritual. Two archaeologists have argued that "research has demonstrated that, within the Blackfoot world, stopping places were chosen for their views of named places where the stories associated with that place could be told, and that these named places figure prominently in the settlement decisions of the region's Precontact inhabitants."[3] Moreover, archaeological evidence suggests that many of the locations featured on these maps were significant to the Indigenous people of the region for many centuries before they appeared on these maps. We also seek to explain that, in the role they played in European mapmaking, they represent only a glimpse of the profound influence that Indigenous geographical knowledge has had on Western maps of North America.

Ted's fascination with the landscape of the Northwestern Plains began when he lived for a time in southern Alberta. He grew to love the stark beauty of the Plains and wondered why so many tourists seemed so eager to get through the region to get to the mountains. For many newcomers, the landscape of the Northwestern Plains is so immense as to be overwhelming and alienating. The landscape and atmosphere often allow a person to stand on a knoll, casting a shadow nearly a mile long, gazing at a landform over sixty miles away. We hope that anyone who comes to appreciate these maps will see how they create from the vastness of the Northwestern Plains something comprehensible, intimate, and magnificent. Ted also brings to this project his perspective as a historian, and his experience of driving many thousands of miles through the region to identify and appreciate firsthand the landforms depicted on these maps.

Heinz views the maps as an archaeologist. He views the maps as glimpses into a certain historic moment in the lives of a hunting and gathering people rooted in many centuries of experience on the Northwestern Plains. These may be wayfaring maps that show how the Blackfoot people navigated and understood their respective territories at the turn of the nineteenth century, but Heinz is convinced that they also contain experience and knowledge accumulated over centuries, and that they reflect fascinating evidence about Blackfoot worldviews.

François has worked as an anthropologist with the Piikani for a decade. His interest in the Fidler maps grew from a project, in collaboration with the Piikani Nation, to collect traditional Blackfoot place names. This project offered an apt avenue to funnel his interests in mapping, language, and archaeology, along with his attachment to the landscape of the Blackfoot traditional territory.

We think these maps are priceless treasures. We are daunted by the prospect of publishing this study of them, but we do so in the hope that many people previously unaware of them will become as fascinated by the maps, their authors, and the territories they depict, as we are. We acknowledge that we are not equipped to explore all facets of these maps, but hope that others will be inspired to make their own contributions to the appreciation and understanding of these extraordinary documents.

The authors offer one "navigational aid" to the book that follows. We have relegated our exploration of Indigenous contributions to European cartography to chapter 7 because we want to emphasize the significance of Indigenous mapping in its own right, and to avoid implying that Indigenous cartography is important because it has contributed to European cartography. However, readers who believe that their appreciation of these maps and of Indigenous mapping generally will be heightened if they are convinced that Indigenous maps have contributed very significantly to European mapping should consider reading chapter 7 before the other chapters of the book.

Acknowledgements

THE AUTHORS ARE DEEPLY INDEBTED to the Blackfeet and Piikani First Nations, and María N. Zedeño. François's participation was partially funded by the National Science Foundation Arctic Social Sciences grant PLR-1827975 to Zedeño and Lanoë. We also thank Andrew Cowell, who generously provided us with his thorough analysis of the Gros Ventre words on the various maps and other documents. We thank Eldon Yellowhorn for reading and commenting on the entire manuscript. His insightful suggestions assisted us in deepening our analysis of these maps. We also thank the press's anonymous reviewers who provided very valuable suggestions for improvement. We also thank copyeditor and proofreader Joanne Muzak for going beyond the call of duty. And we thank Stephanie Cousineau, who scoured the proofsheets for errors. The authors, as usual, assume all responsibility for any errors.

Binnema presented earlier versions of his research as "Two-Hundred-Year-Old Blackfoot Maps, and the Apatóhs-ohsokoi," an invited talk presented at Apatóhs-ohsokoi: A History Conference on Significant Places and Sites along the Old North Trail, Piegan Institute, Blackfeet Reservation, Browning, Montana, on 17 August 2001. We thank the participants of that conference for their insights. Ted also presented an earlier version of chapter 7 at Explorations, Encounters, and the Circulation of Knowledge, 1600–1830, a conference at the University of California, Los Angeles, 15–16 May 2015, and at the Canadian Historical Association Annual Meeting, Calgary, Alberta, 29 May 2016. All three authors also presented "Cartographic Poetry: Five Indigenous Maps from 1801 and 1802" to the Alberta Archaeological Society, Calgary Centre, 18 November 2021. We thank participants in those sessions for their suggestions, encouragement, and feedback.

Maps and Photographs

#	Name	Description	Tents	#	Name	Description	Tents
1	Choque	Mud Houses Indians	150	18	Ne chick a hah soy	a Particular root	60
2	Io sap poo	Crow Mountain	200	19	Shis che tap he	Woody	100
3	ams cps six sue	Sesseer south	70	20	Six six chicts sin na tap he	Sesseer South	50
4	Sip pe tah ke	Wrinkled	90	21	Poo can nam a tup he	Pearl shell	70
5	Rix tah ka tap pee	Beaver	50	22	Six too k tup he	Black	200
6	Choque	go to war with No 1	160	23	Cut tux hee too hen	Flat heads	50
7	Nee coo chies ak ka	Tattoed	80	24	Cum min na tup he	Blue mud	60
8	Sin ne po tup he	Grey fox	40	25	ap pa tup he	Ramen or white	90
9	Ke ta hap rum	Garter	30	26	So he pee tup pee	those that collect shells	
10	So hoo is too ye	Hairy or Beard	50	27	Oc cook sa tap he	Padlory	30
11	Ah hen nix sa tup pe		40	28	At cha tap hee	Small Indn	18
12	Pick et a tup pe	Rib	100	29	Cut tux in mah mi	Weak Bow	18
13	00 apo six sa tup pe	Thigh	20	30	Patch now		10
14	Oc sa tup he	scabby	100	31	Cotton na		22
15	Nac que a tup pe	Wolf	200	32	Pun nus pee tup pin	Long Hair	100
16	Mut tah yo que	Grass Tents	100				
17	mem me ow you	Fish Eaters	20				

From B to C — 2 Days
C to D — 5
D to E — 3
E to G — 3
G to H — 1
H to I — 1
I to 9 — 2
9 to K — 5
K to L — 5
L to M — 9
D to C — 1

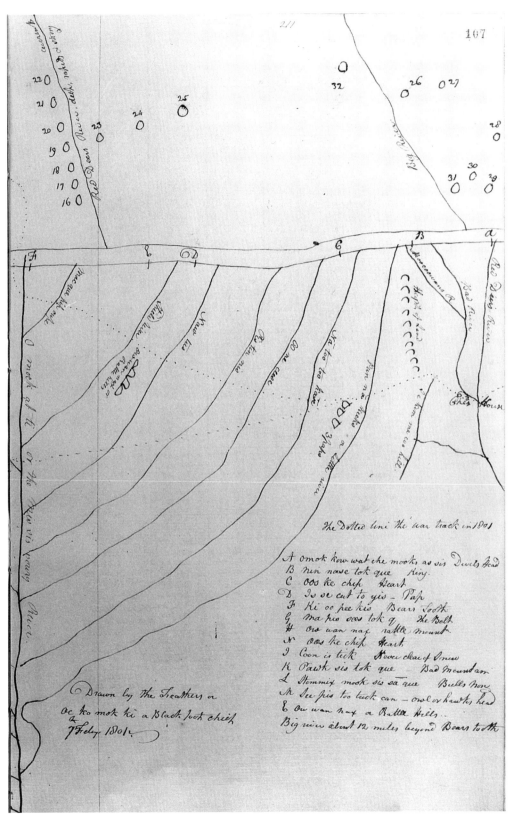

Map 1A. Ac ko mok ki map of 1801. This map, drawn by Ac ko mok ki (Old Swan, Feathers, Painted Feathers) was included in a notebook of journals and maps that Peter Fidler kept in his private collection. The book passed to the Hudson's Bay Company by Fidler's will after Fidler's death in 1822. (Source: HBCA E.3/2, fos. 106d–07.)

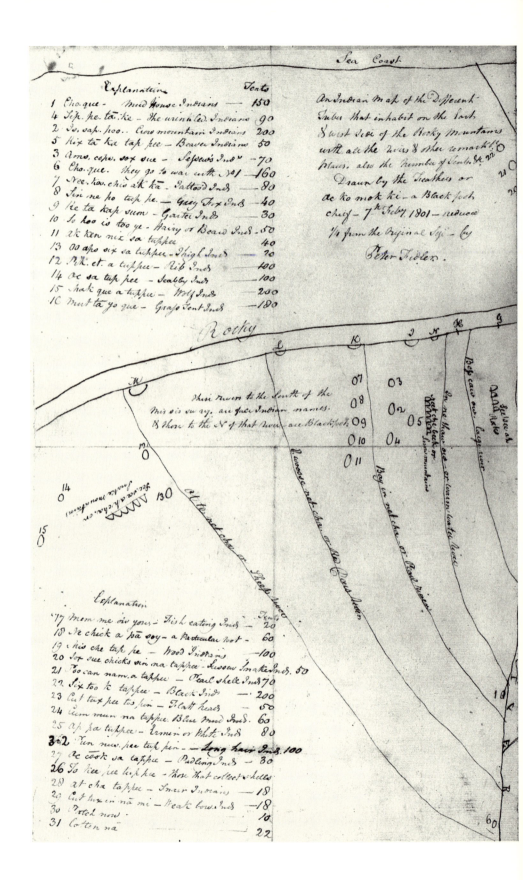

4 CARTOGRAPHIC POETRY

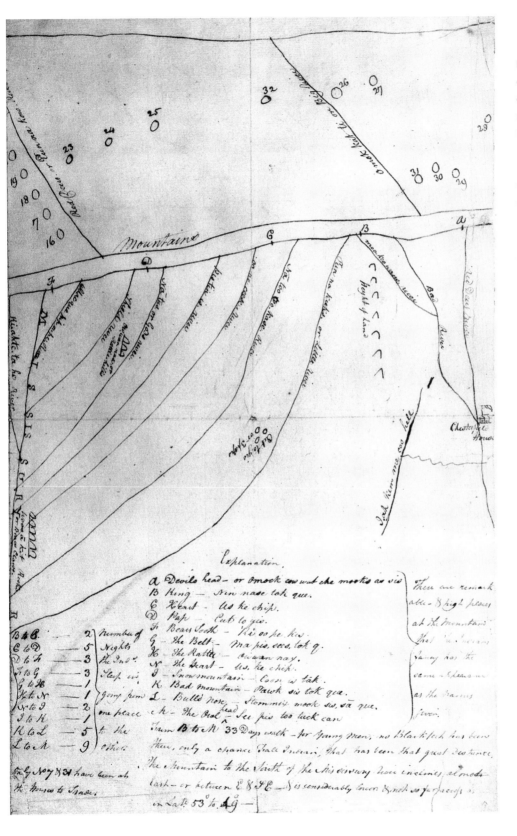

Map 1B. Redrafted copy of Ac ko mok ki's map of 1801. Peter Fidler redrafted Ac ko mok ki's map on a loose paper, and submitted it to the Hudson's Bay Company in 1802. The company shared the map with the eminent London cartographer Aaron Arrowsmith, who incorporated the map into his 1802 map of North America (see Map 14). (Source: HBCA G.1/25.)

Maps and Photographs 5

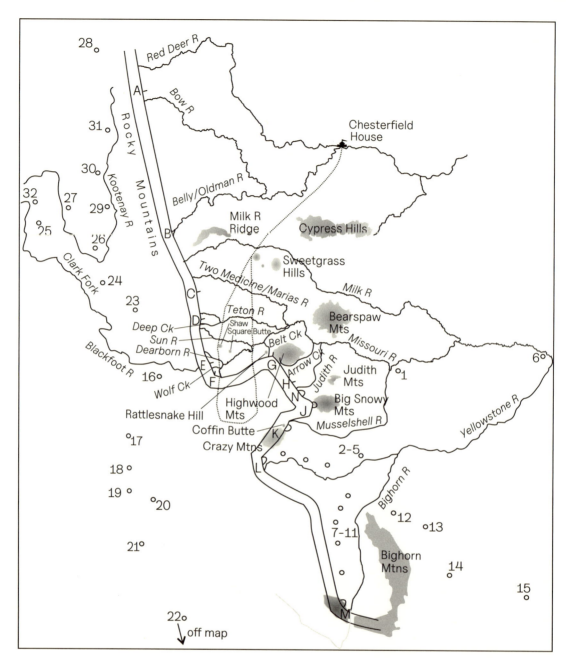

Map 1C. The authors' translation of Ac ko mok ki's map of 1801 into a Western cartographic language. (Map by the authors.)

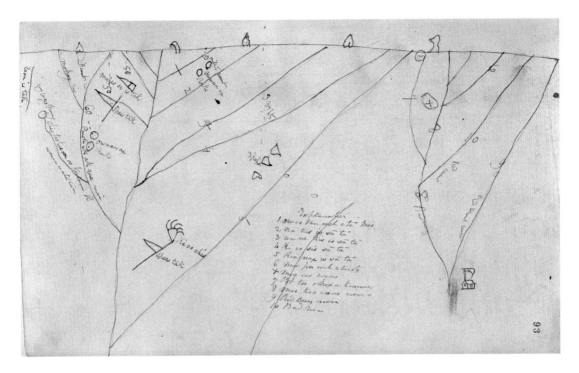

Map 2A. Ac ko mok ki's map of 1802. This map is included in the same notebook in which Peter Fidler kept the rough copy of his 1801–02 journal for Nottingham House (Fort Chipewyan) and other rough notes. It is not clear when this notebook came into the possession of the London headquarters of the Hudson's Bay Company. (Source: HBCA B.39/a/2 fo. 93.)

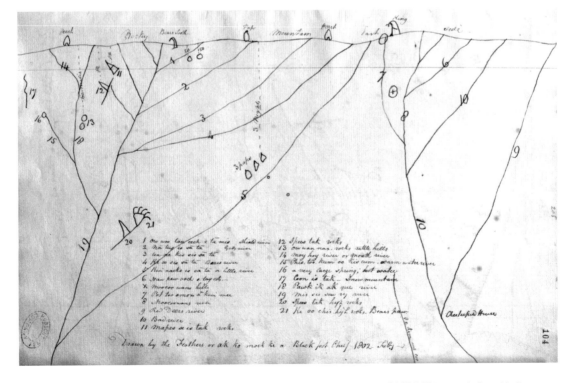

Map 2B. Redrafted copy of Ac ko mok ki's map of 1802. This map is found in the same private notebook as maps 1A, 3B, 4B, and 5A. (Source: HBCA E.3/2 fo. 104.)

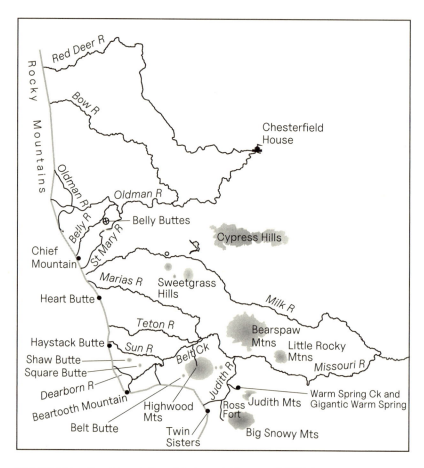

Map 2C. The authors' translation of Ac ko mok ki's map of 1802. (Map by the authors.)

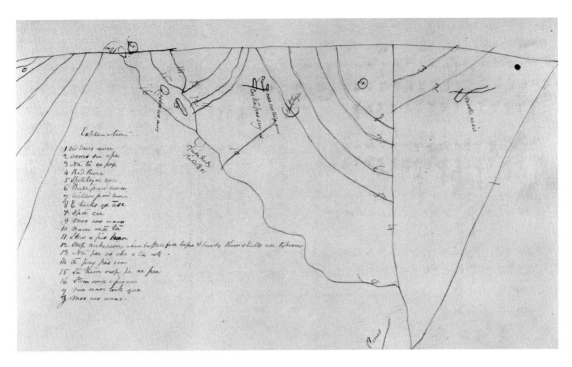

Map 3A. Ak ko wee ak's map. In Fidler's rough notebook for Nottingham House, this map faces Ac ko mok ki's map of 1802 (Map 2A). (Source: HBCA B.39/a/2 fo. 92d.)

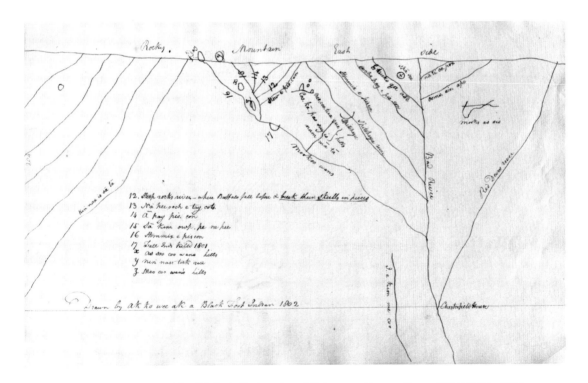

Map 3B. Redrafted version of Ak ko wee ak's map. (Source: HBCA E.3/2 fo. 103d.)

Maps and Photographs 9

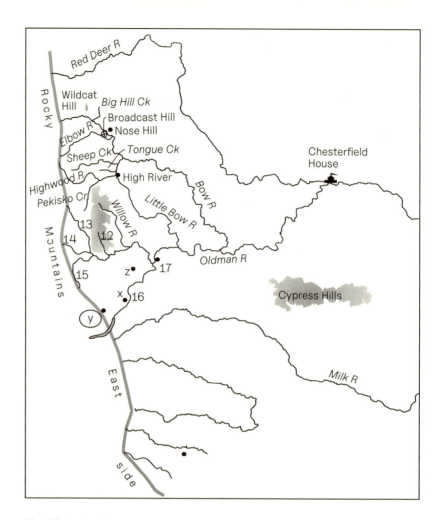

Map 3C. Authors' translation of the Ak ko wee ak map. (Map by the authors.)

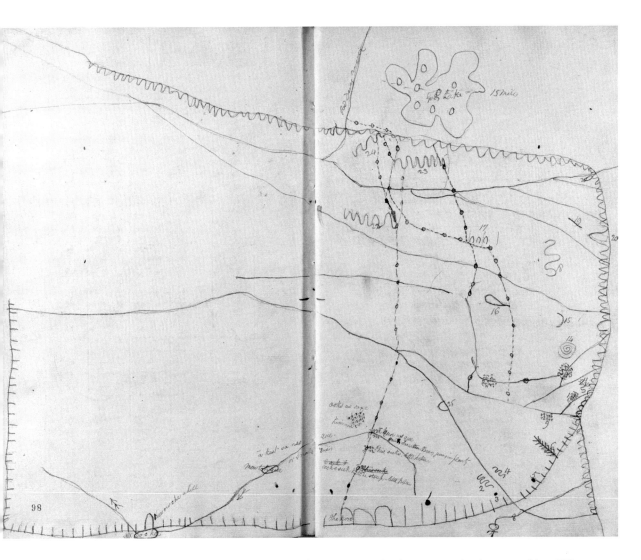

Map 4A. Ki oo cus map. Although inserted in the same notebook as maps 2A and 3A, this map is separated from the other two maps by Fidler's meteorological journal for the period 11 November 1801 to 10 October 1802. (Source: HBCA B.39/a/2 fos. 85d-86.)

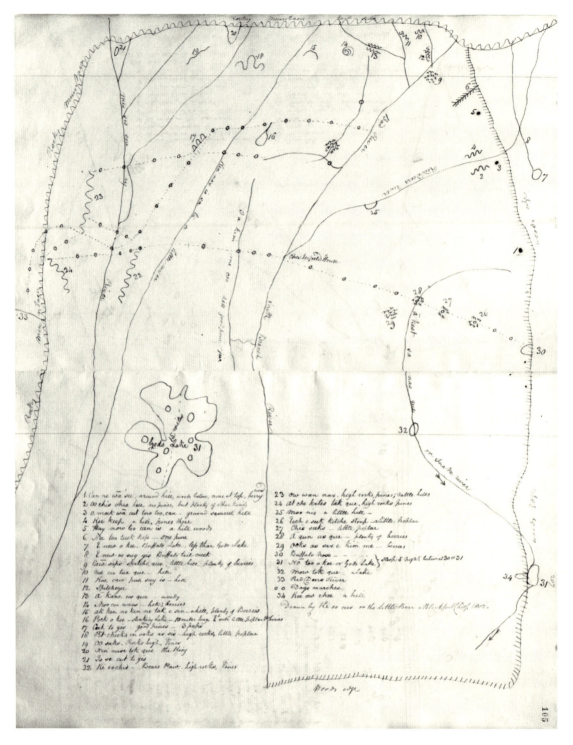

Map 4B. Redrafted Ki oo cus map. (Source: HBCA E.3/2 fos. 104d–105.)

12 CARTOGRAPHIC POETRY

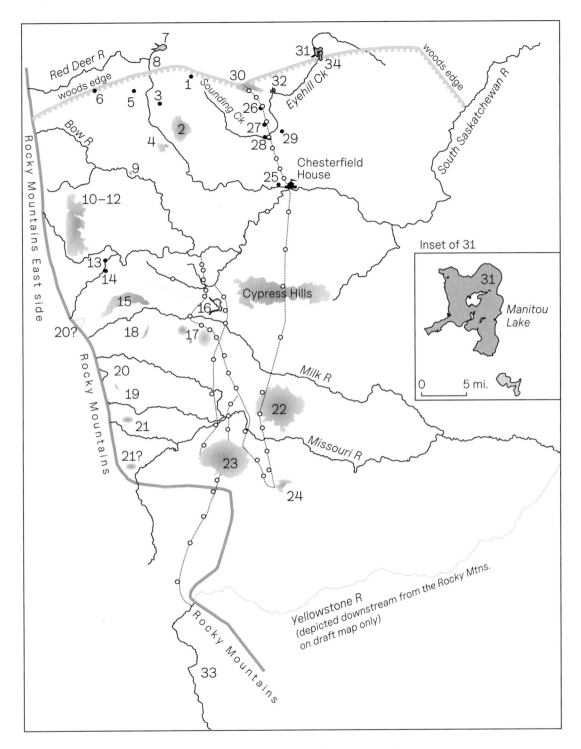

Map 4C. Authors' translation of Ki oo cus map. (Map by the authors.)

		Tents
1	Cock kaw etch — Hatt Head	50
2	Cock kaw yaw etch Do	40
3	See see an nen Snakes Inds	130
4	Ow win nen Crow mount	100
5	Ve tha chee na	30
6	See see an nen	10
7	May aytch at choh	20
8	Nan ni en	100 Free
9	E ta seen	100
10	Sot tan	30
11	Neet chay in in	100
12	Chow win in	20
13	E chaugh a nen	10
14	On now win	10 Free
15	Now wa ben nen nach	10
16	Wa tan nitch	200
17	Now wa se se an nen	300
18	See see an nen ne haud thee — Spanish Settlements	
19	Oth thay in in	100
20	She he nen	100
21	Now watch e ni in	20 Free
22	May aytch e choh	10
23	Chow win nen	8
24	Thot thok ki in in	13
25	Beth thow in in	20
26	Ben eet chaw batch	40
27	Wan nuk ki an	40
28	A. K. thi a wootch	20
29	A beth thoo	15
30	Been nen in	100

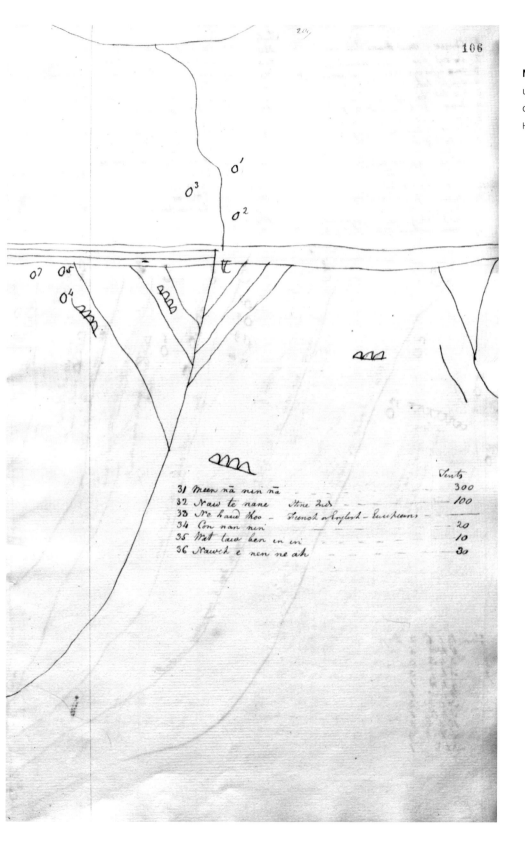

Map 5A. Map by unidentified Gros Ventre cartographer(s). (Source: HBCA E.3/2 fos. 105d-106.)

Maps and Photographs 15

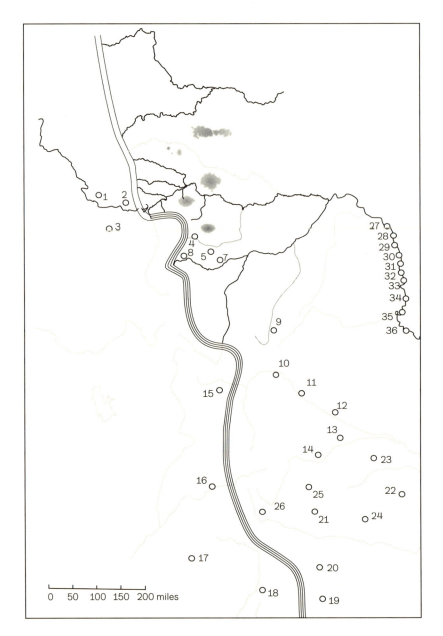

Map 5B. Authors' translation of a map by one or more unidentified Gros Ventre cartographers. (Map by the authors.)

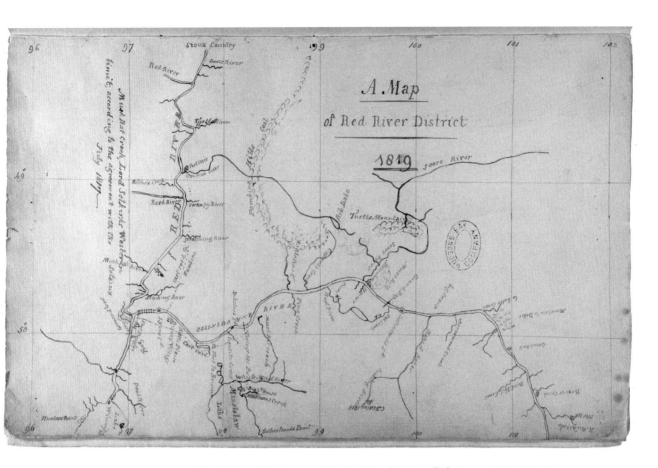

Map 6. Peter Fidler's map of the Red River District, 1819. (Source: HBCA B.22/e/1.)

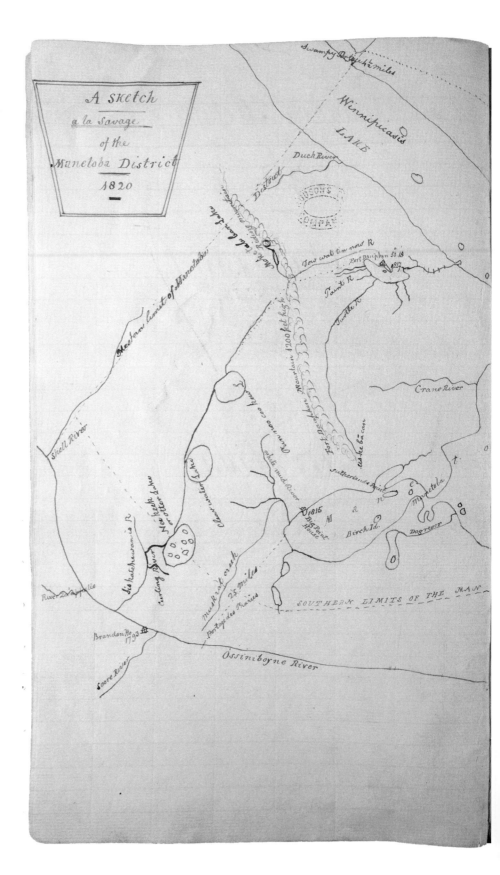

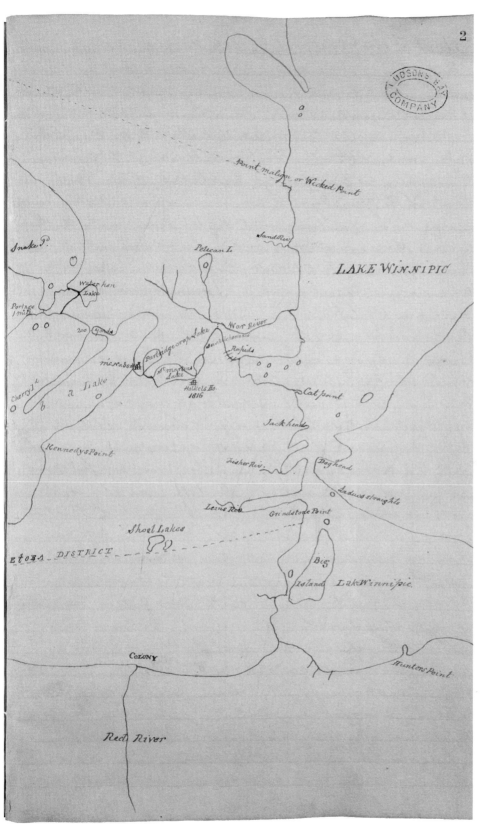

Map 7. Peter Fidler's "A Sketch a la Savage of the Manetoba District 1820." (Source: HBCA B.51/e/1.)

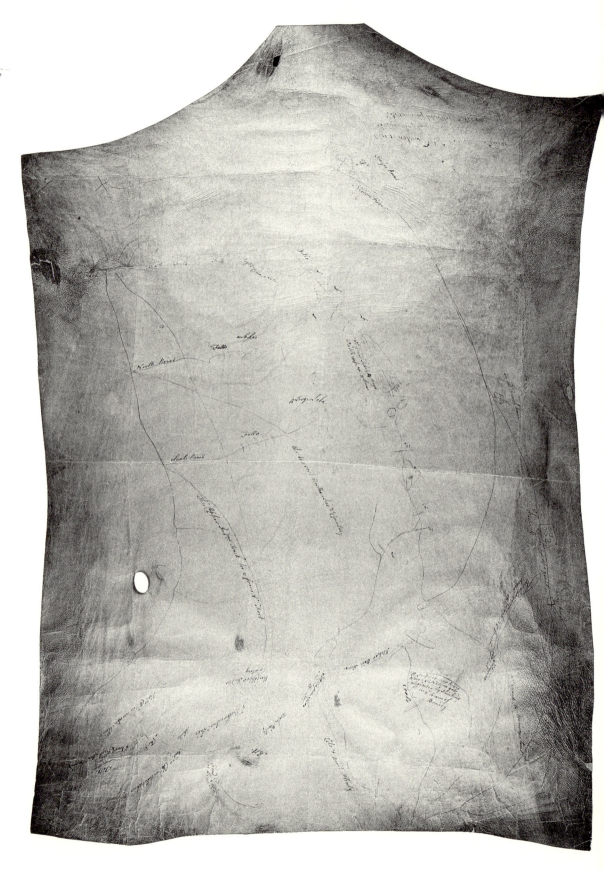

← **Map 8.** "Moses Norton's Draught." Hudson's Bay Company trader Moses Norton obtained maps from Indigenous informants. He copied one of these maps, which subsequently contributed significantly to Hudson's Bay Company knowledge of the northern interior of North America. York Factory (labelled Y.F.) is near the bottom left, Churchill (C Fort) to its right. (Source: Ruggles, *A Country So Interesting*, 132; a copy of the original map, HBCA G.2/8.)

→ **Map 9.** Andrew Graham, "A Plan of Part of Hudson's-Bay, & River, Communicating with York Fort & Severn." This map, drawn by Hudson's Bay Company trader Andrew Graham, betrays obvious characteristics of Cree cartographic conventions. The most obvious is the practice of depicting as one river, two rivers with adjacent headwaters flowing in opposite directions. Anyone familiar with canoe travel in the Canadian Shield region will understand the utility of such a practice. (Source: HBCA G.2/17.)

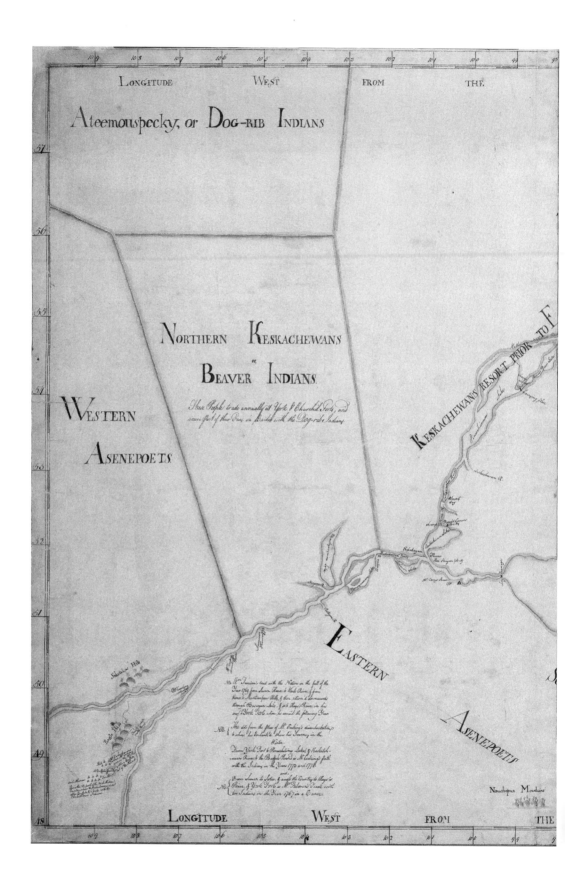

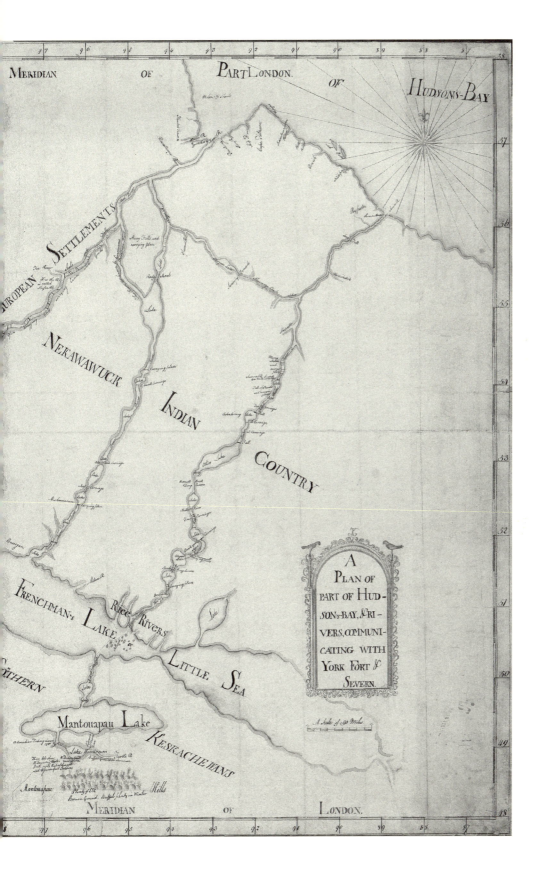

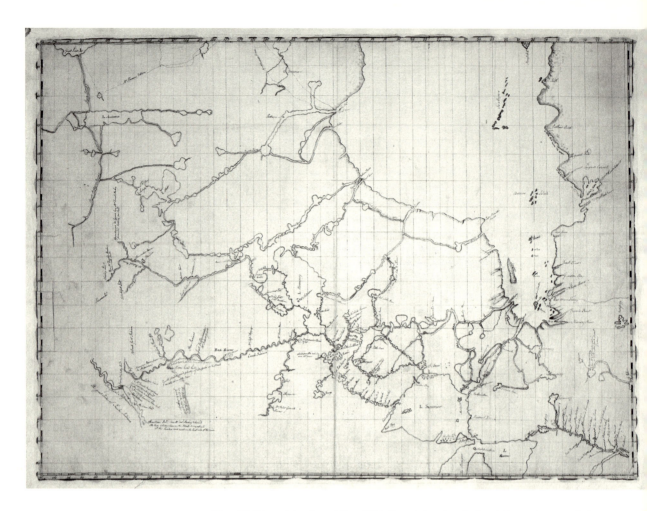

Map 10. Edward Jarvis and Donald McKay obviously relied on information provided by Indigenous people and employed an Indigenous cartographic language when they drafted this map in 1791. (Source: HBCA G.1/13.)

→ **Map 11.** James Swain Sr., *Map of the Severn District Laid Down from Indian Information. Aug[u]st 1815*. This map depicts the waterways used by Indigenous people as travel routes in a vast inland territory between the Severn and Equan (Ekwan) Rivers. Particularly conspicuous is the beads-on-a-string cartographic style common among people who normally traversed the Canadian Shield by canoe. (Source: HBCA G.1/35.)

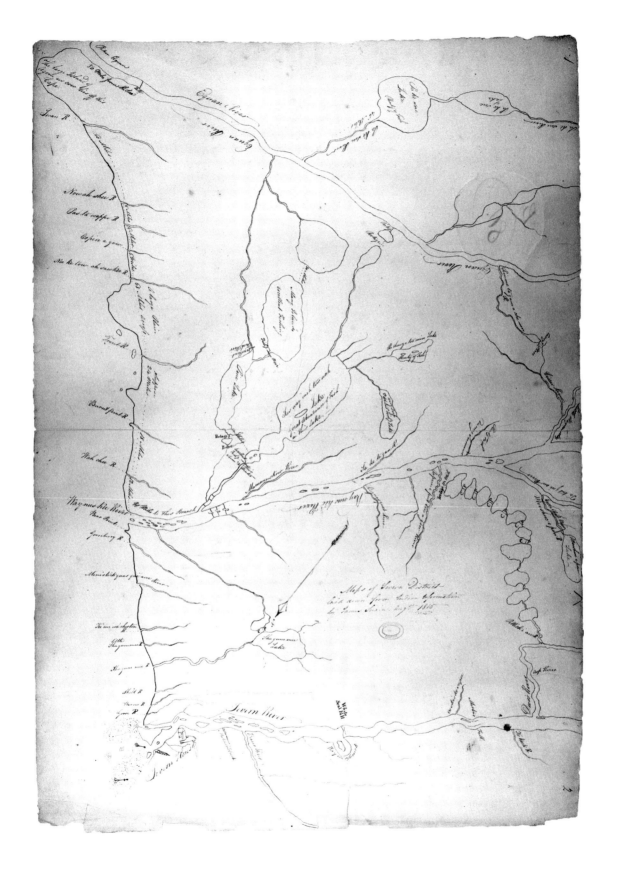

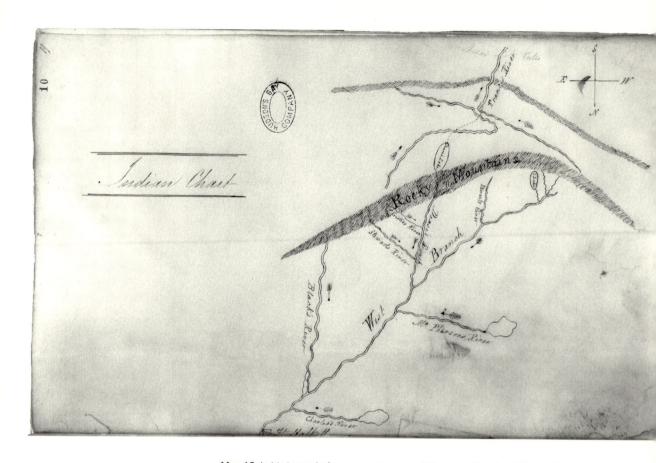

Map 12. In his journal of a reconnaissance of the upper Liard and Dease Rivers in 1834, John M. McLeod preserved this "Indian Chart." Dease Lake, the oval near the top of the map, is shown draining into Dease River through the "Rocky Mountains" into the "West Branch" (Liard) River as far as Fort Halkett at the bottom. The map suggests that Indigenous people of mountainous regions developed unique cartographic styles suited to the landscape. (Source: HBCA B.85/a/6, fo. 10.)

→ **Map 13.** Unless this is a previously unacknowledged Blackfoot map, many lines on the right-hand page of one of Peter Fidler's account books appear to represent Fidler's attempt to draw a map of the region between the North Saskatchewan River and the Sweetgrass Hills in the style of Blackfoot maps. The Sweetgrass Hills, Cypress Hills, and Milk River are unmistakable. (Source: HBCA B.34/a/1, fo. 30.)

North America 1799

Goods

Mens Debts	Sent to McBird	Expenses	Traded	Remains
		50		
		4 2		
		3 4		
		6 ½		
		6 ½		
		2 1		
		6 ½		

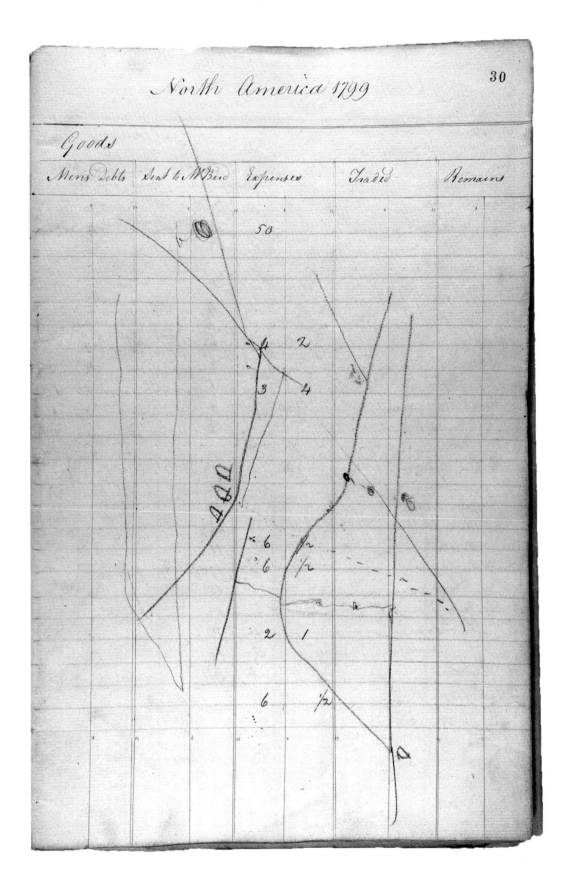

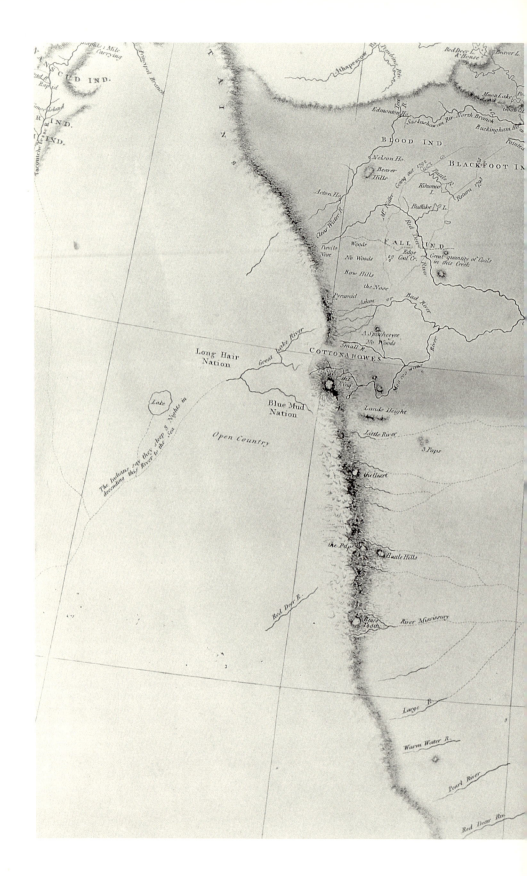

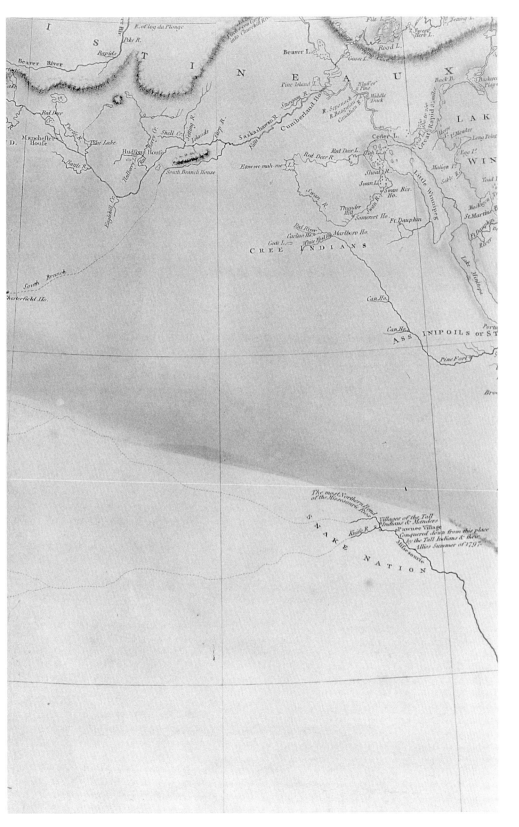

Map 14. Detail of Aaron Arrowsmith's map of North America, 1802. The bottom half of this portion of Arrowsmith's 1802 map of North America represents his attempt to incorporate Ac ko mok ki's map of 1801 (Map 1B), which was conveyed from Peter Fidler to Arrowsmith via the Governor and Committee of the Hudson's Bay Company. Thomas Jefferson, president of the United States, ensured that Meriwether Lewis and William Clark took this map with them when they went up the Missouri River. Lewis and Clark, assuming that Fidler had actually surveyed the region himself, were confused by the map.

Maps and Photographs

Photo 1. {Omok kow wat che mooks as sis} ('Swan's Bill,' Devil's Head Mountain). Devil's Head Mountain is a distinctive nearly symmetrical mountain, the sides of which are often bare of snow, even in winter. Travellers could use this landmark to find their way from the plains into the upper Bow River Valley. The Blackfoot had reason to travel that way to acquire various resources (from lodgepoles and bighorn sheep horns to red ochre for face paint). This mountain is labelled "a" on Map 1. (Photo by T. Binnema.)

Photo 2A. Like Devil's Head Mountain {Nin nase tok que} (Chief Mountain), is an exceptionally suitable guide for travellers. Because of its location in front of the Lewis Range of the Rocky Mountains (and near the divides of the Hudson Bay, Gulf of Mexico, and Pacific watersheds), Chief Mountain appears loftier than nearby mountains that are taller than it. Its distinct flat top and steep sides (which are often bare of snow) also makes it easy to pick out, even from a considerable distance away. The mountain is also among the most revered landforms among the Blackfoot. Chief Mountain can be found at "B" on Map 1, labelled as "King" on Map 2, and at number 20 on Map 5. (Photo by T. Binnema.)

Photo 2B. {Nin nase tok que} (Chief Mountain). Unmistakable on the horizon from more than a sixty miles away, and very impressive from nearby, Chief Mountain must have been iconic for many generations of Blackfoot-speaking people, and has become so for non-Indigenous inhabitants of the region as well.
(Photo by T. Binnema.)

Maps and Photographs

Photo 3. {Oos ke chip} (Heart Butte) (above the horse on the right) overlooks today's Blackfeet Reservation in Montana. Its position in front of the Sawtooth Range makes it prominent compared to other taller peaks. It is located at "C" on Map 1 and signified by a heart shape on Map 2. (Photo by F. Lanoë.)

Photo 4. {Is se cut to yis} (Haystack Butte) is a starkly beautiful nearly symmetrical outlier of the Rocky Mountains. Any plains travellers intending to cross the Rocky Mountains between the Sun River and the Blackfoot River could use this unmistakable landmark to guide them. Haystack Butte is "D" on Map 1, the "Pap" along the Rocky Mountains on Map 2, and probably 21 on Map 5. (Photo by T. Binnema.)

Photo 5. {Ki oo pee ki} ('Beartooth,' Beartooth Mountain). After flowing out of the mountains in front of the unmistakable Beartooth Mountain, the Missouri River flows from right to left through the cottonwood trees in the middle ground. Even from a great distance away, wayfinders could use Beartooth Mountain to find the best way across the mountains at this location. Beartooth Mountain can be found at "F" on Map 1 and is labelled "Bear Tooth" on Map 2. (Photo by T. Binnema.)

Photo 6. It is obvious that {Mapes sis is tak} ('Belt Butte') got its name from the sandstone belt that sets the landmark apart. About twenty-seven miles to Belt Butte's southeast, the nearly symmetrical Wolf Butte (right), an outlier of the Little Belt Mountains (rising to the right) would serve as the perfect landmark for anyone travelling from the photographer's location to the Judith Gap, which is beyond Wolf Butte. Belt Butte and Wolf Butte are "G" and "H," respectively, on Map 1. Belt Butte is number 11 on Map 2. (Photo by T. Binnema.)

Photo 7. In this image, the Musselshell River flows through cottonwoods in front of Coffin Butte (centre), near Harlowton, Montana. The snow-clad Crazy Mountains form the backdrop. Coffin Butte may be the {Pawk sis tok que} ('Bad Mountain') of the Blackfoot ("K" on Ak ki mok ki's map of 1801 [Map 1]). (Photo by T. Binnema.)

Photo 8. Canyon Mountain, which overlooks the Yellowstone River as it flows out of the mountains near Livingstone, Montana, may be the {Stommix mooks sis sa que} (Buffalo Nose) (at "L" along the Rocky Mountains) of Ak ki mok ki's map of 1801 (Map 1). This may also be the location of the northernmost {Chetow} of the Gros Ventre map (Map 5). (Photo by T. Binnema.)

34 CARTOGRAPHIC POETRY

Photo 9. The Wind River emerges from the Wind River Canyon south of Thermopolis, Wyoming. This may be the feature depicted in the more southerly {Chetow} of the Gros Ventre map (Map 5). (Photo by T. Binnema.)

Photo 10. {Ocks as sax e kim me} (The Nose at Neutral Hills). The Nose is the most prominent hill in the long chain of hills known as the Neutral Hills. The Neutral Hills reportedly acquired their name from the fact that they were located near the boundary of Cree and Blackfoot territory, where Cree and Blackfoot people often met to negotiate terms of peace. Today, communications towers are located on many landforms depicted on the Blackfoot maps. The Nose appears as number 30 of the Ki oo cus map (Map 4). (Photo by T. Binnema.)

Photo 11. {E new o kee} (Buffalo Lake). The environs of Buffalo Lake teemed with bison, especially during the winter. The photograph is taken from the tallest hill in the vicinity, Boss Hill, named after the "buffalo boss" (buffalo hump). The hill is also the location of a 7,800 year old archaeological site. The photograph demonstrates that the suggestion made by several authors that the lake acquired its name because of any purported resemblance to the shape of a stretched bison hide is unlikely. Buffalo Lake is number 7 on the Ki oo cus map (Map 4). (Photo by T. Binnema.)

Photo 12A. {Omahkokata} (Gopher Head Hill, Ground Squirrel Hill). Although it rises only about 180 feet above the surrounding plains, Gopher Head Hill was important for wayfinders travelling through the undulating plains of the region because it could be seen from afar. Moreover, those who climbed the hill obtained distant vistas in all directions. This hill is feature 3 on Map 4. (Photo by T. Binnema.)

Photo 12B. {Omahkokata} (Gopher Head Hill, Ground Squirrel Hill). The fact that an ancient stone effigy (destroyed several decades ago) was constructed atop Gopher Head Hill suggests that the location was a destination as well as a landmark. Springs around the base of the hill may have attracted humans and animals to the location. The hill offers unobstructed views in all directions. In this photograph, {Oo chis chis} (the 'Hand Hills') (feature 2 on Map 4) are visible on the horizon about twenty-five miles south. (Photo by T. Binnema.)

Photo 13. The Mud Buttes of central Alberta may be the place identified as {Eech e seek kitche stoup} on Ki oo cus's map (feature 26 on Map 4). (Photo by T. Binnema.)

Photo 14. The Misty Hills, possibly {Chis seeks} of Ki oo cus's map, rise dramatically from the surrounding prairie. The description that the hills supported "a little poplar" seems to fit. There are numerous archaeological sites in the vicinity of these hills. These hills may correspond with feature 27 on Map 4. (Photo by T. Binnema.)

Photo 15. The confluence of the South Saskatchewan and Red Deer Rivers. In this image, the South Saskatchewan River flows from the southwest (left) to join the Red Deer River, flowing from the west. This photograph illustrates that the rivers occupy an underfit valley originally carved towards the end of the last ice age. Peter Fidler stated that Chesterfield House was built on the north (far) side of the confluence, but the remains have never been found, perhaps because the two rivers have shifted significantly since 1802. This location is featured on all of the Blackfoot and Gros Ventre maps (Maps 1 to 5). (Photo by H.W. Pyszczyk.)

Photo 16. {Moo coo wans} (Belly Buttes). The strikingly beautiful Belly Buttes are near the confluence of the Belly and Waterton Rivers on the present-day Kainai Reserve in Alberta. The Belly Buttes are included in each version of Ac ko mok ki's map of 1802 (Map 2), Ak ko wee ak's map (Map 3), and the Ki oo cus map (Map 4). (Photo by T. Binnema.)

Photo 17A: The location of {Cut to yis} (Sweetgrass Hills) near the height of land between the Hudson Bay and Gulf of Mexico watersheds makes them visible from great distances. The three buttes (from left to right Mount Brown, Gold Butte, and West Butte) are between 55 and 60 miles away when viewed from this vantage point on the western shoulder of the Cypress Hills. The spherical sandstones in the foreground bring to mind the "marbles" that the Blackfoot told James Doty about in 1854. These hills are labelled "3 paps" on Maps 1 and 2, numbered 17 on Map 4, and are not labelled on Map 5. West Butte is the one pictured on Photo 17B. (Photo by T. Binnema.)

Photo 17B. {Cut to yis} (Sweetgrass Hills). The Sweetgrass Hills, which appear on Maps 1, 2, 4, and 5, were not only important wayfaring landmarks. They were also important destinations. The hills receive considerably more precipitation in the form of rain and snow than the surrounding plains. For that reason, they support forests of lodgepole pine, luxuriant grasses, and copious springs. The Blackfoot travelled there not only for those resources but because those resources also attracted herds of bison. (Photo by T. Binnema.)

Photo 17C. {Cut to yis} (Sweetgrass Hills). The three distinct sugarloaf Sweetgrass Hills are obvious in this aerial photograph. The many small streams that flow out of the hills into the Milk River (running from right to left in this photograph) speak to the extra precipitation that the hills receive. The photo also shows the deep valleys that offered bison and people shelter in winter. The Highwood Mountains can be seen (about one hundred miles south of the East Butte) in the distance near the horizon, with the Big Snowy Mountains (on the left), Little Belt Mountains (behind the Highwood Mountains), Big Belt Mountains, and margins of the Rocky Mountains (right) on the horizon. The fact that none of the Blackfoot cartographers could ever have had this vantage point, or the benefit of any modern survey equipment, makes their maps of this immense landscape (the highest points of the East Butte and West Butte are about twenty miles apart) very impressive. (Photo by T. Binnema.)

Photo 18. {Ow wan nax} ('Rattle Hills,' Shaw Butte and Square Butte). In this early-morning photograph, Square Butte (right) and Shaw Butte (left) appear to float above the fog that has crept across the land from the nearby Missouri River. These hills may appear as feature E on Map 1A, and almost certainly as two circles on Map 2. (Photo by T. Binnema.)

Photo 19. The clear water of the copious {Phis too keem oo kis cum} ('Warm Water Spring,' Gigantic Warm Springs) (number 16 on Map 2) here joins the cloudy waters of Warm Spring Creek flowing out of the Moccasin Hills in the Judith Basin of Montana. (Photo by T. Binnema.)

Photo 20. Watered by streams flowing from the {At che kates tak que} ('Yellow Mountains,' Judith Mountains), {Coon is tick}, ('Mountain of Snow,' Big Snowy Mountains), Belt Mountains, and {Ow wan nax} (Highwood Mountains), the Judith Basin is a well-watered region. Here, the Judith River (known to the Blackfoot as Yellow River) (number 18 on Map 2) flows from right to left through a deep valley towards the Missouri River. Ac ko mok ki's Map of 1802 (Map 2) is focused on the environs of the Judith Basin, and the Judith Mountains appear as number 24 on the Ki oo cus map (Map 4). (Photo by T. Binnema.)

Photo 21. This photograph shows the eastern edge of the {See see ak} (Highwood Mountains) and the {Ow wan nax} ('Rattle Hills,' Round Butte and Square Butte) to their right looking north from the Judith Basin (numbers 12 and 13 on Map 2B). This {Ow wan nax} (Square Butte) is feature 13 on Ac ko mok ki's 1802 map (Map 2B), and feature 23 on the Ki oo cus map (Map 4). It should not be confused with the feature with the same names near {Ki oo pee ki} (Beartooth Mountain). The two features called {Ow wan nax} are about seventy miles apart. (Photo by T. Binnema.)

Maps and Photographs   43

Photo 22. Manitou Lake figures prominently as number 31 on the Ki oo cus map (Map 4). Although the reason for its inclusion was not recorded, the lake's Cree, Assiniboine, and Blackfoot names imply that each of these peoples attached a spiritual importance to the lake. This view of Manitou Lake taken towards its eastern shore shows that that are several low hills that Ki oo cus might have been thinking about when he included {Kee ow chee} 'a hill' along its shore. The boulder in the foreground is encrusted with the mineral salts to which some people attribute healing properties. Even today, people come to the lake to gather these salts from the lakeshore. (Photo by T. Binnema.)

1 Learning from Early Nineteenth-Century Blackfoot Maps

THE SIKSIKA MAPS of the early nineteenth century are to Western maps as poetry is to prose. Appearing spare and simple, they are ingeniously minimalist. They include the essential information to answer the purpose for which they were created. Poetry is language condensed; Siksika cartography is landscape distilled. With surprisingly few lines and figures, and with accompanying oral information that might be committed to memory, these maps permitted Blackfoot recipients to navigate confidently amongst resource-gathering locations and other significant places on the vast Northwestern Plains. Rosalyn R. LaPier, a member of the Blackfeet Tribe of Montana and an award-winning environmental historian, recently wrote that she could imagine her grandparents "saying *Annóóma*: 'Around here' is where we harvest prairie turnips, 'around here' is where we held our O'kan, 'around here' is where I was born, and 'around here' is where my grandparents are buried. With each mile their lives unfolded, and with each mile our history was told—not by reading a book but from reading the land."[1] Here, we explain this fact by deciphering *what* is depicted on these maps, based interpretations about *how* they convey meaning,[2] supplemented by further linguistic, archaeological, and historical research.

As impressive as these maps are as practical navigational tools, they are also, as all maps are, cultural artifacts rich with evidence about the individuals and societies who created them, and the relationships they had with their surroundings. So, we go beyond deciphering *what* is depicted on these maps, and explaining *how* they work, to exploring them as ethnohistorical sources. Peter Fidler may have collected these maps primarily to fill in a blank space in European maps of western North America, and his contributors may have intended primarily to respond to his queries. The Blackfoot of the time may also have drawn non-navigational maps that included the intersections of the spiritual and material worlds—the Blackfoot, like other Indigenous people, believed that the visible tangible reality was only a small part of the total reality. LaPier has published an excellent contribution to our understanding of "the supernatural world of the Blackfeet."[3] The lines and figures they drew on these maps, and the oral information they conveyed, must have had significance well beyond route planning. They offer glimpses of Blackfoot knowledge and use of resource-procurement sites. Many of the landforms they included were significant for far more than navigation. They were connected with the invisible reality as understood by the Blackfoot. Moreover, although the maps were created within the space of about a year, archaeological evidence shows that many of the locations featured on these maps have ancient histories of human use. Thus, while these maps were apparently intended to represent the tangible Blackfoot world in 1801 and 1802, they also hint tantalizingly at both the ancient and the spiritual and intangible. Indeed, the distinction between the spiritual and physical was blurred. In 1854, James Doty, a member of an American surveying and treaty-making expedition who visited the Blackfoot people, reported that "the Blackfeet have only one Tradition concerning their origin. They say that the first inhabitants of their country were an old man [Napi] and his wife, that this Old Man wandered through the country for many years, creating Mountains, Lakes, Rivers, Plains, etc., and stocking them with game...Finally he created the Blackfeet Nation, as numerous as they at present exist, and then departed they know not where. This tradition is said to have been handed down from their ancestors as is the only idea they have of whence they came or how they were created."[4] Doty's account, flawed as it might have been, shows that the Blackfoot closely associated Napi, their mischievous creator and trickster figure, with the landforms and waters that they included on their maps.

While some cartographers view their enterprise as objective, historians of cartography have shown that maps are prone to misinterpretation when not approached, like any other historical documents, as products of particular people, times, and places.[5] Attempts to study Indigenous maps as if they employed (or should have employed) universal cartographic standards are unsatisfying because the cartographic conventions upon which they are based are foreign to westerners. Barbara Belyea, one student of these maps, has noted that researchers generally portray Indigenous maps as impressive but deficient representations of actual topographical features, noting that scholars have felt compelled to deconstruct, reorient, and correct the "distortions, compressions and 'truncations'" of Indigenous maps to conform to "actual cardinal orientations," to "the actual lay of the land," and to "actual features of topography."[6] This approach is debilitating because if we assume that Western maps provide correct or objective portrayals of landscape, we inevitably judge non-Western maps as flawed or inaccurate; we are bound to transliterate maps rather than translating them. Understanding Indigenous maps requires an acknowledgement that "a single map is but one of an indefinitely large number of maps that might be produced for the same situation or from the same data."[7] Long before Europeans arrived in North America, Indigenous societies developed cartographic languages that produced maps that were readily understood and used by the people of that society, even if they confused outsiders. Today, anyone seeking to understand old Indigenous maps, and to use those maps to better understand the communities that made them, should turn to any available source of knowledge about the cartographers and societies that produced the maps including their language, about the territories their maps portrayed, and about the archaeology of that territory, to understand why the landscape was portrayed the way it was.

The several Blackfoot maps produced for Fidler in 1801 and 1802 provide all students of non-Western maps with an exceptional opportunity because we have several versions of four maps of roughly the same region drawn by three Siksika leaders, and another by one or more Gros Ventre informants. Although the Blackfoot-speaking people and the Gros Ventre spoke distinctly different and mutually unintelligible languages and had very different histories, they were closely associated with one another at the turn of the nineteenth century (meaning that most Gros Ventre spoke Blackfoot as well) and had overlapping territories. Having the ability to compare several maps by different Indigenous people about whom we have some biographical information permits us to arrive at insights that might be impossible to reach if we had only one map by an unknown Indigenous informant. Once translated, they become a valuable source of information for historians of the Blackfoot-speaking people, and for anyone interested in Indigenous cartography.

All maps are products of societies, not just of individuals. Considerable similarities among the Blackfoot maps show that the maps represent the accumulated knowledge of a community. Moreover, the similarities among the Blackfoot and Gros Ventre maps suggest that the Blackfoot and Gros Ventre at that time shared perceptions of the landscape and of cartographic traditions. Finally, the distinctive cartographic style of the Blackfoot maps provides compelling evidence that mapping was a longstanding tradition in Blackfoot society. There can be little doubt that all, or almost all, human communities, including those without writing, engaged in mapmaking. People drew maps (including relief maps) in and with sand, snow, and sticks, and on animal hide, rock, bark, tools and weapons, and even on human bodies.[8] The making of physical maps is all but essential to the communication of spatial knowledge from person to person. It is also, we believe, important to the process of reifying spatial knowledge in the person making maps. If the above assumptions are correct—if the maps represent the knowledge of a community, refined over the years—the maps were probably readily understood and accurate portrayals of the Northwestern Plains. Why would the Blackfoot make maps that were useless navigational aids? We need not assess the quality or accuracy of these maps; we ought to study how the Indigenous cartographers chose to depict their surroundings, what needs these maps might meet, and what the maps might tell us about the society that created them. In contrast to earlier studies, then, this study begins with the dual assumptions that Blackfoot maps ought to be studied together, and that any perceived inaccuracies in them may arise from our inability to understand the unique mapping style rather than from actual error.[9] We examine versions of maps drawn by Ac ko mok ki in 1801[10] (Map 1A and 1B) and 1802[11] (Map 2A and 2B), by Ak ko wee ak[12] (Map 3A and 3B) and Ki oo cus[13] (Map 4A and 4B) in 1802, and a map made by unidentified Gros Ventre informant(s) in 1802 (Map 5A).[14]

The historical geographer D.W. Moodie rightly pointed out that these maps are "bona fide examples of Indian map-making," but he also noted that their creation was influenced by non-Indigenous factors.[15] Unfortunately, few maps drawn by Indigenous people for Indigenous people are likely to have survived. To assess how non-Indigenous factors might have affected the content of any map, one must consider its format, authorship, audience, and purpose. In this case, the fact that we have several examples of Blackfoot maps facilitates this process.

Some have argued that, although these maps were committed to paper, they were probably transcribed by Fidler from the snow, sand, hide, bark, or other medium more familiar to the Blackfoot.[16] We doubt that. Given that most of the maps exist in rough drafts and fair copies, and given that the rough drafts appear to have been drawn originally in pencil with ink tracing, it is more likely that the Indigenous cartographers drew the original maps on paper, with pencil, and that Fidler later used a pen to make the maps easier to read.[17] Still, even if the Siksika authors drew these maps on paper, their cartographic style was influenced by the fact that they were not accustomed to drawing maps on paper intended to be preserved for posterity, and that they normally explained their maps orally. Although preserved on paper, these maps reflect the ephemeral navigational maps that the Siksika probably often sketched in or on any number of media. Moreover, they must include only a small part of the oral information that was conveyed with them. The cartographers would have intended to present efficiently essential information to enable band members to travel through unfamiliar territory, to plan travel schedules and rendezvous points, or to illustrate their stories. The best maps would be ones that would be easily remembered. Under such conditions, the omission of conspicuous topographical features or the inclusion of extraneous information reduced rather than enhanced the effectiveness of the map.

These Indigenous cartographers were aware that these maps were unlike maps they had drawn before. Not drawn for members of their own societies to plan a particular route or rendezvous, but for a trader in response to specific questions, these maps, particularly ones that depict the Pacific Coast, may cover a larger area than a typical Siksika map would. Most of the maps focus on the region southwest of Chesterfield House, not because the Siksika were most familiar with that area, but because Fidler especially sought information about areas that were terra incognita for Europeans. The maps also show Fidler's interpretive hand. Fidler identified and keyed locations by letters and numbers and sometimes indicated distances in miles. Differences between rough versions and final copies of some maps also suggest how Fidler may have reinterpreted the maps. Still, Fidler's additions ought not simply to be interpreted as corruptions, but as his attempts to interpret and incorporate cartographically the oral information conveyed to him by the Indigenous cartographers.

Few people in the Hudson's Bay Company (HBC) were more apt or suited than Peter Fidler to receive and preserve maps drawn by Indigenous people. Soon after the nineteen-year-old Fidler joined the HBC in 1788, he earned a reputation within the company for his intelligence, curiosity, and ability to endure physical deprivation. These characteristics encouraged the company to train him, in 1790, as surveyor. They also made him suitable as an emissary to Indigenous communities. From January to April 1791, Fidler lived with a small Chipewyan band that hunted in the subarctic forests of what is now northern Saskatchewan. Then, in September 1791, a band of Chipewyan led by Thooh, from the Great Slave Lake region, asked for an HBC trader to join them for the winter. On 4 September 1791, Malcolm Ross, Fidler's immediate supervisor at the time, wrote, "I am going to send Peter Fidler with them partly at his own desire, he is very fond of learning their language, which will be very necessary if your Honours settles this Quarter, he is a very fit man for surveying in this quarter, as he can put up with any sort of living, that is in eating and drinking, he is also a very steady sober young man."[18] Sure enough, Fidler stoically endured periods of hunger alongside his hosts during the ensuing winter. Philip Turnor afterward marvelled that Fidler "was glad to take stale Jack fish heads out of the dust to afford some relief to the cravings of nature."[19] But Fidler emphasized the positive. After his stay with the Chipewyan and "having acquired a sufficiency of their Language to transact any business with them," Fidler wrote sanguinely that "upon the whole this has been rather an agreeable winter than otherwise."[20]

After spending the winter of 1791–92 at Great Slave Lake with Thooh's band, Fidler was sent to the HBC's Saskatchewan District, which included the territory of the Blackfoot. Soon after Fidler arrived at the newly established Buckingham House, his supervisor there, William Tomison, noted that "I intend to send Peter Fidler to make some observations at the Rocky Mountains under his [Sakatow's] care as he is one of the Principal Indians from that Quarter."[21] Accordingly, he spent the winter of 1792–93, equipped with surveying equipment, in the company of Sakatow's band of Piikani as they travelled as far southwest as the upper Oldman River region.[22] Then, during the winters of 1800–01 and 1801–02, Fidler supervised the HBC's Chesterfield House (Photo 15) at the confluence of the Red Deer and South Saskatchewan Rivers, one of the very few posts that the HBC ever built south of the North Saskatchewan River. It was there that Fidler collected maps from his Siksika and Gros Ventre informants. At some unknown time, Fidler married, according to Indigenous customs, a Cree woman, with whom he had a large family. He died in 1822 in present-day Manitoba, shortly after wedding "Mary" in an Anglican ceremony.

Fidler was a meticulous observer and an exceptionally inquisitive polymath, constantly seeking knowledge for its own sake.[23] Fidler may have hoped to benefit personally by conveying a redrafted version of Ac ko mok ki's 1801 map to his employer in London, but he probably requested the maps primarily out of personal curiosity. Over the course of his career in the HBC, Fidler collected at least twenty-two maps drawn by nineteen different Indigenous cartographers.[24] Apart from the maps discussed here, Fidler collected maps drawn by Inuit, Chipewyan, Cree, and Ojibwe informants. At least one copy of each of these maps is still preserved in the Hudson's Bay Company Archives (HBCA). Furthermore, Fidler sent only one of the maps discussed here to the company in 1802. The fair copy of each map, contained in Fidler's private papers, reached the company only in 1822 after Fidler's death, and then only because Fidler willed his personal papers to the HBC. Few fur traders or European explorers would have been more likely than Fidler to collect Indigenous maps for their own sake, or to have taken them seriously.

Fidler also carefully recorded the provenance of the Indigenous maps he collected. One is listed as an "Iskemo [Eskimo or Inuit] sketch Drawn by Nay hek til lok an Iskemo 40 years of age 8th July 1809," and another "Drawn by Cot.aw.ney.yaz.zah a young man Jepewyan [Chipewyan] Feby 17th 1810."[25] Sometimes, he also noted in his journals that he acquired maps. In March 1807, Fidler wrote in his rough version of the Cumberland House journals that "Cha cha pay tat te drawed a sketch of the Lower Country."[26] During those years, Fidler also collected at least sixteen maps drawn by HBC and Canadian traders untrained in surveying or cartography. He preserved them as well.[27]

The maps we focus on here are a product of a particular time in the history of the Northern Plains and its peoples, including the Blackfoot and

Gros Ventre. The Siksika and Gros Ventre cartographers shared the maps when the Blackfoot—and to a lesser extent the Gros Ventre—were especially confident and militarily powerful. Having acquired horses around the 1730s and guns and ammunition in the 1780s, they could dominate their rivals (including Shoshone, Crow, and Bitterroot Salish) to the south and west, who would not enjoy steady access to European weaponry until after 1810. Moreover, although Cree and Assiniboine bands to the north and east had better access to European weaponry than the Blackfoot and Gros Ventre did, the relationships between the Blackfoot (especially the Siksika band that supplied these maps) and the Cree/Assiniboine was still mostly peaceful in 1801 and 1802, although deteriorating. The Blackfoot-speaking peoples could still relatively safely visit HBC posts on the North Saskatchewan River until that relationship collapsed after about 1806. By contrast, the Gros Ventre relationship with the Cree and Assiniboine had descended into chronic warfare in the 1790s, forcing the Gros Ventre to gravitate farther south between the 1790s and 1860s. Relationships between Blackfoot and Gros Ventre bands were fraught but mostly peaceful at the turn of the nineteenth century and would not be ruptured until the 1860s. The Blackfoot and Gros Ventre cartographers may have been willing to supply these maps in part because traders at Chesterfield House were their most reliable sources of European goods at the time.[28]

Apparently, in several instances (especially in Ak ko wee ak's map and Ki oo cus's map) Fidler specifically prompted his informants to include places Fidler remembered from his 1792–93 trip with the Piikani. Nevertheless, the same features must have been important to the Blackfoot who travelled the region frequently. Indeed, the maps drawn by Ak ko wee ak and Ki oo cus are particularly likely to include features and locations less valuable as navigational aids than as resource-procurement sites.

Fidler did not explain why he sought maps from these particular individuals, but all of the known authors of these maps belonged to one large Siksika band. This band, led by Ac ko mok ki himself, was the prime Indigenous beneficiary of the establishment of Chesterfield House in 1800.[29] Even before the HBC established the post, members of this band must have informed the traders about the location, for when Fidler made his way up the South Saskatchewan River in August 1800, no trader had ever yet been anywhere near the site.[30] After Fidler established the post, this Siksika band provided the traders at Chesterfield House with an impressive return in wolf and fox furs, and kept them well supplied with meat. Several members of the band, including all known authors of maps, served various functions. Ac ko mok ki, as headman, provided important diplomatic services. Ki oo cus was clearly Fidler's most trusted hunter, horse herder, interpreter, and guide. Ak ko wee ak also served as post hunter, although Fidler had little praise for his hunting abilities.[31] Members of this Siksika band may also have prevented belligerent Gros Ventre bands from attacking Chesterfield House in 1802. In sum, the European traders at Chesterfield House were dependent upon the cooperation of this Siksika band just as this band of Siksika had more to gain from the success of that trading centre than any other Indigenous band.[32]

There is no evidence that Fidler knew whether his informants were more or less able than other Blackfoot people to produce accurate maps of the region. Scholars who study spatial knowledge have confirmed what most of us know intuitively—that spatial acuity differs very significantly from individual to individual.[33] Given that fact, it is intuitive that communities such as the Blackfoot would have esteemed persons with superior spatial abilities, and it is unlikely that the leaders who drew these maps were more directionally challenged than their fellow band members.

If these men were not paid directly for their maps, they certainly expected that they and their kin would benefit indirectly from the gesture that clearly symbolized their commitment to the mutually beneficial relationship that had already been established. The friendly relations between the Siksika cartographers and recipient suggest that it was unlikely that the maps were intentionally drawn incorrectly. On the contrary, the nature of the relationship makes it likely that Fidler was able to persuade his informants to adapt their maps to suit his purpose. This is especially likely in the case of Ki oo cus. None of the Indigenous cartographers, it seems, was a more frequent visitor to the post than was Ki oo cus. His frequent visits and friendly relations may have made it possible for Fidler to introduce Ki oo cus to Western cartographic conventions in an effort to facilitate cartographic communication. Ki oo cus's map suggests that the author tried to adapt to Western cartographic style, and although his map is revealing for this very reason, it also appears to suffer from it in various respects. The fact that the map Fidler conveyed to London closely resembles Ac ko mok ki's 1801 map rather than Ki oo cus's map suggests that Fidler recognized the problems with the latter one.

Just as rhyme, metre, alliteration, and assonance make poetry easier to memorize than prose, Blackfoot maps employ lines, pattern, order, and icons as mnemonic devices. The most obvious characteristic of these maps (although less so for Ki oo cus's) is that straight lines or gently curving lines predominate. There is little doubt that the first line drawn on each map was the straight line (curved in the case of Ki oo cus's) at the top representing the Rocky Mountains as the Siksika perceived them. The cartographer then drew relatively straight lines at right angles to the first, to symbolize main rivers flowing from the mountains through the plains. This sequence of line drawing, which depicted the outside edges of the map first, helped Blackfoot cartographers avoid the bane of countless drawers of sketch maps: running out of space for the intended map.[34] Tributaries to the main rivers were then drawn, almost like veins of a leaf, from the line representing the mountains to the straight line representing the main river. Landforms along the mountains, and notable features between the rivers were probably added last. Foremost among them are Beartooth Mountain (Photo 5) and Chief Mountain (Photo 2), both of which appear prominently along the mountain panorama when viewed from the plains. All the while, the cartographer provided information orally, either on his own initiative or in response to questions. Fidler recorded some of this oral information on the maps but cannot have preserved it all.

The practice of representing with straight lines what are obviously irregular topographical features suggests that these topographical features served the same function as cardinal directions do on Western maps. Cardinal directions serve as abstract reference lines that allow map readers to determine their position and chart a desired course. The Siksika, like many societies, had no need to determine cardinal directions. Topographical features served as concrete reference lines. Rather than setting a course east or north, a Siksika might travel parallel to, or away from, or toward a river or line of mountains. In 1905, Brings-Down-the-Sun, a Piikani, described the Old North Trail in a way that reveals that the Blackfoot used the Rocky Mountains as such a reference line:

> There is a well known trail we call the Old North Trail. It runs north and south along the Rocky Mountains. No one knows how long it has been used by the Indians...It forked where the city of Calgary now stands. The right fork ran north into the Barren Lands as far as people live. The main trail ran south along the eastern side of the Rockies, at a uniform distance from the mountains, keeping clear of the forest, and outside of the foothills. It ran close to where the city of Helena now stands, and extended south into the country, inhabited by a people with dark skins, and long hair falling over their faces (Mexico).[35]

The trail is called *Apatohsóhsokoi* ("north trail") and *Mísmoyai-móhsokoi-aistóhzim-istakisz-awákha* ("old trail passing near the mountains").[36] Clearly, any Blackfoot traveller, familiar with the straight-line cartographic convention, would not be confused or disoriented by the curves and turns of a river or mountain range. The straight lines were a strength, not a weakness, of Siksika maps. The maps illustrate what cartographers understand to be the very essence of successful mapmaking: selectivity. Geographer Mark Monmonier has noted that "to avoid hiding critical information in a fog of detail, the map must offer a selective, incomplete view of reality."[37] Denis Wood has similarly argued that "the map's *effectiveness* is a consequence of the *selectivity* which it brings the past to bear on the present."[38] Indigenous maps resided in the minds of their authors, only occasionally assuming concrete form in the form of sketch maps. That must have been true of many Indigenous Peoples, and that must have persisted among some of them, for many years. In 1891, when reflecting on the fact that some Dane-zaa had shown him the correct way to Fort Dunvegan when his Western map was inaccurate, Warburton Pike noted,

> Indians or hunters, traders and others travelling under the guidance of Indians, do not depend on the latitudes and longitudes of places, or on the respective bearings of one place from another. The Indians follow routes with which they have been familiar since childhood, or, when beyond the boundaries of their own particular region of country, go by land-marks, such as mountains, lakes, and rivers, which have been described to them by their neighbours. Their memory in this respect is remarkable; but it must be remembered that among their principal subjects of conversation when sitting about the camp-fire are the distances in day's journeys from place to place, the routes which they have followed or have known others to follow, the difficulties to be encountered on these, the points at which food of different kinds may be obtained, and the features which strike them as being remarkable in the country traversed.[39]

At about the same time, another man in the same region noted that "In an Indian camp there are only a few topics of conversation, so that they spend much of their time in describing places they have visited, entering minutely into the details of the landmarks, and these things mean more to an Indian than to a white man."[40] These comments are not about the Blackfoot people, but they must have been true about Indigenous communities around the world for thousands of years.

It was essential among oral peoples that maps be easily memorized. The straight-line Siksika maps contain the information necessary to navigate the Northwestern Plains, in a form that is readily committed to memory. Incorporating the sinuosity of topographical features would help neither a person familiar with the terrain (because that person would recognize places by sight), nor a person unfamiliar with the terrain since that person would inevitably forget details of the map, if not the entire map. The use of topographical features such as rivers, mountain ranges, and coastlines as concrete reference lines or points and the related use of the straight-line cartographic style is neither unnatural nor uncommon. According to historian of cartography Gerald Roe Crone, many early Western maps also show little concern with the accurate representation of direction. Depiction of conspicuous landmarks was more important.[41] Similarly, the linguist and anthropologist David Pentland argued that fifteenth-century European maps, eighteenth-century Chipewyan maps, and twentieth-century Cree maps all show rivers as "straight or curved lines, lakes as ovals." He has also noted that contemporary Cree can use stars for navigation but they "prefer to rely on topographical clues rather than the stars."[42] Anyone familiar with present-day maps of urban metro systems should be convinced of the advantages of the straight-line cartographic style.

The inclusion of hills and ridges along rivers and creeks on Ki oo cus's map facilitated finding locations. A map user could easily follow a river, keeping above the valley, to find the hills and resources associated with them. Many such places were visible from a distance. Highlands and hills were important for many reasons for the Blackfoot, so it was important that there was some easy way to find them.

The Blackfoot called the "Rocky Mountains" *mistakis* ('the backbone').[43] The association of the mountains with a backbone may shed light on their tendency to depict them as a straight line on maps. Cartographic convention and perception of the world evidently reinforced one another. The reader must not assume, however, that the Blackfoot's *mistakis* and the Euro-American's Rocky Mountains correspond. They do not. In 1792, Fidler recorded a description of the Rocky Mountains that does not accord well with present prevailing understandings of the Rocky Mountains. Regarding the mountains Fidler wrote that "the [Piikani] Inds say, who have been at war, a great distance to the Southwards that inclining still more Easterly, [the mountain] becomes lower—& that there it is divided into 4 or 5 parallel ridges—with fine plains betwixt them & a small river running thru each of these Vallies—where yew becomes plenty—& 2 or 3 other kinds of wood they describe which I have never seen."[44] Similarly, on the Ac ko mok ki map, Fidler noted that "the Mountain to the South of the Mississury [Missouri] River inclines almost East—or between E & SE & is considerably lower & not so far across as in Lat. 53° to 49°." Finally, the map by Ki oo cus indicates the same thing; the Rocky Mountains swing eastward immediately south of the Missouri River. These descriptions do not correspond to the Rocky Mountains as most people think of them today. The "Rocky Mountains" as described in Fidler's 1792–93 journal and depicted on Siksika maps, however, show that the Blackfoot considered the *mistakis* to include the front ranges of the Rocky Mountains roughly as we know them north of Beartooth Mountain, on the left bank of the Missouri about thirty miles north of Helena, Montana. South of Beartooth, the *mistakis* ran east and then south along the Big Belt, Little Belt, Big Snowy, Pryor, Crazy, and Bighorn Ranges (Maps 1C and 2C). These mountains are much lower than the Rocky Mountains and are separated by the Smith, Judith, Musselshell, Yellowstone, and Bighorn River Valleys, respectively. Only by interpreting the mountains this way can the various features on the Blackfoot (and Gros Ventre) maps be readily identified.

If the "Rocky Mountains" are not what they seem on these maps, it is impossible that the rivers are portrayed as they are on modern Western maps. Modern readers could easily construe the line or lines representing the "Rocky Mountains" on Siksika maps as approximately representing the Continental Divide. They would then assume that all the rivers on the maps are depicted to their headwaters near the divide. The two maps that show rivers west of the mountains would only tend to reinforce this interpretation. Such a reading, however, would make misinterpretation almost inevitable. Rivers on the Northwestern Plains never originate west of the Rocky Mountains as we know them, but rivers must cross the *mistakis* even if they are not shown to do so on Siksika maps. Thus, what might appear to represent the headwaters of the Missouri River, and several other rivers, on these maps are actually well downstream from their sources. The line representing the *mistakis*, then, represents the meeting of plains and mountains, and rivers are depicted only from the point where they emerge from the mountains onto the plains. (The exception is found in Ki oo cus's map, which clearly shows the course of the Missouri and Yellowstone Rivers into the mountains.)

One more straight-line convention is important for understanding these Indigenous maps. Except for Ki oo cus's map, each map depicts river systems with one river drawn in a straight line meeting the backbone at a right angle, and other rivers running, in a straight line or arc, at an angle to the main river. This appears to be a convenient way of indicating which stream was perceived to be the mainstream and which are its tributaries. (On Western maps main streams tend to be drawn wider than tributaries since they usually carry more water than tributaries.) For a modern reader accustomed to seeing maps show the changes in direction of rivers, the Siksika map might seem to sacrifice far too much. For the Siksika, however, such detail was obviously unnecessary. Since suitable water sources were often scarce, the location of water, and the approximate distance between rivers were important in planning Blackfoot travel routes and schedules.[45] Furthermore, river valleys were often the only sources of firewood, shelter, and usable water. Nevertheless, as pedestrian/equestrian people, the Siksika need not have been bothered with the turns of a river, or the shapes of lakes just as, as Plains people, they did not need to portray the changes in direction of mountain chains. The straight-line conventions may seem flawed to modern readers—and may not have worked for the Blackfoot people's Cree or Kutenai neighbours—but Plains people well understood what was and what was not implied by them.

Naming conventions also shed light on Blackfoot perceptions of the landscape. It seems that, according to Blackfoot conventions, the main branch of a river could assume the name of any of its tributaries. For example, Ac ko mok ki's 1802 map includes the {Ki oo sis sa ta} ('Bear River'), which corresponds to the present-day Marias River. It also shows the Teton River flowing into the Marias River just before its confluence with the Missouri. This convention is consistent with modern Western cartographical conventions. On his 1801 map, however, Ac ko mok ki did not depict the Marias River at all. Instead, he included a river called {Na too too kase}. This is the Two Medicine River, a tributary of the Marias River. Ac ko mok ki showed the Two Medicine River flowing directly into the Missouri. Clearly, then, he applied the name {Na too too kase} to part of the {Ki oo sis sa ta}. By modern standards, any map that portrayed the Two Medicine River ought also to show the Marias River to its headwaters. Siksika convention clearly did not require, although it did allow for, this portrayal. Circumstances might dictate which portrayal was most appropriate, and oral communication would have avoided confusion. It is impossible to account conclusively for this convention, but it is worth noting that its flexibility would have facilitated both the production of simple area maps that avoided presenting unnecessary information, and the drawing of more detailed maps.

It is evident that different segments of the same river could also have different names.[46] For example, a river might have several names, each being an apt description of only part of its course. If this was so, a cartographer could draw an entire river, mention one of the names, and his reader would understand that a portion of the river was being emphasized. While these naming conventions might confuse modern readers, and the explanation given here is only tentative, the conventions would have served admirably the goal of producing effective but simple maps. If this convention initially seems odd, consider that on modern maps the Bow and Oldman Rivers "end" where they join. At the same point the South Saskatchewan "begins." Similarly, the "headwaters" of the Missouri River are considered to be at the confluence of the Gallatin, Madison, and Jefferson Rivers. During the eighteenth and early nineteenth centuries, HBC traders had different names for stretches of the Hayes River, which drains into Hudson Bay at York Factory. This naming convention was almost certainly drawn from Cree bands, who also had distinct names for different sections of one river.[47]

These maps reveal that Blackfoot people often named landforms after human and animal body parts. The *mistakis* (backbone) has already been mentioned. Other examples include the Hand Hills, Knee Hills, Belly River, Thigh Hills, Elbow River, The Forehead, Eyebrow Hills, and Nose Hill. Notably, [Buffalo] Boss Hill (the hump of a buffalo was known as the 'buffalo boss') overlooked Buffalo Lake, which drained into [Buffalo] Tail Creek. Some of these names may be both descriptive and metaphorical. The jagged skyline of the Rocky Mountains might resemble a spine, but the name may also metaphorically evoke greater significance. Did those who originally imagined the mountains as a backbone, and their descendants, also imagine themselves living on the broad back of the backbone's owner in ways analogous to the way Iroquoian people imagined themselves on "Turtle Island"? Descriptive names are very common, although many places were named after animals or resources that seem to have been associated with the feature. Some names, such as Beartooth Mountain and Swan's Bill, are a combination in that they seem to use animal parts to describe a feature. It is not difficult to imagine how Beartooth Mountain (Photo 5) and Swan's Bill (Devil's Head Mountain) (Photo 1) got their names. In short, the physical, metaphorical, and spiritual dimensions of place names may have merged imperceptibly in the Blackfoot world.

Only a few place names are obviously related to Blackfoot culture and history. The common Western practice of naming features to commemorate specific individuals is nowhere evident. A few places relate to specific events in Blackfoot history (such as Shield River), although these events are not likely major turning points in Blackfoot history. Some place names are related to Blackfoot mythology (Oldman River, Chief Mountain, "Gods" Lake). These places tended to be well north of the Missouri River, supporting the view that the Blackfoot in 1800 already had a long history in the Oldman River basin. They were very familiar with the resources of that region and appear to have held a strong attachment to it. The fact that Ac ko mok ki gave Gros Ventre names, rather than Blackfoot names, for the rivers south of the Missouri suggests that the Blackfoot were less familiar with that region in 1802 than they were later in the century.

In many cases, Blackfoot and their neighbours had similar names for the same geographic feature. The Crow knew the Yellowstone River as *E-chee-dick-karsh-ah-shay* ('Elk River'). The Blackfoot named the river after the same species. Likewise, as noted below, the names for many Indigenous groups were identical in the Blackfoot and Gros Ventre languages. This should not be surprising. Indigenous people communicated with each other often, and many spoke more than one language. They often camped together, intermarried, and adopted each other's children. Even those who did not know each other's languages often communicated by sign language, and their names for Indigenous communities were often related to sign-language designations.

The Siksika maps were evidently primarily navigational. If so, they are superlative examples of cartography; for they can readily be used to navigate an immense area. The success of the maps is related to the consistent conventions they employ. Scrutiny of these maps of the Northwestern Plains makes it clear that the most important criterion that the Indigenous cartographers used to select topographical features for inclusion in their maps was their visual impact when viewed from the plains. Fidler explained to the HBC officials in 1802 that on the map he was sending them, "The places marked the Devil's Head, Pyramid, King, Heart &c &c are parts of the mountain that considerably overtop the rest."[48]

Fidler was wrong. The mountains on the maps did not "overtop the rest," but were the most prominent or distinctive mountains when viewed from the plains. On clear days, the distinct flat-topped Chief Mountain (Photo 2) is readily seen on the horizon from the vicinity of Lethbridge, Alberta, to the northeast, and from many hilltops to the east and southeast. But Chief Mountain obscures the view of several taller nearby mountains. Beartooth Mountain can be discerned from hills as far away as the Fort Benton vicinity, a hundred miles to the northeast, and from the Three Forks of the Missouri about seventy-five miles to the south. Because of its location near the Missouri-Saskatchewan-Pacific heights of land, for anyone travelling south from Calgary, Chief Mountain becomes visible once the Porcupine Hills no longer obstruct the view. Travellers can then repeatedly catch sight of the mountain for more than two hundred miles as they make their way southeast. The mountain made an immediate impact upon many people, including non-Indigenous people. In 1882, surveyor Otto J. Klotz wrote that "Chief Mountain, with its broad shoulders, towers toward the skies, a monument of nature's work." He first caught sight of Chief Mountain at a distance of "about 100 miles. It appeared like a huge trunk rising above the horizon."[49] It is no surprise that people who lived most of their days beneath its imposing silhouette, and that pedestrian and equestrian travellers who used it to orient themselves for days on end, formed emotional and spiritual attachments to the mountain. Chief Mountain must have seemed like a constant companion. Newcomers to the region also quickly formed an attachment to the mountain. Annora Brown, born in 1899, the daughter of a North-West Mounted Police officer, recalled that, although it was sixty miles from her home, the "massive, square-topped bulk of Chief Mountain" was an important part of her world.[50] Brown, like countless non-Indigenous people on the Northwestern Plains, followed generations of Indigenous people in forming an attachment to the iconic Chief Mountain.

Once Chief Mountain is no longer visible, travellers headed southward could scan the mountains to the south for the distinct form of Beartooth Mountain (Photo 5), which they could use either to find their way to the upper Missouri River region or as a guide to the Judith Basin or the Musselshell Plains. The residents of Helena, Montana, have formed an attachment to the Sleeping Giant (of which Beartooth Mountain is the nose), much as others have to Chief Mountain. However, even on high points as far away as the vicinity of Fort Benton, people who know what to look for can find Beartooth Mountain on the horizon.

The landforms between the rivers, particularly from the Oldman River south, also served as wayfinders. Travellers climbing any of the region's hills are likely to find at least one of the landforms on the maps. The unmistakable three "sugarloaf" buttes of the Sweetgrass Hills (Photo 17), which rise almost 3,000 feet above the surrounding plain very near the height of land separating the Hudson Bay/Gulf of Mexico divide, can be seen from as far away as Nobleford, Alberta, almost a hundred miles to the northwest, especially when the hills are snow-covered. They are also visible from the Cypress Hills and Bears Paw Mountains. In 1855, James Doty reported that the Sweetgrass Hills represented a "lofty Land Mark—visible in clear weather at a distance of more than 100 miles."[51] From the vicinity of the unmistakable Belt Butte one can easily find Wolf Butte (Photo 6), which, because it is so symmetrical, acts as a fail-safe marker to the entrance to the Judith Gap, whether the traveller approaches the Gap from the northwest or northeast. Most of the other features are also remarkable for their conspicuous appearance, and many are strikingly symmetrical. A traveller standing on some of these high points would also be able to discern the course of valleys that had to be traversed. The flatter landscape with fewer prominent uplands north of the Sweetgrass and Cypress Hills is more difficult to navigate this way than the more southerly region, but the Blackfoot clearly navigated the vast plains confidently. On 8 December 1792, when he was travelling with Sakatow's band of Piikani south of Bow River, Fidler remarked that "springs of fine water" were "of very great service on passing these great plains," and that "it is very surprising how straight the Indians go to them altho there is no woods to direct their way."[52]

A mountain is particularly likely to be on these maps if it could guide travellers towards a specific place, a convenient place to cross mountain ranges or a culturally significant place. These criteria applied both to mountains along the mountain chain, and other highlands on the plains. Thus, the Siksika might easily overlook tall mountains included on modern maps but include smaller, culturally important, neighbouring mountains. Beartooth Mountain, likely to be included only on the most detailed Western maps, was obviously prominent in Blackfoot mental maps. If both cartographer and reader understood that features were selected for inclusion on maps according to their appearance from the plains, Siksika cartographers must certainly have aimed to include all conspicuous features if their omission was likely to lead to confusion or disorientation. The Siksika maps are very effective by this standard. They select from the hundreds place names known to have been in use among Blackfoot people, as recorded by the Canadian Dominion Land Surveyor J.C. Nelson, American writer and explorer James Willard Schultz (Apikuni), enigmatic Jean L'Heureux, and the Canadian geologist George Mercer Dawson.[53]

The historian of cartography J.B. Harley has argued that "both in the selectivity of their content and in their signs and styles of representation maps are a way of conceiving, articulating, and structuring the human world which is biased towards, promoted by, and exerts influence upon particular sets of social relations."[54] Siksika cartography was influenced by

Blackfoot ways of thinking, but also must have itself tended to promote, reify, and influence these ways of thinking. The fact that the maps depict the *mistakis* as a straight line may well have been influenced by the Blackfoot perception of it, but its depiction as a straight line certainly promoted that perception. It has been shown that most of the features on these maps have remarkable value as navigational aids; it is also clear, however, that many of these features also are significant in other ways. For example, the maps and Fidler's travels show that features were both landmarks and frequent destinations and resource-procurement sites. Because hills and mountains on the Northwestern Plains attract more snow and rain than surrounding plains, they supported luxuriant grasses that attracted buffalo herds (Photo 17B). The Canadian scientist George Mercer Dawson recalled from his first visit to the Sweetgrass Hills in 1874 that "the height and mass of the Buttes is sufficient to cause the formation and arrest of clouds in their immediate vicinity, where the rainfall is in consequence much more copious. These mountains and the broken ground around them form a favourite haunt of the buffalo where they find abundance of food and water. The springs arising from some parts of the Buttes are very copious, and form streams, which, on leaving the shelter of the wooded valleys and issuing on the plains are rapidly absorbed by the dry soil and atmosphere, at least in the summer season."[55] Hills provided surface water, trees suitable for use as fuel and lodge poles, berries and roots, and stones suitable for tool production (the importance of which Ki oo cus's map suggest historians of the Blackfoot may have underestimated). Many locations portrayed on the Ki oo cus map have a very high archaeological site density going back thousands of years. The Misty Hills (Photo 14), Mud Buttes (Photo 13), and "Buffalo Nose" (Photo 10) have unique micro-environments and rare (and visually striking) geological features. All three contain the fine-grained pebble cherts highly sought after for making stone tools, uncommon in this vast landscape. For thousands of years, these resources were crucial. At the time the maps were drawn, the Siksika only relatively recently replaced stone tools with metal tools, but the maps suggest that the Siksika continued to identify with places that their ancient ancestors relied upon.

Landmarks such as Chief Mountain, the Sweetgrass Hills, and the Cypress Hills are also important in Blackfoot religion and mythology.[56] Maybe places became sacred to the Blackfoot because of their appearance (conspicuity, shape), utility (position along travel routes, source of resources), and their connection to important events. But most identifiable landforms included on maps are visually striking from many directions, easy to find or to describe, and often relatively symmetrical. It is probably no coincidence that stone effigies, medicine wheels, and ribstones were often built on high prominent places. Canadian surveyor George M.

Dawson noted that a prominent hill east of the Porcupine Hills that J.C. Nelson named Sundial Hill, had "a cairn with concentric circles of stones and radiating lines. I have not seen it, and therefore cannot describe it in detail. It is named *Onoka-katzi*, and regarded with much reverence."[57]

Of all locations on these maps, Chesterfield House (Photo 15) may seem least "Indigenous." It was the first European trading post built in the core of the territories of the Blackfoot-speaking and Gros Ventre peoples. However, the evidence already noted that the Siksika themselves must have invited the traders to establish Chesterfield House, combined with archaeological evidence of the significance of the confluence of the Red Deer and South Saskatchewan Rivers for the Blackfoot, show that the confluence of the two rivers had long been a very significant place. The location is remarkable for many reasons. Visually, it offers some of grandest river-valley views in the Siksika territory. Although the two rivers normally carry considerably less water than the North Saskatchewan or Missouri Rivers, the lower eastward-flowing portion of the Red Deer River, and the portion of the South Branch River included on this map occupy so-called "misfit" or "underfit" streams—rivers occupying valleys far deeper and wider than the present-day rivers could have carved. The valley at the confluence of the Red Deer and South Saskatchewan Rivers is about four miles wide from rim to rim and more than three hundred feet deep. It, like that of the Battle River and Sounding and Eyehill Creeks to the north, the Milk River to the south, and the Qu'Appelle Valley to the east, was created at the end of the last ice age by massive meltwater rivers that drained eastward along the southern edge of the Laurentide icesheet.[58] The lower Red Deer River and South Saskatchewan River follow this underfit valley until the South Saskatchewan River turns northward at a low divide near today's Elbow, Saskatchewan. The valley continues eastward, occupied thereafter by the underfit Qu'Appelle and Assiniboine Rivers. From many locations, the view of the forks of the Red Deer and South Saskatchewan Rivers is impressive.

The depth and breadth of the valley helps explain the location's second important characteristic. The rivers, the deep forested valley, and the adjacent grasslands, provided water, food, and thermal cover for bison herds in winter and summer. The Chesterfield House journals show that bison abounded in the vicinity of the forks during the winter. People, of course, were drawn to the area for the reliable water, protection from winter weather, and the large herds. The valley sides also provided excellent landforms for bison jumps and pounds. Although the confluence may not have been as important during summer, the valley also supported berries. As a resource-gathering site, the confluence was extraordinary.

Archaeological evidence shows that the forks were important for centuries before the maps were drawn. During the 2010s, archaeologists Brian

Reeves and Margaret Kennedy conducted four seasons of archaeological investigations in the vicinity of the confluence of the rivers.[59] They found myriad human-made features that speak to the ceremonial importance of the forks, including thousands of anthropogenic stone constructions—cairns, stone circles and arcs, and a medicine wheel—in the vicinity of the confluence and two other nearby locations. Reeves and Kennedy argued that people built these features at least in part because of the expansive and outstanding views and remarkable landscape there. In a stretch from five miles upstream and two and a half miles downstream of the forks, Reeves and Kennedy found many human-made stone features built in locations with good views of the confluence, but very few on locations without such views. Pointing to evidence that some Indigenous people believed that river confluences marked entry points into other worlds, Reeves and Kennedy speculated that the same may have been the case with those who built these stone structures.[60] At the very least, the archaeological evidence shows that the forks had great significance to the inhabitants of the region for centuries. When Ac ko mok ki's band encouraged the NWC, HBC, and XY Company traders to establish posts at the confluence of the Red Deer and South Saskatchewan Rivers, they were encouraging the traders to settle at an ancient and favourite location, probably used by the Blackfoot at any time of the year for any number of reasons related to subsistence and ceremony, although the traders, who abandoned the location in summer, were particularly interested in settling in locations where the Blackfoot could provide provisions and furs during the winter, and where wood for fuel and building purposes was abundant.

Indigenous maps reveal how culturally bound cartographic conventions are. Indigenous people can be as baffled by Western maps as westerners are by non-Western maps. In the 1970s, David Pentland explained that "the overwhelming detail of a topographic map causes more confusion than enlightenment for a Cree guide. He will become disoriented even in areas he has known since childhood, attempting to get his bearings by counting off the creeks along the course of a river, not realizing that the cartographer may have omitted his favorite landmarks while including others he has never given any attention to."[61] Pentland argued that Western cartographic conventions are the outliers: "the Eskimo, the tribesmen of Siberia and central Africa, and the Cree all have agreed on a set of conventions for map making—it is the modern cartographer with his satellite photographs and computers who is out of touch with the rest of the world."[62] Western cartographers today, like Siksika cartographers of the early nineteenth century, unwittingly but unavoidably reveal much about the societies for which they are produced. Those who initially assume that Western maps of the same region are the scientific and unbiased counterpart to idiosyncratic

Indigenous maps should recognize that Western maps are as freighted with cultural assumptions as any other maps are, and that Western maps not only reflect culturally specific ways of thinking about landscape, but also influence human perceptions of the landscape.

To appreciate the distinctive cartographic style of Siksika maps, each map is discussed individually in chapters that follow. Our analysis of the maps is influenced by the fact that Fidler attempted to render into British English words spoken by Siksika informants. Others, such as Schultz, Grinnell, and Doty rendered into American English words spoken by Kainai and Piikani informants. L'Heureux understood English, but his renderings were influenced by the fact that French was his first language.[63] Pronunciation may have varied; in the case of Fidler, pronunciation should in general render "e" as [i], "c" and "q" as [k], "u" alternatively as [u] or [w], "ch" alternatively as [k] or [x]. We should also remember that names for features may have differed from group to group, and may have changed after significant events. These maps are the product of members of a particular Siksika band, and an unidentified Gros Ventre contributor(s) in 1801 and 1802. They are not timeless.

2

The Ac ko mok ki Map of 1801

PETER FIDLER OBTAINED ONLY ONE SIKSIKA MAP IN 1801, but he preserved two versions of the Ac ko mok ki map of 1801. One version (Map 1A) may have been drawn by Ac ko mok ki himself on 7 February 1801 at Chesterfield House. Fidler probably prepared the second version (Map 1B) as late as July 1802 for submission to the London Governor and Committee of the Hudson's Bay Company (HBC). This second version is the most studied because of its historical importance. The prominent British cartographer Aaron Arrowsmith incorporated it into his 1802 map of North America (Map 14). The versions appear very similar but have some significant differences.

The interpretation of places on these two very similar maps elaborates upon and refines earlier publications.[1] The names and descriptions given below are drawn from the first version, but where the second version differs, information from that map is added and underlined. Our translation is portrayed cartographically in Map 1C.

Streams

Given that Fidler rendered the Blackfoot word for "river" as {is sā tā}, and Doty as {sis-sah-ti}, his informants probably often used the word *a'siítahtaa*, which literally means 'young river' and was apparently a more general term for a stream than *niítahtaa* ('river').[2] In some maps, Fidler included the specifier *is sā tā* or *sis sā tā* at the end of the names of rivers, but in other cases, including on this map, he recorded only the unique portion of a river's Blackfoot name. Thus, as we will see on page 67, Fidler's {Pistin is} and James Willard Schultz's {Pístun Isisakta} are obviously the same stream (Deep Creek).

On this 1801 map (but not the 1802 version) names of the tributaries on the right (south) side of the Missouri River, as well as some of the mountains, are given in the Gros Ventre language. In contrast to the method

Fidler used with Blackfoot river names, with Gros Ventre names Fider tended to include the specifier "river" {net chay} (*niiceeheh*) on the 1801 map.³

Red Deer's River = Red Deer River, Alberta

The Red Deer River is known to the Blackfoot as {Ponoka-sis-sok-tey} ('Elk' or 'Red Deer River'), as recorded by L'Heureux.⁴ The parkland environment along northern portions of the river would have been ideal habitat for elk (*ponoká*), which much have been rare farther south.

Bad River = South Saskatchewan/Bow River, Alberta

None of the maps indicates the Blackfoot name for this river, but in his 1792 journal Fidler recorded the Cree name for the river as {as kow seepee}, from *ahcâpiy* ('bow') and *sîpiy* ('river'), and the Blackfoot name as {Nā mā kay sis sā tā}.⁵ L'Heureux similarly recorded the name of the river as {Na-ma-kanis}.⁶ The Blackfoot name (and English translation) apparently alludes to the fact that bows (*náámaa*) were made from wood (especially of large choke cherry bushes) collected there.

Moocoowans River = Belly/Oldman River

The name of the Belly River derives from *móókoan* ('belly,' 'stomach'). For this river, as for most Blackfoot place names collected by Fidler, the Blackfoot version is limited to the name of the place ("Belly" instead of "Belly River"). Thus, James Doty's rendering of "*Mo-ko-un* or Belly river" was appropriate.⁷ Until 1915, the Belly River was considered to run from its source just west of Chief Mountain, Montana, to its confluence with the Bad (or Bow) River. In 1915, those who sought a more polite name for the river succeeded in having the portion of the river passing through Lethbridge renamed the Oldman River.⁸ Alan Rayburn's assertion that the name "Belly" refers to the Gros Ventre ("Big Bellies"), however, is erroneous. The name of the river was probably taken from the Belly Buttes (see further discussion on page 107) rather than from the Gros Ventre tribe, whom the Blackfoot referred to as *Atsíína* ('Fat People'), a name that was derived from the hand sign for the Gros Ventre, not from any thought that they were actually corpulent.

Pun nā keeks or Little River = Milk River, Alberta and Montana

This name does not conform to the known Blackfoot name for this river, unless Fidler's "P" should have been a "K" (see further discussion on pages 73, 78, and 93), but it is unmistakably a depiction of the Milk River.

Nā too too kase = Two Medicine/Marias River, Montana

The name combines *naato'ki* ('two') and *okan* ('medicine lodge'). The name of the Two Medicine River was recorded by others as {Mátoki Okás} and {Ná tokiokasi}.[9] In 1905, Brings-Down-the-Sun explained that this river was called the Two Medicine River because "we once had a double piskun [buffalo jump] there. We drove the buffalo over one, or the other, as we chose."[10]

Oo ne ceese = Teton River, Montana

The identity of this river is obvious given that *mónnikis* (the initial *m* or *n* in Blackfoot words was often not pronounced) means 'breast' in Blackfoot, just as *teton* refers to the breast/nipple in French. Schultz gave the name as 'Breast River' {Múnikis Isisakta}.[11] See further discussion on page 77.[12]

Pistin is = Deep Creek, Montana

The Blackfoot word for 'deep' is *ipisttanisii*. Moodie and Kaye argued this was "possibly Deep Creek" and the fact that Schultz identifies Deep Creek as {Pístun Isisakta}, confirms it.[13] Note that Deep Creek is a tributary of the Teton River, although they are both shown on Ac ko mok ki's map to flow directly into the Missouri River. This is an example of a convention that would not have confused a Blackfoot person who would have received oral information along with the physical map.

Naw tus or God's River = Sun River, Montana

The Blackfoot used the same word, *naató'si*, interchangeably to mean 'god/sacred' and/or 'sun.' Thus, "God's River," as Fidler named it in English on the 1802 redraft of this map, and the present English name are both translations of the Blackfoot name. The river was also known as "Medicine River" ("medicine" connoting "power").[14] These names reflect the centrality of the Sun River for the Blackfoot.

Shield River = Dearborn River, Montana

This name comes from *awo'taan* ('shield'). According to Schultz, the Blackfoot called this river {Áhwotan Ótsitamisti} ('Where the Shield Floated Down'). He explained that "The Pikunis [Piikani] were moving camp, and while crossing the river a shield fell and floated down the river."[15]

Mac que pip oupe = Wolf Creek, Montana

This name combines *makoyi* ('wolf') and *isttohkohpi'yi* ('falling down'). According to Schultz, Wolf Creek was known as {Mahkwíyi Istikiop} ('Where the Wolf Fell Down'). He explained that "there was a buffalo fall [jump] here, and a buffalo at the end of the herd went over taking a wolf with him."[16] This name and story, then, predate 1801. They also offer a hint that names could derive from unusual events, but ones that would not necessarily warrant mention in present-day history books. Wolf Creek is a very short creek that flows into the Missouri at the present-day town of Wolf Creek. It rises near Rogers Pass, the route of present-day Highway 20 in Montana.

O mock at ti or the Mississoury River = the Missouri River in Montana and North Dakota and as far upstream as Beartooth Mountain near present-day Helena

From *omahk* ('big') *iítahtaa* ('river'). It is crucial to understand that Ac ko mok ki made no effort to depict the Missouri to its headwaters over 250 miles upstream from Beartooth Mountain. Ac ko mok ki depicts the river only from the point where it exits the mountains and enters the plains—a location now commonly known as the "Gates of the Mountains." Unless the reader appreciates this fact, misinterpretation of other features is very likely. J.C. Nelson shows that the name was also applied to the North Saskatchewan River, whereby the Missouri River may go as 'Big River of the South' {Amiskapo'omakaty}.[17] The American soldier James H. Bradley recorded the Blackfoot name for the Missouri as {O'-much-Ha'-tuch-tah'-I}.[18]

Kiahte ta he = probably Belt Creek, Montana

{Kiahte ta he} translates as 'Belt Butte.' George Bird Grinnell gave the Gros Ventre name for this stream as {kā yā' tī hē'} ('belt') and {nī tsēh} ('river').[19] There is no record of a Blackfoot name for Belt Creek. Moodie and Kaye also suggested the creek depicted was possibly Belt Creek, Montana.[20]

Bess caw ow, Large River = Arrow Creek, Montana

From *beeth* ('large') and *koh?owu* ('creek'). Schultz gave the Blackfoot name of this stream as {Ápsisakta} 'White River.'[21]

In ne thaw ow or Warm Water River = Judith River, Montana

This name is attributable to the Gros Ventre *iniith-oowu-h* ('warm water').[22] Moodie and Kaye suggested it was "possibly the Judith River,"[23] but the identity of this stream is further discussed in our interpretation of Ac ko mok ki's 1802 map on page 82.

Bay in net chay or Pearl River = Musselshell River, Montana

The name combines *byeei* ('pearl') and *niiceeheh* ('river').[24] According to Schultz, the Blackfoot knew the upper portion of this river as 'Shell River' {Otsistsi Tuktai} and the lower portion as 'Bear River' {Kaíyi Tsisísakto}.[25]

E woosse net chay or Red Deers River full of rapids & very strong current = Yellowstone River, Montana

In Gros Ventre, *iwosiihi* means 'elk,' and *niiceeheh* means 'river.' Grinnell gave the name as {Ĭ wăs' sĭ' nī tsēh}.[26] Schultz indicated that the Blackfoot also knew the river as the 'Elk [Red Deer] River' {Ponoká Isisakta}.[27]

Otte net chay or Sheep River = Bighorn River, Montana

The fact that *otei* means 'bighorn sheep' seems to make this interpretation obvious. Grinnell rendered the name as {Ŏt tē' ī nī tsēh} ('Wild Sheep River').[28] According to Schultz, the Blackfoot also named the river {Amúkikini Isisakta} after bighorn sheep (*miistáksoomahkihkinaa*).[29]

Red Deers River or *Pun na kow* River deep, rapids & strong current = the Blackfoot and Clark Fork Rivers, Montana and Idaho

This name derives from the Blackfoot, *ponoká* ('elk'). Moodie and Kaye argue that this is a schematic version of the Snake River "erroneously shown as flowing directly to the Pacific."[30] However, the proximity of the river to Wolf Creek and the Missouri at Beartooth Mountain (to be discussed later) suggests that, close to the *mistakis*, this represents the Blackfoot River that rises near Flesher and Rogers Passes, Montana, joining the Clark Fork at Missoula, Montana. Fidler's notes on Ac ko mok ki's 1801 map indicate that this was a "Big river about 12 miles beyond Bears tooth." The Flesher Pass and Rogers Pass are just under and over 15 miles from Beartooth Mountain, respectively. Further downstream, the river may indeed be meant to represent a larger waterway, or a set of waterways, including the Clark Fork (of which the Blackfoot River is a tributary) and the Salmon River (a tributary of the Snake River), on which sides the Shoshone and Flathead groups lived.

O mok kat ti or Big River = Kootenay/Kootenai River, British Columbia, Montana and Idaho

This was apparently one of at least three rivers that the Blackfoot referred to as ('Big') *omahk* ('River') *iitahtaa*. Moodie and Kaye argued that this is "undoubtedly a schematic version of the Columbia River,"[31] but its direction of flow suggests that it is the Kootenay River, a tributary of the Columbia. The Blackfoot were apparently occasional visitors to the Paint Pots (*Estae-sachta*, or 'paint place') along the upper Kootenay River. Like the nearby "Red Deers River," it may have been meant to represent a set of rivers further downstream, including the Clark Fork, as suggested by the placement of Indigenous tribes.

Mountains

A. *Omok kow wat che mooks as sis* = Devils Head = Devil's Head Mountain, Alberta (Photo 1)

The Blackfoot name combines *iimahkáyii* ('swan') and *mohksisís* ('beak'), thus "Swan's Bill." When Fidler was with the Piikani in 1792 he described {*O mock cow ate che mooks as sis*} as "a sharp cliff" that was "conspicuous" and "remarkable."[32] The name "Devil's Head" is apparently derived from the Cree name of the mountain. Devil's Head Mountain (9,174′) is just north of the Ghost River and north of Lake Minnewanka, near the present-day Ghost River Wilderness area. Anyone wishing to enter the Rocky Mountains via the Bow River or Lake Minnewanka, particularly from the north or west would find it a helpful marker.

B. *Nin nase tok que*, King = Chief Mountain, Montana (Photo 2)

Chief Mountain is one of the most remarkable and important landforms in the Blackfoot world. Its name is drawn from the Blackfoot *ninaa* ('chief') and *iisták* ('mountain'). The mountain is a conspicuous landmark, visible far onto the plains, even beyond Lethbridge, Alberta. From there it is the most remarkable mountain even though other nearby mountains are taller. John Palliser described Chief Mountain in the 1850s as "a high prominent mountain, called the Chief's Mountain, in full view of which the Indians meet in the autumn, and perform some characteristic dances."[33]

C. *Oos ke chip*, Heart = Heart Butte, Montana (Photo 3)

In Blackfoot, *osskitsipahp* means 'heart.' Schultz gave the Blackfoot name of 'Heart Mountain' as {Úskitsipupi Istúki}.[34] It is a noteworthy landmark on today's Blackfeet Reservation in Montana.

D. *Is se cut to yis*, Pap = Haystack Butte, Montana (Photo 4)

Given that Fidler never saw this hill, his use of the word *pap*, an archaic English word for a breast-shaped hill, suggests that his informants described this feature to him this way. Haystack Butte is a very prominent landform between the Sun and Dearborn Rivers. For anyone intending to cross the Continental Divide between the upper Big Blackfoot River and the Sun or Dearborn Rivers, Haystack Butte was an ideal landmark. It was important to people other than the Blackfoot. Nez Perce people told Meriwether Lewis and William Clark to use Shishequaw Mountain (Haystack Butte) as a landmark when they arrived on the plains from the west. Their journals reveal that they did so on 8 July 1806, a day after crossing the Continental Divide. The journals describe the mountain as "a high insulated conic mountain Standing Several miles in advance of the Eastern range of the rocky Mountains."[35] The name appears to derive from *katoyís* ('sweet pine'), here as in other Blackfoot place names a reference to the local stands of subalpine fir (*Abies lasiocarpa*).

E. Ow wan nax, Rattle Hills [not indicated on 1802 map] = likely the Square and/or Shaw Buttes (Photo 18), but possibly an unidentified prominent landmark lying between the Dearborn River and Wolf Creek, in Montana

In Blackfoot, *awanaan* means 'rattle.' If this was not a reference to Square and/or Shaw Buttes, it could refer to Coburn Mountain, which would serve as a helpful marker for those travelling south from Haystack Butte towards the Missouri River above the canyon country around Craig.

F. Ki oo pee ki, Bears Tooth = Beartooth Mountain, Montana (Photo 5)

The name combines *kiááyo* ('bear') with *ikin* ('tooth'). Moodie and Kaye proposed that this landform was the "Beartooth Mountains in the Absaroka Range in northwest Wyoming."[36] The fact that this mountain is indicated on every Siksika map that shows the Missouri River suggests that it was one of the most important landmarks for the Siksika. Careless misplacement of this landmark by any of the Siksika was unlikely; the fact that the maps consistently place this mountain on the true left bank of the Missouri makes an error almost unimaginable. Beartooth Mountain (elevation 6,792') is indicated on only the most detailed modern maps, there being four mountains over 7,000' within twenty miles of it, these being Sheep Mountain (7,368'), Hogback Mountain (7,813'), and Rock Slide Mountain (7,093'). Beartooth Mountain is located at W 112° west, just north of N 47°, about 30 miles north of Helena, Montana. For those approaching the Rocky Mountains wishing to travel towards the Three Forks of the Missouri, it would have served as a good marker.

G. Ma pis sees tok q, the Belt = Belt Butte, Montana

From *amaiipssim* ('belt') and *iiståk* ('mountain'), the name of this hill located between the Highwood Mountains and Big Belt Mountains is certainly apt (Photo 6). Anyone told to look out for it would recognize it immediately. Moodie and Kay proposed that the Little and Big Belt Mountains as a whole were intended, but such an interpretation assumes various incongruities in the map. Schultz indicated that the Blackfoot did refer to the Belt Mountains as {Mapsí Istuk} ('Belt Mountain'), but adds that "the mountain range is named from a butte at the Head of Belt Creek which has a circular rim of rock around it part way to the top."[37] The icon on the map must be meant to evoke that specific butte. Also see the discussion of this feature on pages 80–81 and 84–86.

H. *Ow wan nax*, Rattle Mountain = Wolf Butte, Montana (Photo 6)

Wolf Butte, a prominent symmetrical conical butte somewhat detached from the Little Belt Mountains, is unmistakable from the west, north, and east. It seems to be the best candidate for this landform.[38]

N. *Oos ke chip*, Heart = unidentified

There is no obvious candidate, but it must be a landform near the eastern extremity of the Little Belt Mountains or the headwaters of the Judith River in Montana, for instance the Twin Sisters.[39]

J. *Coon is tick*, Mountain of Snow = the Big Snowy Mountains, Montana, or a prominent point therein

The name comes from *kóónssko* ('snow') and *iisták* ('mountain').[40]

K. *Pawk sis tok que*, Bad Mountain = the Crazy Mountains in Montana, generally, or Coffin Butte specifically (Photo 7)

In Blackfoot, *paahk* means 'bad,' and *iisták* ('mountain'). Moodie and Kaye did not identify this landmark. Schultz indicated that the Blackfoot knew the Crazy Mountains as {Pahtsís Stuksi}, writing that "so many of the Pikuni were killed near these mountains that they came to call them the 'Unfaithful Mountains.'"[41] Possibly, as was the case with the Belt Mountains, the name was derived from a particular landmark. That the Blackfoot would travel from the Big Snowy Mountains to the Crazy Mountains proper in one day seems unlikely. Furthermore, since Ac ko mok ki places the landmark on the right bank of the Musselshell River, the actual feature was likely used to guide the Blackfoot to the place where the Musselshell River emerged from between the Little Belt and Crazy Mountains. Coffin Butte (6,400′) west of Harlowton or less likely the nearby Twodot Butte matches such a description. This was country that might have been travelled by Siksika warriors, but not by entire bands. When travelling south of Judith Basin, Blackfoot warriors must have preferred to stay off the open plains. By travelling south along Coffin Butte, they would have been near the rocks and trees of Coffin Butte, should they need to hide from the Crow. Continuing southward along the base of the Crazy Mountains, they would have been near hiding places most of the way. Today, antelope and rabbits are plentiful there.

L. *Stommix mooks sis sa que*, Buffalo Nose = perhaps Canyon Mountain near Livingstone, Montana (Photo 8)

Stumik means 'bull' and *mohksisís* means 'nose.' The identification of this landform is uncertain. Moodie and Kaye suggest the Bull Mountains, which are south of the Musselshell River downstream from Harlowton.[42] Schultz identified the Bull Mountains as {Istúmik Istukiks} ('Snake's Nose'),[43] which does not support this interpretation but does not rule it out either. But the Bull Mountains are in the wrong place. Given its location where the Yellowstone River emerges from the mountains, Canyon Mountain seems a more likely candidate. It is an obvious landmark as one travels up the Yellowstone River, but also as one travels the Shields River Valley.

M. *See pis too tuck can*, the Owl Head = probably a landform overlooking or in the vicinity of Wind River Canyon, Wyoming

The Blackfoot words for 'owl' and 'head' are *sipisttoo* and *o'tokáán*, respectively. The landform was probably used as a guide to the Wind River Canyon. There are any number of candidates in the vicinity. The shape of T-Hill, a symmetrical flat-topped hill near present-day Thermopolis, Wyoming, can possibly suggest the head of an owl. Moodie and Kaye proposed the Owl Creek Mountains of west-central Wyoming, south of Wind River Canyon, but the similarity in names may be purely coincidental. Schultz mentions the Blackfoot name for a Round Butte as {Sisístotokis} ('owl's ears') but without disclosing its location.[44] An alternate possibility is that Owl's Head is associated with the Pryor Mountains, but that would make it more difficult to interpret the location of the Indigenous groups on the map. Today, there are many landforms named "Round Butte" in the region; two are located near the Pryor Mountains, near Bridger and Rockvale, respectively.

Features on the Plains
Heyt of Land = the Milk River Ridge, Montana and Alberta

Moodie and Kaye identified this simply as the divide between the Hudson Bay and Gulf of Mexico drainage, but it is likely that it refers more specifically to the Milk River Ridge, a prominent ridge along the divide, visible from a considerable distance.[45] Although not high, it collects greater precipitation (including snow in winter) than the surrounding plains—thus its grasses may have attracted buffalo. The topography of the ridge also facilitated its use for buffalo jumps. The Blackfoot knew the Milk River Ridge as 'Big Ridge' {amuh-pow-ekwi}[46] or 'Little River' [Milk River] 'Ridge' {Kinúk'si-sakta Pahwakai}. Based on surveys conducted in 1882 and 1883, George Mercer Dawson described the ridge as "a rough irregular plateau varying in width from six to twelve miles, and extending from near St. Mary River, eastward, parallel to the Milk River for about forty miles. Its northern edge is rather abrupt, and rises in some places as much as 600 feet above the plains. Its southern border is not so well defined and is worn into a succession of deep bays by small streams which flow into Milk River."[47]

***Iah kim me coo* Hill = Cypress Hills, Alberta and Saskatchewan**

The identity of this landform is obvious. Fidler's rendering of the name is probably from *kááyih* ('gap') and *kimiko* ('hill'), sometimes translated as 'striped earth hills,' 'divided mountains,' or "the hills of whispering pines." Other spellings include {Ai-ékun-ékwe}, {A-iki-mi-kooy}, and {Ahya Kimikwi}.[48] Moodie and Kaye agree on the location.

***Cut to yis* 3 Paps = Sweetgrass Hills, Montana (Photo 17)**

There is no doubt about the identity of this landform. The name evokes *katoyís* ('sweet pine'), also spelled as {Kutoyísiks}, {Katoyis} and {Kat-e-is}, and {Kato-wis}.[49] The Sweetgrass Hills are low hills, but the surrounding topography renders them visible from a great distance away, especially to the north. They are also well enough treed to have supplied lodge poles.

***Woos ā kit* Rocks or Bears Claws [only on 1802 map] = Bears Paw Mountains, Montana**

These mountains, detached from others, are remarkable as landmarks and resource-gathering locations.

***Ow wan nax* or Rattle Hills = probably Square Butte, Shaw Butte, and perhaps Cascade Butte, all in Montana (Photo 18)**

These distinctive and nearly symmetrical buttes would have been very useful navigational aids. They are also near the hills associated with the Ulm Pishkun (Buffalo Jump), one of the largest buffalo kill sites in the United States.[50]

***See see ak* Rocks, Snake Mountains = the Highwood Mountains, Montana (Photo 21)[51]**

Siisiiyee means 'snake.' This could refer to Rattlesnake Hill and englobe the nearby Highwood Mountains.

***Neetche beek* or Snowy Mounts Rock = Little Snowy and/or Judith Mountains, both in Montana (Photo 20)**

This name derives from *niichibiik* ('never summer'). This depiction might reflect confusion by a Gros Ventre/Arapaho informant and/or by Fidler himself, as the Big Snowy Mountains are already depicted on the map by Ac ko mok ki. The Big Snowy Mountains seem to have been alternatively considered part of the Rockies or as an independent range.[52]

***See see ah cha* or Snake Mountains = perhaps the Bighorn Mountains, in Montana and Wyoming**

Like the depiction of the Big Snowy Mountains on this map, this representation may result from confusion and/or a late addition by a Gros Ventre/

Arapaho informant for whom the Bighorn were an independent range, whereas they were considered part of the Rocky Mountains to Ac ko mok ki. Alternatively, this could be a depiction of the Wolf Mountains around the Northern Cheyenne Reservation.[53]

Chesterfield House = Chesterfield House, located near the confluence of the South Saskatchewan and Red Deer Rivers, although the remains have never been found (Photo 15)

Archaeologists have used Fidler's recorded coordinates for the post, aerial photographs of possible locations, ground proofing to search for the post. One location does have historical archaeological deposits, but further testing is required before determining whether they are related to Chesterfield House.[54]

The Revised Ac ko mok ki Map of 1801

We are fortunate to have Fidler's redrafted version of the original map (Map 1B) because it includes much information that allows us to interpret the other maps. Fidler certainly produced the 1802 map for submission to company officials in London. Superficially, it appears to represent Fidler's attempt to copy, very carefully, the map of 1801, except for a few changes, probably to explain and accentuate to his superiors the usefulness of the map. But the maps are significantly different. In the first place, the revised map has a noteworthy omission. The omission of the 1801 "war track" leaves out the feature that might explain why Fidler sought the map in the first place. Fidler replaced {O mok at ti}, the Blackfoot name for the Missouri River, with "Mississury" in upper-case letters, the name that would be familiar to his London audience.

Fidler also made significant additions on the second map. These additions are so useful to scholars today because most of these additions must represent his effort to incorporate aspects of the 1801 map that were conveyed only orally. For example, he added the label "Rocky Mountains" to the revised map. He also inserted a note regarding the places identified along the Rocky Mountains that "These are remarkable & high places at the mountains that the Indians fancy has the same appearance as the names given." The note that "the Mountain to the South of the Mississury River inclines almost East—or between E & SE & is considerably lower & not so far across as in Lat. 53° to 49°," which Fidler had known as early as 1793, is also very valuable, because it clarified the cartographic convention—deliberately portraying as a straight line a feature understood not to run in a straight line—that would be counter-intuitive to Fidler's audience in London and to most map readers today. It was also a note that Aaron Arrowsmith ignored when he tried to incorporate this map into his own.

The second map includes a line labelled "Sea Coast" at its top. The first map might easily be interpreted to imply that only the upper portions of the western rivers are depicted. And so, at least notionally, one might argue that the second map might pretend to depict twice the area of the first. It is impossible to know whether this addition was Fidler's attempt to add information conveyed orally, or if Fidler added it because of his own knowledge. The revised map also includes the Bears Paw Mountains. Fidler may have first learned of the Bears Paw Mountains in February 1802, when he collected a second map from Ac ko mok ki. Fidler also noted that the names of rivers to the south of the Missouri were in the Gros Ventre language, rather than in Blackfoot, and that no Siksika person had ever been as far as the southernmost point on the map, "only a chance Fall [Gros Ventre or Arapaho] Indian."

The revised map also includes something of a title absent on the draft map: "An Indian Map of the Different Tribes that inhabit on the East & west side of the Rocky Mountains with all the rivers & other remarkable places, also the number of Tents &c." Fidler must have anticipated that people in London would be most interested in this map for its depiction of territories unknown or little known to Europeans at the time, but Fidler chose to emphasize the map as an ethnographic map. To emphasize how new this information was, Fidler inserted a note to say that of all of the groups identified, "only No 7 [Tattood] and 31 [Cotton nā] have been at the Houses [HBC posts] to Trade."

Three Indigenous Maps Drawn in 1802

Ac ko mok ki's Map, 1802

Fidler acquired a second map (Map 2B) from Ac ko mok ki a year after he acquired the first (Map 2A). Unlike the first, this second map contains no obvious clues as to what Fidler was looking for when he obtained the map. It covers a much smaller territory, centred on the area from the Bow River to the Judith Gap. It also employs more distinctive icons to designate the more remarkable places.

The interpretation of this map is presented cartographically on Map 2C.

Numbered Features

1. *Ow woo tan each e tā mis*, Shield River = Dearborn River, Montana
Unlike on his 1801 map, here Fidler recorded his rendering of the Blackfoot name of the river, which Schultz gave as {Áhwotan Ótsitamisti} ('Where the Shield Floated Down').[1]

2. *Nā tus is sā tā*, Gods River = Sun River, Montana
In contrast to his practice on the 1801 map, on this map Fidler incorporated {is sā tā}, the Blackfoot word (*a'síítahtaa*) for 'river' into most river names.

3. *Un ne kis sis sā tā* = Teton River, Montana
Having rendered *mónnikis* as {oo ne ceese} in 1801, Fidler did so differently here. Note that Ac ko mok ki suggests a confluence of the Teton and Marias Rivers just before they flow into the Missouri. This is consistent with the depiction on good modern maps.

4. *Ki oo sis sā tā*, Bears River = Marias River, Montana
From *kiááyo* ('bear') and *sisaahtaayi* ('river'), this is consistent with Schultz's information {Káiyi Isisakta} as well as Nelson's {Kyo-eis-úghty}

and L'Heureux's {Ka-ye-sis-sok-tey}.² When he crossed the Marias River in 1855, James Doty, emissary of the United States government to the Blackfoot, wrote that the river's valley about thirty miles north of Fort Benton was "from one half a mile to two miles in width, well timbered with cottonwood, and having a soil of reddish or ash coloured loam, which in many places appears well adapted to agricultural purposes. Maria's river is here about 70 yards wide, and 2½ feet deep at the ford with a three mile current. The Indian name of the river is *Kay-i-you-sis-sah-ti*, or Bear's river."³

5. *Kin nacks is sā tā* or Little River = Milk River, Montana and Alberta
Notice how differently Fidler wrote the name on Ac ko mok ki's 1801 map. Here he clearly records a name based on the Blackfoot *i'nak* ('little') and *a'síitahtaa* ('stream'). Compare with Schultz {Kinuk Sisakta} ('Little River'),⁴ Nelson {kinok-kxis-ughty} and {ki-nuh-si-suht},⁵ and L'Heureux {On-ni-ki-sis-sok-tey}.⁶

6. *Naw pew ooch e tay cots* = the upper reaches of the Oldman River, Alberta
From *inaapim* ('old man') and an unknown name for ('bowling green'). It was also recorded as 'Old Man's Gambling Place' {napia-otzi-kagh-tzipi} and 'Two Medicine Lodges' {natok-kiokas} by Nelson.⁷ The first two names refer to the Oldman Gap, associated with myths related to the creator and trickster figure Napi ('Old Man'). Fidler's Piikani hosts had taken him to the Oldman Gap in December 1792, when Fidler learned that {Naw peu ooch eta cots} was a particular place from which the river acquired its name. He elaborated by explaining that

> Indians formerly assembled here to play at a particular Game with by rolling a small hoop of 4 Inches diameter & darting an Arrow out of the hand after it & those that put the arrow within the hoop while rolling along is reckoned to have gamed. This is on a fine level grass plain very little bigger than the enclosed space—one side is within 10 yards of the river—& the direction of this curiosity is directly due North & South—all those peaces [sic] that compose the outer & inner parts are small stones set close together about the bigness of a persons fist above the ground—& they are so close set & neatly put together that it appears one entire ledge of stones—there are 11 piles of stone loosely piled up at regular distances along the outsides about 14 Inches Diameter & about the same height—these I imagine to have been places for the older men to sit upon to see fair play on both side & to be the umpires of the Game. On my enquiring concerning the origin of this spot the Indians gave me surprising & ridiculous accounts—they said that a White man—(what they universally call Europeans) came from the South many ages ago—& built this for the Indians to Play at that is different nations whom he wished to meet

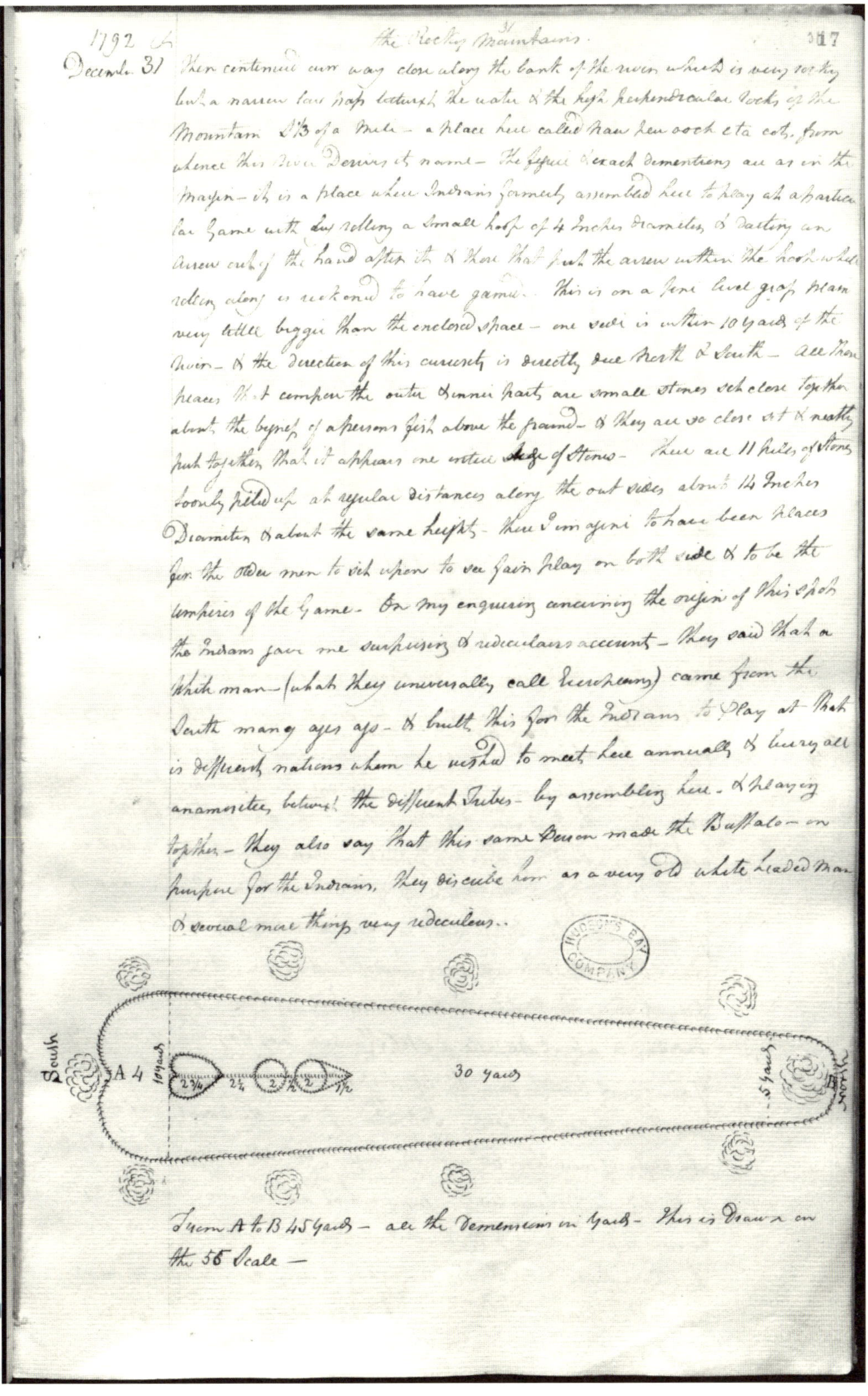

Figure 1. The Old Man's Bowling Green as found in Peter Fidler's journal (Source: HBCA E.3/2, "Journal of a Journey," fo. 17.)

here annually & bury all anamosities [sic] betwixt the different Tribes—by assembling here & playing together—they also say that this same person made the Buffalo—on purpose for the Indians, they describe him as a very old white headed man & several more things very ridiculous.[8]

Fidler included a diagram of the Old Man's Bowling Green in his journals (see Figure 1). In 1854, Jame Doty reported that the Blackfoot informed him that it was Napi's "amusement to play at marbles with enormous boulders or nodules of sand stone and they point out several places said to be his play-ground" (Photo 17A).[9]

To the Blackfoot, the Oldman River extended only as far as its confluence with the Crowsnest River near present-day Cowley, Alberta. See the discussion of the Belly River on Ac ko mok ki's 1801 map (page 66).

7. *Pot too amox ā kim mi* = St. Mary River, Alberta and Montana

The name derives from *paaht* ('inside') and *omahksikimi* ('lake'). Compare with Schultz: 'Lakes Inside River' {Puhtomuksi Kimiks Atuktai} and Dawson 'Banks damming the river' {*pa-toxi-a-pīs-kun*}.[10] Nelson gave the name of St. Mary River as 'South Big Lake River' {opoghto-maxi-kimi-'tughty}, and Dawson as {*puh-to-mux-okin*}.[11] Note that Ac ko mok ki depicted St. Mary Lake at the river's headwaters. The name alludes to the fact that that St. Mary Lake lies in part inside the mountains.

8. *Moocoowans* River = Belly/Oldman River, Alberta

See the discussion of *móókoan*, the {Moocoowans} River, on Ac ko mok ki's 1801 map (page 66).

9. Red Deers River = Red Deer River, Alberta

Richard G. McConnell, who acted as an assistant to George Mercer Dawson on his survey of the Canadian prairies, reported in the 1880s that "The Red Deer River varies in width from 150 to 300 yards; its bed is usually sandy, and sand-bars and sandy islands occur at intervals, all the way down."[12] The Red Deer River {Ponoka-sis-sok-tey} is discussed on page 66.

10. Bad River = South Saskatchewan/Bow River, Alberta

As noted in chapter 1, the Cree name for the Bow River is {as kow seepee} from *ahcâpiy* ('bow') and *sîpiy* ('river'), and the Blackfoot name is {Nā mā kay sis sā tā} from *náámaa* and *a'síítahtaa*.

11. *Mapes sis is tak* = Belt Butte, Montana (Photo 6)

The way that the landform is rendered, and Fidler's note that the Belt is fifty miles from the mountains suggests that the very distinctive Belt Butte itself, not the Belt Mountains more generally, is the landmark Ac ko mok ki was thinking about. Also see the discussion of this feature on Ac ko mok ki's 1801 map (page 71).

12. *Spees tak*, rocks = Highwood Mountains, Montana (Photo 21)

The Blackfoot word *sspii* denotes 'high' or 'tall' and *iisták* means 'mountain.' This identification is consistent with Fidler's note that these mountains are fifty miles from the "Rocky mountains." Schultz indicated that the Blackfoot called these mountains 'Middle Mountains' {Sitosis Tuksi} because they were surrounded by other mountain ranges.[13]

13. *Ow wan nax*, rocks, Rattle Hills = Square Butte and Round Butte, near the town of Square Butte, Montana (Photo 21)

A Square Butte (5,684') and Round Butte are located just northeast of the Highwood Mountains southwest of the town of Square Butte, Montana. Schultz provided the Blackfoot translations for four different "Square Buttes" without indicating which name refers to this butte. One of the four, however, was known as {Ahwanáhksa} ('Rattle Butte'). Schultz wrote that "there are three buttes in this vicinity all named for the rattles used by the Pikunis [Piikani] in religious ceremonials. They are all made of rawhide withling handles and have gravel inside."[14] Given the similarity in shape of various Square Buttes, we regard it as possible that there was more than one {Ow wan nax}, just as several landforms in Montana carry the name "Square Butte" today. Since Square Butte is about fifty miles from Twin Sisters (Heart?), and is near the Highwood Mountains, it is consistent with information provided on Fidler's map.

14. *Moy hoy* River or Mouth River = perhaps the Ross Fork of the Judith River, Montana

Maoó means 'mouth.' The Ross Fork Creek, a tributary of the Judith River, leads toward the Judith Gap (between the Little Belt and Big Snowy Mountains). It appears to be the best candidate for this river.

15. *Phis too keem oo kis cum*, Warm Water River = Warm Spring Creek, Montana (Photo 19)

The name appears to combine *iksistokomi* ('warm water') with *maksísskomm* ('spring'). Warm Spring Creek is a small tributary of the Judith River, which has its headwaters in the Judith Mountains.

16. A very large spring, hot water = Gigantic Warm Springs, Montana (Photo 19)

Gigantic Warm Springs are very copious warm springs. The water is warm, not hot (a steady temperature of 68°F), but has a remarkable average flow of about 50,000 US gallons per minute. It is situated between the North and South Moccasin Mountains just west of the Judith Mountains. The spring must have attracted people for many years for many reasons, and was developed commercially in the 1930s. On a cold winter's day, the steam that rises from this ample spring can be seen from a considerable distance.

17. *Coon is tak*, Snow Mountain = Snowy (and Judith?) Mountains, Montana (Photo 20)

18. *Pawk ik ak que* River = Judith River, Montana (Photo 20)
Probably from *paahk* ('bad') and *aohkíí* ('water'). This name is not consistent with Schultz's rendering of the Blackfoot name for this river, 'Yellow River' {Otokwi Tuktai},[15] but the location seems to suggest that river.

19. *Mis sis sou ry* River = Missouri River, in Montana
Fidler's informants would not have referred to this river as the Mis sis sour ry, but as the {O mok at ti} 'Big River.' The first reference to this river by a name resembling "Missouri" is on a map drawn by French explorers Jacques Marquette and Louis Jolliet in 1673.[16]

20. *Spees tak,* high rocks = Little Rocky Mountains, Montana
The Blackfoot name is simply a descriptive name (see description in #12 above), but the location of these mountains reveals them to be what Schultz identified as 'Wolf Mountains' {Mahkwyi Stukists}, also recorded by Nelson by that name {Muck-kwyé-stokkis}.[17]

21. *Ki oo chis*, high rocks = Bears Paw Mountains, Montana
In current Blackfoot, *kiááyo* means 'bear' and *mo'tsís* means 'paw' or 'hand." Fidler used {oo chis}, which is another Blackfoot word for 'hand."[18] Compare with Schultz: 'Bear Hand Mountains' {Kyai Ochisistukiks}, Nelson {Kyo-'tsis}, and L'Heureux {Ka-ye-otis}.[19] According to legend, the mountains acquired their name from an Indigenous story of "a lone hunter in search of deer to feed his clan. He killed a deer but, while returning to the prairie, encountered a bear. The bear held the hunter to the ground, and the hunter appealed to the Great Spirit to release him. The Great Spirit filled the heavens with lightning and thunder, striking the bear dead and severing its paw to release the hunter. Looking at Box Elder Butte, you can see the paw, and Centennial Mountain to the south resembles a reclining bear."[20]

Mountains along the "Rocky Mountains"[21]

The landforms along the "Rocky Mountains" are discussed in chapter 2 in connection with Ac ko mok ki's map of 1801.

King = Chief Mountain, Montana (Photo 2)

Heart = Heart Butte, Montana (Photo 3)

Pap = Haystack Butte, Montana (Photo 4)[22]

Bears Tooth = Beartooth Mountain, Montana (Photo 5)

Heart = unidentified landform in the Snowy Mountains or the Little Belt Mountains, perhaps the Twin Sisters

Other Features

⊗ = Moocoowans Ridge (Belly Buttes) (Photo 16)

Chesterfield House = Chesterfield House (Photo 13)

I e kim mee coo = Cypress Hills

"3 paps" 3 nights from the mountains = Sweetgrass Hills (Photo 17)

Two small circles near the Sweetgrass Hills = possibly Writing-on-Stone and Pakowki Lake
The rough draft (HBCA B.39/a/2) of this map places the three paps, the first circle, the second circle, and {I e kim mee coo} differently than the finished map does. The placement of these features on the rough draft is more consistent with the interpretation that they represent the Sweetgrass Hills, Writing-on-Stone, Pakowki Lake, and Cypress Hills, respectively.

Two circles near the Bears Tooth = probably Square Butte and Shaw Butte (Photo 18)
The rough draft of this map identifies these circles as "*Ow wan nax*, rocks." Thus, they are the same landforms (presented quite differently) on Ac ko mok ki's 1801 map.

Discussion

It is difficult to guess what Fidler made of this 1802 map. He recorded nothing of his impressions of it. He appears to have seen enough congruities between this 1802 map and Ac ko mok ki's 1801 map that he assumed that Ac ko mok ki's 1801 map was not deliberately deceptive. Fidler, after all, did convey a revised version of Ac ko mok ki's 1801 map to London several months after acquiring this one, not something he likely would have done if he had concluded that Ac ko mok ki was misleading him. On the other hand, except that Fidler may have added the Bears Paw Mountains to his revision to Ac ko mok ki's map of 1801 because of its inclusion on this map, Fidler appears to have been at a loss as to how to "merge" the two maps. If Fidler had doubts about the 1801 map, Ac ko mok ki's depiction of Beartooth Mountain and several other landforms along the Rocky Mountains would have pleased him. On both maps, Beartooth is placed in the Rocky Mountains adjacent to the Missouri River. {Mapes se is tak} (Belt Butte) might have been reassuring and confusing at the same time. It appears on both maps in what was plausibly the same place, but in 1801, Ac ko mok ki placed it along the Rocky Mountains while in 1802 Fidler noted that it was fifty miles from the Rocky Mountains. From our knowledge of the territory, we can reconcile the difference by concluding that Ac ko mok ki's line of the Rocky Mountains ran across Belt Butte in the 1801 map (Map 1), but about twenty miles south of Belt Butte in the 1802 map (Map 2). This variable placement of landmarks in relationship to the *mistakis* mirrors the treatment of the Big Snowy Mountains on Ac ko mok ki's 1801 map. And we can understand how, with appropriate oral information, a person attempting to navigate the territory would not be confused. But we can only guess what Fidler made of the apparent discrepancy. Fidler could once again be reassured by the placement of the "Heart" near the "warm water river," on the top left side of the map. But the warm water river itself, shown to flow directly from the vicinity of the "Heart" to the Missouri in the 1801 map, is depicted flowing from the "Snow mountain" to another Missouri tributary in the 1802 map. Now able to compare the five Blackfoot maps with known territory, we can surmise that Ac ko mok ki did something in these maps similar to what other Blackfoot cartographers appear to have done. In 1801, he attached the name of one tributary (warm water river) to the entire river, but in 1802, drawing the Judith Basin in more detail, he showed various branches of the Judith River system. Thus, in 1802, Ac ko mok ki attached the name "warm water river" only to what is now known as "Warm Spring Creek." He included two other rivers, neither of which he appears to have identified as "Yellow River," the presumed equivalent of "Judith River." In fact, Ac ko mok ki was likely attaching the name of another tributary to most of the river. If "Heart" is Wolf Butte, Ac ko mok ki's map would have been an especially useful map for finding the Judith Gap from any number of directions, ending with finding the Ross Fork Creek (14). If that is correct, perhaps Ac ko mok ki was attaching the Blackfoot name for one of the several left-bank tributaries of Ross Fork Creek to most of the Judith River, just as he had attached the name of

Warm Spring Creek to the entire river in 1801. The Gros Ventre also appear to have used "Warm Spring" and "Yellow River" to refer to the same river.[23] But, it is understandable that Fidler, unfamiliar with the territory and Blackfoot cartographic conventions, made few changes to the 1801 map before sending it to London. The depiction of the Teton River on the 1802 map might have alerted Fidler to Blackfoot conventions. On the 1801 map, Ac ko mok ki depicted it, without any tributaries, running from the Rocky Mountains to the Missouri River. In the 1802, in keeping with an evident intention to provide more detail of that region, Ac ko mok ki showed the Bears (Marias) River and Teton River joining, as they do about a mile before flowing into the Missouri River. Historians cannot help but wonder what would have happened if Fidler had added to his map sent to London, information that the two rivers joined just before they flowed into the Missouri, and if Arrowsmith had incorporated this information in his 1802 map. Members of the Lewis and Clark Expedition may have been spared the confusion, indecision, and delay they did in June 1805 at the confluence of the Missouri and Marias Rivers.[24]

Perhaps in his effort to understand this 1802 map, Fidler asked Ac ko mok ki about distances between landforms and the Rocky Mountains, including the distance between Belt Butte and the mountains, which Ac ko mok ki had placed along the mountains in 1801. If we assume that Ac ko mok ki was not familiar with miles as a measurement, we are left wondering how Fidler translated the information Ac ko mok ki gave him into miles. At any rate, it is difficult to understand how Belt Butte, one of the most obvious features on the map, was fifty miles from the Rocky Mountains, or even how the various landforms estimated to be fifty or sixty miles from the Rocky Mountains were all roughly the same distance away. In one case, Fidler included "nights," rather than miles. It is plausible that a fast-moving party could make it from the western slopes of the Sweetgrass Hills to the nearest base of foothills of the Rocky Mountains in three nights, since the terrain between the two is forgiving. The fact that Fidler estimated some distances in miles suggests that Ac ko mok ki did not estimate those distances in days' travel. Perhaps that suggests that, while Blackfoot-speaking people routinely travelled back and forth between the Sweetgrass Hills and the Rocky Mountains (in three days, according to Ac ko mok ki), they normally traversed the valleys between Belt Butte and the mountains.

The region covered by Ac ko mok ki's 1802 map has exceptionally long viewscapes, thanks to the generally undulating landscape, the very prominent landforms both in the mountains and on the plains, and the atmospheric clarity that prevails for much of the year. For example, the Rocky Mountain panorama, including Chief Mountain, can be discerned easily from the slopes of the Sweetgrass Mountains, just as the Bears Paw Mountains and Cypress Hills can be seen from the eastern slopes of those hills. Beartooth Mountain can be seen from well beyond Square and Shaw Buttes. The unmistakable shape of Belt Butte (Photo 6) is obscured by the Highwood Mountains for those travelling from the northeast, but serves as an excellent landmark for those travelling from the northwest or southeast.

Ak ko wee ak's Map of 1802

Fidler probably acquired Ak ko wee ak's map at about the same time as Ac ko mok ki's 1802 map. There are enough similarities between Ak ko wee ak's map (Map 3) and maps by Ac ko mok ki to have convinced Fidler that the Siksika had a well-developed cartographic tradition, even if the complexities of their cartographic conventions still escaped him. The cartographic style was ideal for pedestrian and equestrian people who inhabited the plains adjacent to the Rocky Mountains. Whereas the beads-on-a-string cartographic style typical of maps drawn by Indigenous communities such as the Cree (see Maps 9, 10, and 11), was ideal for those who typically travelled by canoe, the straight-line convention used by the Siksika is typical of maps drawn by plains dwellers who typically travelled by horse and on foot. Although Ak ko wee ak's map appears to be a genuine and authentic Blackfoot map, its contents were certainly influenced by the fact that Fidler was the map's recipient. Fidler almost certainly had a draft of his 1792–93 journals with him at Chesterfield House, and almost certainly prompted Ak ko wee ak to include places Fidler had visited, for some of the place names on Ak ko wee ak's map are spelled in the same way as they are spelled in Fidler's journals. If this is correct, although Fidler preserved no record of his opinion of this map, he must have been struck by at least one discrepancy in the map. Fidler had paid off Ak ko wee ak as a hunter in December 1801, "as he is a very expensive man to employ and no hunter."[25] Perhaps he came to the same opinion of the man's cartographic skills. Still, it is probably true that Ak ko wee ak attempted to provide an accurate map, but that he was not familiar with all of the locations Fidler asked him about.

Probably thanks to Fidler's prompting, Ak ko wee ak's map is particularly detailed for the region near the foothills of the Rocky Mountains and the Porcupine Hills between the Bow and St. Mary Rivers. The entire area on both sides of the Porcupine Hills was a major travel route of the Old North Trail, is archaeologically dense with bison jumps, and is prominent in Blackfoot mythology. The map includes several features that Fidler had seen or visited during his time in late 1792 and early 1793 travelling with a Piikani band. It is also remarkable in that it includes several locations that would not have served as navigational aids, but as bison-procurement sites. The emphasis on bison jumps is more striking when we consider that

Ak ko wee ak appears to have drawn streams, but rather than give Fidler the Blackfoot name for those streams, he gave Fidler the names of bison jumps and pounds associated with those streams (the Blackfoot word that Fidler rendered as {piscon}—*pisskan* in modern Blackfoot—refers to buffalo jumps).

Fidler had been struck in 1792, precisely when travelling through this region, by bison jumps. Fidler and other Hudson's Bay Company (HBC) traders were familiar with bison pounds (enclosures) constructed where there was enough wood to build corrals into which bison could be coaxed or driven for slaughter, but he was obviously not previously familiar with bison jumps, in which cairns made of rocks or bison dung were used to lure herds towards precipices over which bison were driven. On 5 December 1792, when just north of the Bow River, Fidler noted that his Piikani hosts "crossed a creek a little above a high steep face of rocks on the East Bank of the Creek, which the Indians use occasionally as the purpose of a Buffalo Pound, by driving whole heards [*sic*] before them & breaking their legs necks &c—in the fall—which is perpendicular about 40 feet—vast quantities of Bones was laying there, that had been drove before the rock."[26] Although he used the same term—"pound"—for bison jumps and pounds, Fidler understood that bison jumps were distinctive:

> This kind of Places in the Plains are very useful for the Indians, where no wood is to be had to make one [bison pound] off.—dry Buffalo dung is piled up about knee high & about the distance of 30 yards from each other, & at the rock the 2 sides are not more than 20 yards asunder, but they spread gradually wider all the way from the rock that at the other end the piles of Dry Buffalo dung will be 1 or 2 miles wide—The men drives the Buffalo within this kind of fence all the way to the rock & by the great way the Buffalo makes they are at the very brink of the precipice before they are aware of the Danger—& some men ly down flat on the ground near the Dead men & rise up as the Buffalo passes them & follows them with all speed, to keep them constantly on the run—was not that the case, the Buffalo by going along easily would perceive the danger & avoid it by turning upon one side or the other—all thro' these extensive plains, several of these steep perpendicular rocks are to be seen, which the Indians never fail to make proper use off for Killing the buffalo—they seem to have been designed by nature for that purpose where no woods are to be seen.[27]

Fidler's descriptions of bison jumps are among the most evocative written descriptions of the period. In a passage written on Christmas Day in 1792, he explained how he and his companion were fooled—thus hinting at how bison were fooled—by the lay of the land around bison jumps. At a bison jump near {Spitcheyee}, we saw a small heard of Buffalo running very hard & 2 men on horse back galloping after them which in an Instant we lost sight of the Buffalo; and as there was a few inequalities tho small in the ground we constantly imagined that we should every moment see them run over some small eminence or other & as when we saw them at first before they disappeared, they was at no great distance & running in a direct line towards us—we both prepared to meet them & have a shot—not seeing any thing of them after staying a little time we proceeded forwards & found that the Inds had drove them before a perpendicular rock 29 of which was killed on the spot & only 3 escaped, but with legs broke—that the Inds soon overtook & killed with arrows—as the Indians are always very anxious never to let a single Buffalo escape that has been in a Pound—the reason they assign for this is that should these that escape be at any future time be in the Band of Buffalo, that they might be bringing to the Pound, by their once being caught in the Trap they would evade going into it again—for in general when ever a single one breaks out of the Dead Men—all the rest will follow.[28]

The number of words Fidler devoted to his descriptions of bison jumps must reflect his fascination with them. Of course, that this map features so many places near the foothills between the Bow and Oldman Rivers (and that Fidler spent so much time there) also reflects the fact that the region was a favourite wintering grounds of the Piikani. Bison gravitated there in the winter because the frequent chinook winds ameliorated winter weather and helped cure the nutritious fescue grasses of the region. The broken terrain and springs provided water sources. The Piikani gravitated there for many of the same reasons, but also because the broken terrain offered countless opportunities for bison jumps.

Another interesting feature of the Ak ko wee ak map is a reference to a location at which "Fall Indians" [Gros Ventre] were killed in 1801. Fidler knew about that devastating attack. During the summer of 1801 he noted that "the Southern [Cree] and Stone [Assiniboine] Indians had made war upon them [the Gros Ventre], killing 76 men women & children—in two different places up toward the Stony Mountain in the Moocoowans river & at the Ie kim me coo hill."[29] Fidler likely asked Ak ko wee ak to show him where the attack took place because he attributed Gros Ventre belligerence at Chesterfield House during the 1801–02 season (when this map was drawn), partly to this event.[30] The site indicated on Ak ko wee ak's map seems to be near present-day Lethbridge, Alberta.

The interpretation of this map is presented cartographically on Map 3C. That some of the the features on this map can be identified with certainty makes it easier to limit the possibilities of some of the others, but several pose interpretive challenges. In fact, there may be one or more errors, perhaps because Siksika such as Ak ko wee ak must have been less familiar with the territory featured in this map than the Piikani were, and perhaps because Fidler asked Ak ko wee ak to include places that Ak ko wee ak was not familiar with.

Rivers

1. Red Deers River = Red Deer River, Alberta

2. *Ooms sin ape* = Big Hill Creek
From *sina* ('picture'), Nelson recorded the name as {omisinah}. The name refers to rock art located on the Cochrane Ranche Historic Site, at the base of Big Hill.

3. *Nā ti oo pox* = Wildcat Hills, or Grand Valley Creek at their base
From *natayo* ('lynx') and *sspahko* ('hills'), Nelson recorded the name as {Natayo-paghskin}. The Wildcat Hills are linear in shape and oriented transversally to the Bow River, so the line could represent the hills rather than Grand Valley Creek at their base.

4. Bad River = Bow/South Saskatchewan River, Alberta

5. *Spitcheyee* River = Highwood River, Alberta
The name of this unmistakable place combines *sspitaa* ('tall') and *iistsis* ('trees'). Fidler travelled there in 1792 with his Piikani host band and camped very near the location of present-day High River, Alberta, with about 150 tents of other Piikani and accompanied by visitors: some Cree, four Shoshone men, and a "Flatt head boy, that was caught stealing horses."[31] According to Fidler, the river was "from 25 to 30 yards wide—pretty good current—very clear water, but several small rapids or shoals in it.—This falls from the rocky mountain & empties itself into the Bad river—it runs nearly NEbN to that river—no woods to the Eastwards—& very little to the westwards only." He continued by describing the environs: "here, 2 Good Hammocks of pretty large Poplars—one here & the other about 3 miles to the NEastwards down the river—called by these Indians oo oose spitcheyee—signifying a small hammock of poplars—the hammock that we now encamp at is about 4 miles long close along the Banks of the river."[32] The river's upper reaches apparently had a different name.[33]

6. *Stommix e piscon* = a tributary of the Bow or Highwood River, possibly Tongue Creek (Tongue Flag Creek) or Pekisko Creek, Alberta, apparently connected with a buffalo jump with the same name
It is difficult to be definitive about the identity of this stream. The name combines *stumik* ('bull') and *pisskan* ('bison jump'). On the rough draft of

this map, Fidler correctly translated the name as 'Bull pound River.' The name, however, is not very helpful, because there may have been several streams with this name. For example, David Thompson's map of the northwest shows a river labelled {Stumuk ske piskon}, but that river appears to be near the Lower Oldman and St. Mary Rivers (see page 93). According to Fidler's journals of 1792–93, on 25 December 1792, Fidler and his Piikani hosts "put up at the Bull pound river—or Stommix e pis con about 8 or 10 yards wide—midling water—runs a SE course about 10 miles, where it falls into the Spitcheyee River."[34] Because of Fidler's explicit information that this river flowed into the Highwood River, we can attribute Ak ko wee ak's portrayal of the river as flowing directly into the Bow River to known Blackfoot cartographic conventions already discussed. Thus, the possibilities can be limited to tributaries of the Highwood River despite the portrayal on the map. James MacGregor asserted that Stommix e pis con is Pekisko Creek, while Randolph Freeman proposed Sheep River.[35] Pekisko Creek is a possibility because Fidler's 1792 journals suggest that his party travelled south from {Spitcheyee} before reaching this stream, and the size of Pekisko Creek plausibly fits Fidler's description. Pekisko Valley is replete with potential bison jumps, and is archaeologically rich.[36] However, Ak ko wee ak's maps show Stommix e piscon as flowing between two rivers about which we can be certain, the Highwood River and the Bow River. Pekisko Creek does not do so, and there is no evidence of a Blackfoot cartographic convention that would permit placing the Pekisko River there. So, if Ak ko wee ak was not mistaken, he intended to portray a left-bank tributary of the Highwood River. The terrain between the Highwood and Elbow Rivers is dissected by several small streams. Tongue Creek and the Sheep River are the most prominent candidates, although Sheep River seems too large to fit Fidler's description. Tongue Creek was the place where Napi got his food stolen.[37] Nelson knew it as 'Tongue Flag' {Matsin-awastam}.[38] The river could correspond to Thompson's {I too kai you}, of unclear meaning.

7. *Ooche pay e piscon* = a tributary of the Bow or Highwood River, probably Sheep River, Alberta, apparently connected with a buffalo jump with the same name

This is the most perplexing feature on Ak ko wee ak's map. Fidler must have asked Ak ko wee ak to include this feature on the map because his journal entry for 6 March 1793 mentioned that on this day he and his Piikani hosts "came to 12 Tents of Blood Indians who has been here at a Pound all winter & is now nearly full of putrified carcasses of Buffalo... This Pound is made of Wood all round about 25 yards square...where we put up formerly an old Buffalo Pound here—called oo che pay e pis con— or the Willow Pound."[39] The interpretive challenge posed by this entry is that this Willow Pound was in the vicinity of Buffalo Lake, nearly 125 miles north of {Spitcheyee}. If Ak ko wee ak was thinking of that bison pound, he should have placed it on the far right of his map. Given the plethora of bison jumps in the {Spitcheyee} area and given that multiple features could have the same name, Ak ko wee ak may have been thinking of a Willow Pound near {Spitcheyee}, or he may have been mistaken. Or perhaps Fidler was mistaken when he transcribed what Ak ko wee ak told him. At the very least, Fidler's journal entry of 6 March 1793 offers no help in identifying the feature on the map. Ak ko wee ak's placement of the Willow Pound may have caused Fidler to doubt the accuracy of the map, but other congruencies with Ki oo cus's portrayal of Porcupine Hills area could have reassured him that the map was generally accurate.

Fidler was correct in his journal and on the rough draft of the map that *otsipiis* means 'willow' and *pisskan* means 'bison jump.' If Ak ko wee ak intended to place a river there (whether or not he intended it to be Willow Pound), he must have intended a tributary of the Highwood River located between Tongue Creek and the Elbow River. Sheep Creek is an obvious candidate, but the name does not agree with any known name for the Sheep River, recorded as "Rock River" by Nelson {okotokxi-etughty} and L'Heureux {oko-tox-si-etook-tey},[40] certainly because the most famous glacial erratic, known to the Blackfoot as *Óóhkotok* (Big Rock, Okotoks), is located near the Sheep River. It could correspond to Thompson's {ho kaik she}, possibly meaning 'moose' (*sikihtsisoo*).[41] Interestingly, Thompson's portrayal also shows it flowing directly into the Bow River rather than into the Highwood River. Perhaps Thompson's portrayal derives from a Blackfoot map, rather than from his firsthand knowledge.

8. *E tucks qu āse* = a tributary of the Bow River, probably the Elbow River, Alberta

The Blackfoot name for the Elbow has been given as {O-too-kwa na}.[42] This probably relates to Nelson's name for Shaganappi Point near the Elbow River's Mouth, given as "Half Point" {eh-naok-keet-tox-kway}, in which {eet-tox-kway} would refer to 'point.'[43] The Elbow River was recorded by Nelson and L'Heureux as 'Elbow,' rendered {moki-nist-sis} and {okinistis-etook-tey}, respectively.[44] It probably relates to Thompson's {Hapik-she}, of unclear meaning.

9. *Moo coo wans* = the Oldman River in Alberta, apparently only downstream to its confluence with the St. Mary River

See the note on Ac ko mok ki's 1801 map (page 66) regarding the {Moocoowans} and Belly Rivers. The upper {Moocoowans} River (the current Belly River) seems to have been omitted from this map.

10. *Nam mā tā* = Little Bow River, Alberta

The name comes from *naamaa* ('bow') and *iitahtaa* ('river'), although the name has also been translated as 'naked river' and 'poor river.' The name was recorded as {namagh-ty} by Nelson, and {na-mak-tey} by L'Heureux.[45] It must have been a very convenient connecting route between {Spitcheyee} and the Oldman River, for though it flows into the Oldman River, its headwaters are exceedingly close to the Highwood River at {Spitcheyee}. In fact, the geological evidence suggests that the Highwood River formerly flowed south to the Oldman River through the valley now occupied by the Little Bow River. The upper Highwood River, subject to flash floods, probably deposited sufficient debris on the flat land at {Spitcheyee} over the years to divert its course towards the Bow River.

11. *Stow e pis con* = Willow Creek, Alberta

From *stá'ao* ('ghost') and *pisskan* ('bison jump'), the name may allude to rare "white" buffaloes whose hides were highly valued among Indigenous people. Barb Tilander-Mack gave the name as {stiapiskan}, and Nelson as {stai-a-pis-kun} and {staow-piskan}.[46]

12. Steep rocks river, where Buffalo fall before & <u>break their skulls in pieces</u> = Beaver, Alberta

(Emphasis is on the 1802 final draft of this map.) This is probably the earliest documentary reference to Head-Smashed-In Buffalo Jump. A bison jump known by that name located just north of the present-day Oldman River about halfway between Beaver Creek and Willow Creek is now a UNESCO-designated World Heritage Site, although it is not certain that the present name is attached to the same jump known by that name in 1802.[47] It is now the site of an interpretive centre. At that centre, visitors are always told that the name of this buffalo jump is related to a young man whose skull was crushed by falling buffalo. Ak ko wee ak's reference appears to differ with this reference. The two, however, do not necessarily contradict. The Siksika may have had a slightly different name than other groups did. Alternatively, Ak ko wee ak may have given the name by which the jump was known in 1802. It is possible that sometime later, after the mishap, the name was amended to commemorate the death. Tilander-Mack gave the name as 'Where his head smashed in' {Estipah-kikikikni-kots}, similar to Nelson's {ehtzi-pák-si-kini-kawts}, 'where we smashed their heads in the mud.'[48]

13. *Nā pee ooch e tay cots* = the Oldman River in Alberta, above its confluence with the present-day Crowsnest River

14. Ā (p/k)ay pis con = perhaps the Crowsnest River, Alberta

The location of the river suggests the Crowsnest River, and the name as given here may refer to a buffalo jump associated with the river. Freeman translates {a pay} as 'winter-coat weasel' (*áápaiai*).[49] It may also translate to 'Women's Bison Jump' (*aakíí-pisskan*). Lindsay Amundsen-Meyer indicated that this name seems to have applied to several places. Those include two archaeological sites located near Claresholm and Cayley, the latter of which is officially designated as the Women's Buffalo Jump in the Alberta Register of Historic Places.[50] Walter McClintock mentioned a potential third "Women's Jump" near the Crowsnest River, either along the Crowsnest River valley itself or on the Oldman River between the mouths of the Crowsnest and Belly Rivers, a combined stretch of water he referred to as "Crow Lodge River."[51]

15. Sā kim owp pe ne pee = perhaps the Castle River, Alberta

Etymology uncertain, the name may refer to prairie turnips (*Pediomelum esculentum*), which are known as *saukas* in the Blackfoot language. There was a *Akai-saukas* ('many turnips place') at Cowley, Alberta.[52] Freeman interprets this course as Pincher Creek; however, the latter only took prominence with Euro-American settlement, and seems to have been known to the Blackfoot as 'Small Trees' {*in-oks-spit-zi*}.[53]

16. Stom mix e pis con = St. Mary River, Alberta and Montana

This seems to be unmistakably a depiction of the St. Mary River and Lake (indicated to be "1 Day" away from Chief Mountain and on the east side of Belly Buttes). The name does not agree with the name Schultz and Ac ko mok ki gave for the river, which emphasizes the river's source region. Ak ko wee ak's name agrees, however, with Thompson's {stumuk ske piskon}, which may also have been used for the Lower Oldman River of which the St. Mary River is a tributary. It also compares to a name recorded by Nelson that refers to a bison jump {pa-toxi-a-pīskun}, with the first element {pa-toxi} probably translating to 'high banks' or 'enclosed water' (*paaht-aohkíí*).[54] In any case, both Ak ko wee ak's and Nelson's names for the river suggests that these river bluffs may have been the site of an important buffalo jump. Yet another name recorded by Schultz is 'Many Chiefs Gathered River' {Ahkai'nuskwona Iye'túktai}.[55]

Kin nas is sā tā = Milk River, Alberta and Montana

Ak ko wee ak also drew in but did not identify what appear to be the upper Marias/Two Medicine, Teton, Sun, and Dearborn Rivers.

Other Features

Mooks as sis = Nose Hill, in present-day Calgary

Mohksisis is the Blackfoot word for 'nose.' Nelson gave the name of "the Nose" as {mōk-sis-sis}.[56] Nose Hill forms an eastern extremity of the foothills, a remarkable landmark and vantage point on the north side of the Bow River, from which Devil's Head Mountain is easily seen.

Spā sis = the plateau in present-day SW Calgary upon which communications towers and Canada Olympic Park are built

Portions of this plateau that overlook present-day Calgary are known as Broadcast Hill and Signal Hill, although the present Tsuut'ina Reserve is also situated on this plateau. Of uncertain etymology, Nelson gave the Blackfoot name of this plateau as {spas}.[57] Like Nose Hill, it represents the eastern extremity of the foothills. It offers expansive views in all directions, from the Rocky Mountains (including Devil's Head Mountain), well onto the plains. It was also apparently on a trail along the south side of the Bow River.[58]

I e kim me coo = Cypress Hills

Nee coo tux que = probably a reference to specific hills in the northern Porcupine Hills

Of uncertain etymology, the name could be connected with Pekisko (*pikisko*, meaning 'hills'), or alternatively to the 'Middle Highlands' {sitook-spagkway} west of Cayley as recorded by Nelson.[59]

Cos kā pas suy is = the Porcupine Hills north of Willow Creek, Alberta

From *kai'skaahp* ('porcupine') and *ohsoyís* ('tail'). Nelson gave the Blackfoot name for the Porcupine Hills as {Ky-es-kaghp-oghsuyiss}, and L'Heureux as {Ka-yes-pah-osoyis}.[60] The Piikani may have used these landmarks to find the headwaters of the Oldman River from the north, and one section of the Old North Trail seems to have gone between the Porcupine Hills and the Rocky Mountains.[61] Fidler's party of Piikani went to the important ritual site "Old Man's Bowling Green" (see pages 78–80) on the upper Oldman River by approaching it from the north.[62]

17 [on final draft] Fall Inds killed 1801

The battle referred to here is already discussed on page 88.

y *Nin nase tock que* = Chief Mountain, Montana (Photo 2)

z *Moo coo wans* hills = Moocoowan Ridge, (Belly Buttes), Alberta (Photo 16)

17 [on rough draft (marked with an "x" on final draft)] *as soo coo wans hills* = perhaps the rocky ridge at the confluence of the Drywood Creek and Belly River, near Hill Spring, Alberta

This is the most remarkable landmark in the region. An alternative across the Waterton River are the two hills known as Twin Butte {Natsikapaitomo}, in which *astsikap* translates as 'double.'

Chesterfield House

The circle between the Sun and Dearborn Rivers seems to correspond with the {ow wan nax} hills of Ac ko mok ki's maps. It probably represents Square Butte (Photo 18), the most recognizable, nearly optically symmetrical flat-topped butte in the area.

The 1802 Map by an Unidentified Cartographer(s)

Aspects of the map by the unidentified cartographer (Map 5) suggest that that map was drawn by a Gros Ventre, even though the circumstances at Chesterfield House in 1802 suggest otherwise. The map appears to focus on a region farther east and south than the others. Moreover, the Indigenous groups noted on the map are identified in the Gros Ventre language, and in three cases groups are specifically noted as being "Fall Indians," thus as kin of the Gros Ventre who visited Chesterfield House regularly. Still, especially during the 1801–02 season, the Gros Ventre constantly threatened to attack and kill every fur trader they could lay their hands on. True to their word, they killed ten Iroquois trappers and two North West Company men during the winter, although they never attacked Chesterfield House itself. It is difficult to imagine how, under these conditions, one of the Gros Ventre men would have drawn a map for Fidler. It is conceivable, although unlikely, that one of the Siksika men who knew the Gros Ventre language (like Ki oo cus did), could have provided Fidler with the information for this map. Another possibility is that the map was drawn by a Gros Ventre woman. Fidler's journals mention a Gros Ventre woman who, although scalped, survived an attack by Cree and Assiniboine bands in the summer of 1801.[63] During the following winter, Fidler outfitted her to trap in the Cypress Hills. It is not inconceivable that this woman drew the map for him. A final possibility is that Fidler did not record the name of the cartographer because the map was made by more than one Gros Ventre cartographer. The cartographer or cartographers, however, are unlikely ever to be identified.

As mentioned, this map was drawn by one or more Gros Ventre informants, perhaps informed by knowledge gained from Arapaho kin. Documents apart from this map make it clear that the Arapaho were familiar with New

Mexico, certainly by 1811.[64] The Indigenous groups are identified in the Gros Ventre language and the map shows a region farther south than the other maps. The Gros Ventre were kin to the Arapaho, and Gros Ventre and Arapaho bands did occasionally visit one another, sometimes for months—perhaps years—at a time. As early as 1790, HBC William Walker trader remarked that the Gros Ventre had "been off from" any HBC posts for two years previously because of conflicts with the Cree.[65] And in 1801, some Gros Ventre guided an Arapaho band to the vicinity of Chesterfield House. On 30 October 1801, Fidler noted that "Three Tattood [Arapaho] Indian chiefs came with their families consisting of four young men, five women and seven children: this is part of a nation that never saw Europeans before. They inhabit on the eastern borders of the mountain far to the south of this, they have been forty-four days in coming, they speak nearly the same language as the Fall Indians [Gros Ventre] and are at peace with them, who have escorted them here."[66] Fidler also mentioned on 27 February 1802 that "the whole nation of the Fall Indians" was at Chesterfield House. He mentioned the presence of the Arapaho for the last time on 1 March 1802, when he noted that "The Tattood Indians [are] assembled about the house."[67] So Arapaho people were near Chesterfield House when the Gros Ventre map was drawn.

Some members of the Gros Ventre had also clearly been to Spanish settlements in the south. The map suggests that the Gros Ventre had a similar cartographic style as did the Blackfoot. None of the rivers and landforms is labelled by name, although some are clearly identifiable, thanks to the existence of the other maps. To the right, the cartographer has shown the Bow and Oldman Rivers and the Cypress Hills. The main stream of the Missouri River and Beartooth Mountain, Montana, are obvious. The Sweetgrass Hills and the Bears Paw Mountains are also readily identifiable. The placement of the Sweetgrass Hills to the right of all the left-bank tributaries of the Missouri suggests that the Milk River is not depicted. The rivers that are depicted, then, are probably three of the following four: Marias, Teton, Sun, and Dearborn.

The right-bank tributaries on this map are more difficult to identify with certainty, although the most likely possibilities do not alter the possible locations of the various Indigenous communities very much. Comparison with the Siksika maps offers guidance. One of the right-bank tributaries is shown joining the Missouri near what must be the Bears Paw Mountains. The Judith River answers this description well. If it is the Judith River, the landform indicated on its right bank must represent the Snowy Mountains and perhaps the Judith Mountains. This interpretation would also agree exactly with aspects of Ac ko mok ki map of 1801. In 1801, Ac ko mok ki indicated that the Mountain Crow (No. 2) were located near the Judith Mountains. On the present map, group 4, the Mountain Crow, are located in nearly the same place. The upstream tributaries, then, might be the Arrow and Smith Rivers, with the Highwood or Little Belt Mountains shown between them.

The map is spare enough that other possibilities are apparent. The river across from the Bears Paw Mountains might be the Musselshell River, not the Judith River, in which case the next river might be the Bighorn. That possibility should be considered because a combination of the lower Musselshell and Bighorn River would be a convenient route between the territories of the Gros Ventre and their Arapaho kin. However, if the Musselshell and Bighorn were intended, the identity of the hills near the Musselshell is unknown.

The two downstream tributaries are each associated with a feature labelled {chetow} located, in one case, along the river as it exits the mountains, and in the other case on the other side of the mountains. This word appears to contain the noun final -ɔ'ɔwuh 'land.' A likely meaning is ciit'ɔwuh 'inside land' or 'entering land,' used in reference to a pass through the mountains or a canyon allowing such passage. The Arapaho place name ciitoowuu' 'inside' is used for an area of Rocky Mountain National Park in Colorado that allows passage to the inner meadows and hunting grounds of the park, as one exits the canyon of the Big Thompson River.[68] If {chetow} refers to a landform such as a canyon or gap, the rivers depicted are probably the Yellowstone and Bighorn Rivers. The upper {chetow} would represent the Grand Canyon of the Yellowstone where the river flows out of the Rocky Mountains (Photo 8), and the lower {chetow} would represent the Wind River Canyon at the headwaters (in its western acceptance) of the Bighorn River (Photo 9), and far upstream from where the Bighorn River enters the plains, on the other side of the Bighorn Basin. As in Ac ko mok ki's 1801 map, both rivers are shown to flow directly into the Missouri. Given that the Yellowstone River and Bighorn Rivers could provide a convenient north-south travel route into present-day central Wyoming, it would be only natural that these two rivers are depicted. In that case, the landforms on the right bank of the Bighorn River would be the Bighorn Mountains. This interpretation also reconciles with the placement of the "Fall Indians." On Ac ko mok ki's 1801 map the "Tattood [Arapaho] Indians" are placed between the Musselshell and Yellowstone Rivers. On this map one of the "Fall" groups, the {Nan ni en} are at the same place. This reference is to the Arapaho who were Algonquian-speaking kin of the Gros Ventre (Fall).[69] The only Pacific-watershed river indicated seems to be a reference to the Blackfoot River, which rises near Beartooth Mountain. If this interpretation is correct, fourteen of the Indigenous groups identified, (9–14, 19–26), including two additional groups related to the Gros Ventre, were in present-day Wyoming; ten were located on the Missouri downstream from its confluence with the Yellowstone River, and three more on the apparent route to the "Spanish Settlements." This interpretation is portrayed cartographically on Map 5B. It must be remembered, however, that this interpretation is uncertain. Experts in the Gros Ventre language and ethnohistorians interested in the human communities of the lower Missouri River and what is now Wyoming may be able to shed greater light on the map. Because human communities move in ways that geographical features do not (and some Indigenous territories changed significantly after 1801), we faced challenges in deciding where to place the Indigenous communities on the map. Our challenges were deepened by the fact that we believe that the cartographer(s) may not have been familiar with the territories and peoples located a great distance from their own territory. We have attempted, in the first place, to reflect the intentions of the cartographer(s) as much as possible by placing the circles near the known features as portrayed on the map. However, where the locations of communities as of 1801 are known and documented, we have placed them at these known locations. Still, for most communities, our portrayal does not represent our opinion on where each of these communities was centred in 1801.

4

The Ki oo cus Map of 1802

THE TWO VERSIONS of the Ki oo cus map (Map 4A and 4B) differ significantly from the other Siksika maps. It is impossible to know why that is the case, but we entertain the possibility that Peter Fidler, who apparently had more repeated contact with Ki oo cus than any other Siksika leader, introduced Ki oo cus to certain Western cartographical conventions and asked him to draw a map he could understand more easily. Perhaps, after collecting the other maps, Fidler was frustrated by his inability to extract more useful information from them. He may also have been more familiar with some of the regions depicted on the Ki oo cus map, having probably travelled part of it himself. At any rate, the map seems to exhibit a mix of Blackfoot and Western cartographic conventions. For example, the map clearly shows the "Rocky Mountains" as Fidler knew the Siksika and Piikani perceived them, turning east south of the Missouri River. If the map was influenced by Fidler's interventions, the results are mixed, for the map seems easier to reconcile with Western maps, but also contains some inaccuracies that might be related to Ki oo cus's unfamiliarity with Western cartographic conventions. Whether or not Fidler asked Ki oo cus to modify his map, the map includes tremendously valuable evidence about the Siksika and their territory at the time. Unlike Ac ko mok ki's 1801 map (Map 1A and 1B), Ki oo cus's map appears to have included Blackfoot territory as of 1801, and little more, but little less. Furthermore, unlike the other maps, which seem oriented towards territory with which Fidler was unfamiliar but about which he wanted more information, Ki oo cus's map emphasizes the Siksika portion of Blackfoot territory.

Ki oo cus's map depicts areas farther north than any other Siksika map. However, although it would have been easy for Ki oo cus to include the North Saskatchewan River and the various Hudson's Bay Company (HBC) trading posts that then existed along it, the map shows only a few features beyond the "woods edge" to the north and west of the Great Plains.

Perhaps Ki oo cus, whose band particularly benefitted from Chesterfield House, wished to convey the importance of that post by suggesting that, for the Blackfoot people, the North Saskatchewan River and the HBC posts there were on the margins of their world, too far north for them to visit regularly.[1] Ki oo cus did not intend *woods edge* to refer to the edge of the boreal forest. Few, if any of the Blackfoot had been to the boreal forest, the edge of which was 120 to 125 miles farther north, well beyond the North Saskatchewan River. Ki oo cus was referring to the edge of the discontinuous parkland forests comprising groves of mostly fire-hardy deciduous trees and shrubs such as aspen (*Populus tremuloides*) and willows (*Salix* spp.), although spruce (*Picea engelmannii*) and lodgepole pine (*Pinus contorta*, suitable for lodge poles) could be found in wetter and cooler north-facing slopes and valley bottoms, and high hills. Known in Alberta now as the parkland forests, this was a qualitatively different environmental region from the Great Plains. In the parkland, saskatoon (service) berries (*Amelanchier alnifolia*), chokecherries (*Prunus virginiana*), pin cherries (*Prunus pensylvanica*), and other edible fruit were abundant. It was also where bison and humans sought thermal cover in cold spells during winter. Elk were common in the parkland forests, but virtually absent on the prairie. Ki oo cus's line would not have confused Fidler because Fidler was familiar with the edge of the boreal forest, had himself crossed Ki oo cus's woods edge in 1792–93, and remarked upon it. On 20 November 1792, when in the vicinity of Buffalo Lake, Fidler noted that that "all to the Westwards of us is a woody country, all the Way to the Rocky Mountain particularly more woody the nearer to that place—but to the Eastwards of us the woods extend but a short distance, & then nothing else but one intire plane, for several hundreds of miles to the South & Eastwards—except along the banks of rivers or Creeks that intersect in that direction some few Poplars—& a chance soletary pine is to be found."[2] The line also roughly conforms to the line between what HBC fur traders at the time often referred to as the "large plains" and the "small plains."

The parkland forests were important to the Siksika because they had resources that were uncommon on the Great Plains, but also for other reasons. The woods edge served a navigational function. In 1793, during their return to Buckingham House from the Oldman River region, Fidler's Piikani hosts travelled north by keeping the woods to their west and prairie to their east.[3] When the Piikani went to the North Saskatchewan River to trade, they also tended to leave their families at the woods edge. In 1792, when the men of Sakatow's Piikani band went to Buckingham House to trade, they left most of their families at the Red Deer River, exactly at the woods edge as shown on this map. Then in March 1793, Fidler noted that when just south of Buffalo Lake, the men once again "left here their Tents & families as usual."[4]

Ki oo cus also omitted other features north of the woods edge. He did not include the Battle River. He did not include the Neutral Hills proper, but according to J.C. Nelson, the term "Nose" may have applied to the Neutral Hills in general.[5] He did include minor features such as Tail Creek and Sounding Creek. Tail Creek and Buffalo Lake might have been included because Fidler passed that way with the Piikani in 1793. Fidler had never been to Sounding Creek, so Ki oo cus may have included it, together with the many resource-procurement sites along it, because of the travel route extending south from the Nose.

Just as Ak ko wee ak's map seems oriented towards the locations of bison jumps, Ki oo cus's reveals Blackfoot interest in plant resources. Apart from depicting the woods edge, Ki oo cus's map shows places where berries, pines, and poplars could be found. The map may serve as a reminder that, although famous as a bison-reliant people, the Blackfoot economy was broader than that.

The reason for the inclusion of a small-scale map of the amoeba-like God's Lake (31) (Manitou Lake) may remain forever a mystery. Ki oo cus must have considered it significant because it is the only feature on any of the Blackfoot maps that is presented in a small-scale inset map. When Ki oo cus drew it, he must have conveyed a lot of oral information to Fidler, but Fidler recorded none of this information and he nowhere indicated that he or other traders had seen it. However, the Siksika, probably more than the Piikani or Kainai, must have been very familiar with the large lake. The lake's Blackfoot name, like the Cree name (Manitou Lake) by which it is now familiarly known, both allude to the intangible and spiritual. It is easy to understand why the lake might have instilled wonder. The lake, fed by Eyehill Creek and mineral springs, normally has no outlet, so its waters have become very salty and mineral rich, causing promoters to dub it "Canada's Dead Sea." Today, people gather evaporated mineral salts from rocks along the shore for their supposed healing properties. Given how fascinating non-Indigenous people have found this lake over the years, it is not surprising that Indigenous people who had never visited the ocean were intrigued by it. In 1882, James F. Garden, Canadian Dominion land surveyor, indicated that Manitou Lake was "very picturesque, and in its main part has an average breadth from east to west, of from 6 to 7 miles, extending north and south about 9 miles. Including the long narrow inlets, it stretches from the south-east to the north-west about 18 miles. The banks vary in height from 80 to 130 feet, and are in many places thickly wooded. Several high islands were observed in the lake. The water is saline, but good water is found in the adjoining sloughs."[6]

Ki oo cus's depiction of the lake, like Garden's, offers some valuable historical environmental information because it has been decades since Manitou Lake has drained to the Battle River via that valley. Manitou Lake's water level has dropped for most of the last century. If Fidler's indication that it was fifteen miles across, and if Ki oo cus meant to indicate that the lake was studded with small islands, the lake is very much smaller—perhaps seven and a half miles across—now than it was at the beginning of the nineteenth century. In recent times, the lake has only one large island, but if the water level were higher, it would have several islands. Ki oo cus also indicated a creek flowing out of Manitou Lake to the Battle River. Only on extremely rare occasions in the past century has the water level in the lake been high enough for water to drain from Manitou Lake to Battle River. It is normally a closed-basin lake.

Labels on the Ki oo cus map are more likely than those on the other maps to be descriptions rather than evident place names. Moreover, the English words after the Blackfoot words are more likely to be descriptions, rather than translations of the Blackfoot words. The descriptions reflect the fact that many of the landmarks, even those that were obviously navigational aids, were often also important resource-procurement sites. For example, Ki oo cus indicated that the Cypress Hills, Sweetgrass Hills (Photo 17), and Bears Paw Mountains had pine forests or stands, including "sweet pine," actually subalpine fir (*Abies lasiocarpa*) and lodgepole pine, from which the Blackfoot often obtained their lodge poles. Ki oo cus also indicated where berries were abundant.

Other places refer to animals or parts of animals, either because those animals were abundant there, or because the landform resembled a feature. For example, on the Ki oo cus map Buffalo Lake, Buffalo Tail Creek, and Buffalo Nose all occur roughly along the parkland–prairie transition in Alberta. This area of Alberta was a very important wintering ground for the plains bison and thus there are several places, creeks and lakes that refer to bison in this region. Buffalo Lake (Photo 11) may have received its Blackfoot name because it was a favourite wintering ground for bison, or because from some vantage points, its shape resembles that of a stretched buffalo hide.[7] Other features, such as the Beartooth Mountain and Swan's Bill clearly had less to do with resources that could be procured than with the physical appearance of a landform.

This map is interpreted cartographically on Map 4C.

Labelled Rivers

Ākest sa nas que or Snake River = Sounding Creek/Eyehill Creek, Alberta and Saskatchewan

Just as Fidler's English name for "Swan's Bill" (Devil's Head) was not derived from the Blackfoot name, his English name for this creek may not have been a translation of the Blackfoot name. In Blackfoot, *aká* means 'many,' *[p]iksííksiinaa* means 'snake,' and *ssko* means 'place.' The construction *aká...ssko* is common in Blackfoot place names. It is difficult to see how

Ak ko wee ak's name can be translated as "Snake River." This region at the parkland boundary has fewer snakes than the adjacent prairie. An alternative may thus be 'place of many Cree' ('Cree': *asinaa*). "Snake" was a common way to refer to enemy tribes and this was a time when Blackfoot and Cree tribes started going to war against each other.

Ki oo cus's map indicates that the Blackfoot understandably thought of Sounding Creek and Eyehill Creek as one stream flowing into Manitou Lake. On current English maps, Sounding Creek flows into Sounding Lake (a small alkali lake that dries up completely in dry periods), while Eyehill Creek flows from Sounding Lake to Manitou Lake. The map includes an arrow correctly indicating the direction of the flow of this stream. It also shows a stream (with another arrow) flowing out of Manitou Lake. There is indeed a coulee that runs from Manitou Lake (at nearly 2,000 feet above sea level) to the Battle River (at a place about 1,700 feet above sea level). Nelson and L'Heureux recorded the Blackfoot name for the Battle River as 'Little River' {Kinok-kxis-sis-ughty} and {Kenox-si-si-sok-tey}, respectively.[8]

Red Deers River = Red Deer River, Alberta and Saskatchewan

Bad River = Bow River/South Saskatchewan River to its confluence with the Red Deer River, in Alberta and Saskatchewan

South Branch River = the South Saskatchewan River beginning at Chesterfield House, in Saskatchewan
"South Branch River" was the traders' term, not the Siksika's.

***Kin nax is sa tā* or Little River = Milk River, Alberta and Montana**

***Mis sis sou ry* River = Missouri River, in Montana**
"Mis sis soury" is not a Blackfoot term, but originates from a different Algonquian language. The Blackfoot term is given in Ac ko mok ki's 1801 map.

Numbered Features
1. *Can ne wā see* — a round hill, woods below, none at top, berry wood = a hill in the Stettler area, Alberta
It may be impossible to identify this location. The meaning of the Blackfoot words is uncertain, although it could refer to the Kainai. If archaeological evidence offers any clues, this could be Leithead Hill, just west of Sullivan Lake and north of Endiang, Alberta. Two ribstones (site FaPa-1) formerly sat on top of this very prominent hill. A stone pipe from the prehistoric era, and historic glass beads and other trinkets were found beneath the

ribstones.[9] There is another prominent hill north of Sullivan Lake, but no archaeological remains are associated with it.

2. *Oo chis chis* — hill, no pines, but plenty of other kinds = the Hand Hills, Alberta (Photo 12A)

On 28 February 1793, when he was west of the Red Deer River, Fidler remarked on a "long range of hills about 40 miles off—this is called the oochis chis or the Hand—being seen a long way off & directs the Indians thro these extensive plains—behind this hill at a good distance the Red Deers & Bad rivers join."[10] The name derives from *o'tsíístsi* ('hands') and/or *ootsistsiin* ('strawberry')—the latter may be a translation error by later authors. The hills seem a little out of place this far upstream but they clearly are the Hand Hills east of Drumheller, and were recorded as such by L'Heureux {ot-tis-tis} and Nelson {Oht-tchis-tchis}.[11] The Hand Hills are among the most prominent landforms in southeastern Alberta and were well known to the Blackfoot and other people, including the Cree. The Cree likewise called them *Michichi Ispatinan* ('Hand Hills'), apparently because they remined the Cree of the fingers of an outstretched hand (*micihciy*).[12] The Hand Hills had an important navigational function even when they were not actually visited.

3. *O mock wā cut too can* — ground squirrel hill = probably Gopher Head Hill, Alberta (Photo 12)

Omahkokata means 'gopher' or 'ground squirrel' and *o'tokáán* means 'head.' The hill is 14 miles east of present-day Rumsey, Alberta. When Fidler was with the Piikani in 1793, his Piikani hosts must have pointed it out to him from the west side of the Red Deer River. He mentioned "A small hill in the Plain bearing from here ESE½E about 14 miles called by these Inds A mok wa cut tow too can or the Ground Squirrel Hill."[13] L'Heureux identified it as {omako-kotah-tokan}.[14] MacGregor described it as an "unmistakable landmark" from the vantage point Fidler would have had of it in 1793.[15] Although it appears on only the most detailed topographical maps, it is unmistakable on these maps where it is shown to rise over 175 feet above the surrounding level plain. From the summit of the hill, viewers can see at least 30 miles in all directions, including to the Hand Hills to the south. According to Eric Holmgren and Patricia Holmgren, Gopher Head Hill got its name from being the shape of a gopher's head, but they cite no authority for this information.[16] This hill is very close to the present-day prairie–parkland transition zone at approximately 51° 52' N 112°31' W. It is near the eastern edges of a larger knob and kettle complex located immediately to the west. It is not likely a coincidence that both the Ki oo cus name and local name refer to a rodent, and there is a chance that the Blackfoot name was passed on to later settlers. According to the archaeological records, in the early 1960s this hill had a stone effigy on top of it (Borden #ElPd-44) in "the figure of a man laid out in stones which are now displaced and set into initials. H. Walters and friends did this as kids, also a circular hole about 1 ft deep and 4 ft across, some stones contiguous to it may be part of original mosaic."[17] Like so many of the high prominent places, this hill also contained archaeological remains and was probably of considerable spiritual importance. Several springs can be found around the base of the hill. The Wolf Hill Ribstone site (ElPc-3) was located very close to Gopher Head Hill. A ribstone was also present on this prominent hill, which was rolled down the hill leaving a prominent depression on top of the hill, similar to the one described at Gopher Head Hill. Ribstones (*she-soo-wa-taghs*) were likely carved by and/or sacred to the Blackfoot.

4. *Kee keep* — a hill, pine there = the Wintering Hills southwest of Dalum, Alberta

Nelson recorded the Blackfoot name for the Wintering Hills as {kegh-keep}, L'Heureux as {ke-kip} and {kakip}, and Holmgren and Holmgren as {kikichep}.[18] According to Nelson and Holmgren and Holmgren, the meaning may have been "leaning hill" or "propped up hill." That name may be explained by Richard G. McConnell, who reported that towards the north from Blackfoot Crossing on Bow River, "the country gradually rises until the summit of the Wintering Hills is reached. These hills although their slope southward is very light, presents a steep escarpment to the north."[19] According to L'Heureux, however, the name equated to 'flint knife' or 'broken knife.'[20] Today's name, "Wintering Hills," of more recent origin, stems from the fact that Métis communities established winter villages in these hills in the 1860s.[21]

5. *Hay now too can is* — a hill woods = possibly the hills near Pine Lake, Alberta

In Blackfoot, *i'ni* means 'dead man' and *o'otokáán* means 'head.' L'Heureux records the place as {ini-otokan} and notes it is south and east of the city of Red Deer, without disclosing its exact location.[22] Pine Lake (formerly known as Ghostpine Lake) is the locale for an Indigenous story in which a headless ghost haunts the woods. The legend allegedly originates from a battle between the Blackfoot and Cree occurring in the early nineteenth century,[23] but it may conceivably have been combined with earlier stories contemporary of Ki oo cus.

6. *Nee too tuck kess* — one pine = a reference to the "Lone Pine," Alberta

This name comes from *ni't* ('lone') and *ahtóók* ('pine'). Also recorded as {nitoks-kaskway} and (probably) {olokan-exi} ('head pine') by Nelson.[24] This location has a poignant story behind it. There was a remarkably large pine tree growing far into the grasslands in the eighteenth century. However, it was apparently largely destroyed by a despondent Blackfoot man after the smallpox epidemic of the early 1780s. David Thompson saw the tree in 1787 while visiting the Piikani. He wrote,

> About the tenth day we came to the "One Pine." This had been a fine stately tree of two fathoms girth, growing among a patch of Aspins, and being all alone, without any other pines for more than a hundred miles, had been regarded with superstitious reverence. When the small pox came, a few tents of Peegans were camping near it, in the distress of this sickness, the master of one of the tents applied his prayers to it, to save the lives of himself and family, burned sweet grass and offered upon its roots, three horses to be at it's [sic] service, all he had, the next day the furniture of his horses with his Bow and Quiver of Arrows, and the third morning, having nothing more, a Bowl of Water. The disease was now on himself and he had to lie down. Of his large family only himself, one of his wives, and a Boy survived. As soon as he acquired strength he took his horses, and all his other offerings from the "Pine Tree," then putting his little Axe in his belt, he ascended the Pine Tree to about two thirds of it's [sic] height, and there cut it off, out of revenge for not having saved his family; when we passed the branches were withered and the tree going to decay.[25]

Peter Fidler's journals seem to corroborate Thompson's account. Fidler did not see the tree, but in 1792 his Piikani hosts told him when they were between twelve and fifteen miles from it that "there is a single very large Pine, called {Nee tuck kis}."[26]

7. *E new o kee* — Buffalo Lake, less than Gods Lake = Buffalo Lake, Alberta (Photo 11)

The Blackfoot name for this lake combines *iinii* ('bison') and *aohkíí* ('lake'). L'Heureux called it {in-niw-ow-ki}, and Nelson as {ini-'oghke}.[27] This is one of the few places on the map that is in the parklands, past the "woods edge." In the early 1880s, C.A. Magrath, a Dominion land surveyor, indicated that, in earlier days "buffalo were plentiful in this locality." He described the lake as "a beautiful sheet of water; in size about 12 miles long, and from 2 to 5 miles wide. The beach (sand and gravel) presents a lovely appearance. The water in this lake is excellent, and abounds in large pike and suckers."[28] Since the Blackfoot did not eat fish, the pike and suckers would not have been important to them, but they probably were to the Métis who formed a settlement alongside the lake in the 1860s. There is a large archaeological site dating back about 7,800 years on Boss Hill, on the east side of the lake.[29]

8. *E new oo suy yis* — Buffalo Tail Creek = Tail Creek, Alberta

Named from *iinii* ('bison') and *ohsoyís* ('tail'), this creek's valley was probably a convenient travel route.

9. *Caw sapis spatche que* — little hill, plenty of berries = Drifting Sand Hills near Blackfoot Crossing, Alberta

From *kaatsi* ('drifting') and *spatsiko* ('dunes'), Nelson recorded the name as {kasapō-spatchikway}.[30]

10. *Nee coo tux que* — hill = a prominent point in the Porcupine Hills north of Willow Creek, in Alberta

See the discussion of *Nee coo tux que* on Ak ko wee ak's map (page 94).

11. *Kos caw pus suy is* — hill = the Porcupine Hills north of Willow Creek, in Alberta

See the discussion of *Cos kā pas suy is* on Ak ko wee ak's map (page 94).

12. *Spitcheyee* = Blackfoot name for a point along the Highwood River very near present-day High River, Alberta

See the discussion of {Spitcheyee} on Ak ko wee ak's map (page 89).

13. *Ā kane us que* — woods = probably the stretch of the Belly River southeast of Fort Macleod, in Alberta

From *aká* ('many'), *iin* ('berry'), and *ssko* ('place'), this place name may refer specifically to the wooded stretch of the Belly River around Fort Slide-Out (near Highway 511), between the mouth of the Belly River and the Belly Buttes. The two squiggly lines on the map could refer to the hills on both sides of the Belly River, recorded by Nelson as {mas'-etomo} ('turnip hill') and {sitoko-pawaghko} ('middle ridge').[31] Nearby Fort Whoop-Up (near present-day Lethbridge) was known as {Ākka'-inow-skway} ('Many Kainai died,' in Nelson).[32] While we might assume that that name refers to the Kainai/Piikani–Cree/Assiniboine battle of 1870, the similarity of the name suggests a possible relationship.

14. *Moo coo wans* — hill, berries = Belly Buttes, Alberta (Photo 16)

The name comes from 'belly,' and appears to have gotten its name from the nearby river, but since Fidler indicated that it was a hill, it must refer to the Belly Buttes, which were identified as {mō-kō-an-etōmō} by Nelson (*i'tómmo* meaning 'hill'),[33] {mokowan'etomo} on the survey of the Kainai Reserve, and Mokowans Ridge on topographical maps. This is a conspicuous hill especially when viewed from the west, just east of Stand Off.

15. *Ak ken ne kin ne tak e sin* — a hill, plenty of berries = Milk River Ridge in Alberta and Montana, or a specific hill therein

Joachim Fromhold gave the same name {ukskuni kini tuksin} to the Whiskey Gap that opens through the Milk River Ridge. Meaning is uncertain; Fromhold proposes "valley through the ridge."[34] {Kin ne tak e sin} may refer specifically to the Milk River, using the form *iítahta* for 'river' rather than the usual *sisaahtaayi* (see discussion on pages 73, 78, and 93). Based on surveys conducted in 1882 and 1883, George Mercer Dawson described the ridge as "a rough irregular plateau varying in width from six to twelve miles, and extending from near St. Mary River, eastward, parallel to the Milk River for about forty miles. Its northern edge is rather abrupt, and rises in some places as much as 600 feet above the plains. Its southern border is not so well defined and is worn into a succession of deep bays by small streams which flow into Milk River."[35]

16. *Pock o kee* — Stinking Lake — 10 miles long. Et [east] side little poplar and berries = Pakowki Lake, Alberta

One of the larger lakes in Blackfoot territory, the name stems from *paahk* ('bad') and *aohkíí* ('water'). Nelson gave the name as {pā-kow-k} and {pák-oghkee}, and Doty as {Pah-kah-kee}.[36] The lake is fed by Etzikom Coulee, but usually has no outlet, leaving brackish and greyish water. In the early 1880s, Otto J. Klotz, a surveyor, offered a description of "Lake Pakoghkee, or Bad Water Lake, the former being the Blackfoot name." He wrote that it was

> a large expanse of water with numerous islands, large and small. The extreme length of the lake is about fifteen miles and width six miles. The water is milky in appearance, sweetish of taste, but by no means unfit for use. It is very shallow, no place having been found more than about six feet in depth across the whole lake. The bottom of the lake is a tenacious clay, so much so that it is only with the greatest difficulty that one can extricate himself from its firm grasp. There are a few willow bushes on the islands and shore, and the beach is covered with willow seed capsules, dry weeds, and myriads of dead lizards... The western beach of this lake is stony; the eastern one soft and clayey. On the eastern side a number of deep cut banks (10 to 15 feet) creeks (now only pools) empty into the lake...The islands in the lake are visited by buffalo as they are strewn with bones and fresh droppings. A small rise in the water will cover a large tract on the east side of the lake.[37]

17. *Cut to yis* — good pines, 3 paps = Sweetgrass Hills, Montana (Photo 17)

See the discussion of the Sweetgrass Hills on pages 59–60 and 74.

18. *Pit chicks in ooks as sis* — high rocks, little poplar = Rocky Spring Ridge, west of Sunburst along Interstate 15, in Montana

The name must originate in *pitsííksiinaa* ('snake') and *aksísskomm* ('spring'). James Willard Schultz provided the same name {Piksáksin Otsiskum} for Cutbank Creek that goes along Rocky Spring Ridge ({ahkó ksikumiks} or 'many springs' according to Schultz), suggesting the name of the creek and the highlands may have been conflated.[38] The Old North Trail and Whoop-Up Trail pass at its foot.

19. *Oo saks* — rocks high, pines = unnamed hills north of Blackleaf, Montana

The name refers to *oosak* ('backfat'). Schultz indicated that the Blackfoot knew Dupuyer Creek, which originates in these hills, as {osaks ituktai} ('Backfat River').[39] The hills are wooded and of striking shape. Brian Reeves's archaeological survey of the region shows that a branch of the Old North Trail passed at the foot of those hills.[40]

20. *Nin nase tok que* — the King = Chief Mountain, Montana (Photo 2)

Chief Mountain appears near the headwaters of the Milk River on Ac ko mok ki's 1801 map, but it is placed in the wrong location in both the rough and final drafts of Ki oo cus's map, although the rough draft also includes a large lobe where Chief Mountain ought to be, and where Ki oo cus may have intended it. The actual location of Chief Mountain is shown in grey on Map 4A.

21. *Is se cut to yis* = Haystack Butte, near Augusta, Montana

As with Chief Mountain, this feature poses some interpretive challenges. The name conforms exactly to what we interpreted on Ac ko mok ki's map as Haystack Butte. If that was intended, the adjacent river is the Sun River, with the Teton and Marias also depicted. The location of the landform, however, implies Beartooth Mountain (shown in light grey on our map).

22. *Ki oochis* — Bear's Paw, high rocks pines = Bears Paw Mountains, Montana

The placement of the Bears Paw Mountains on this map is consistent with that of Ac ko mok ki's 1801 map.

23. *Ow wan nax* — high rocks, pines, rattle hills = probably the Highwood Mountains, and the outlying Square Butte, in Montana (Photo 21)

See the discussion of feature 13 on Ac ko mok ki's 1802 map (page 81).

24. *At che kates tak que* — high rocks pines = probably the Judith Mountains, Montana (Photo 20)

Probably from *otahko* ('yellow') and *iisták* ('mountains'), Schultz recorded the name of the Judith Mountains as {Otokwi Istuki}.[41]

25. *Moo nis* — a little hill = probably "Bull's Forehead," about six miles upstream of Chesterfield House associated with medicine wheels, but perhaps Hunting Hill

Mooni'si means 'forehead' in Blackfoot. This name is consistent with a landform described by Brian Reeves and Margaret Kennedy as the "Bull's Forehead," which is "a visually prominent 2 km long ridged and benched landform standing 107 m above the Red Deer River valley. From the west, the upper ridge profile resembles the forehead of a buffalo bull." Reeves and Kennedy explain that from a medicine wheel constructed across the river from the Bull's Forehead, a person can see both the Bull's Forehead and the forks of the Red Deer and South Saskatchewan Rivers.[42] Nelson {moh-nisey} and L'Heureux {mo-nice} also noted the existence of a 'forehead' in this vicinity.[43] Its location on the map appears too far upstream from the mouth of the Red Deer, but that might be attributed to the use of an "elastic" scale, as is the case elsewhere on the map. Terry Beaulieu has argued that *moo nis* refers to Hunting Hill, located along the Red Deer River directly across from the mouth of Matzhiwin Creek, about nine miles west of Steveville, Alberta.[44] The location seems correct, and Hunting Hill is archaeologically dense. However, Nelson recorded Hunting Hill as {sah-a-misapi}.[45] Specifically, Nelson indicated that there are three hills called {sah-a-misapi} or "Spy Hill." One is "between Coal Banks [Lethbridge] and Rocky Coulée," probably near the Hunting Hill Coulée.[46] Another {sah-a-misapi} is "N. of Red Deer River," and we argue that this is the location known as Hunting Hill today. *Sáami* means "go hunt meat," and appears to have been transcribed by Nelson indifferently as "Spy Hill" and "Hunting Hill."[47] Nelson lists {sah-a-misapi} as meaning "spy hill."[48] He also identifies the modern Hunting Hill (on the Red Deer River) as "Hunting Hill" on the accompanying "Geological Map."

26. *Eech e seek kitche stoup* — a little poplar = probably the Mud Buttes southeast of Consort, Alberta (Photo 13)

This name may combine *a'síítsik* ('poplar') and *ki'tsi* ('plateau') or its derivative *ki'tsóóht* ('on top'). The Mud Buttes are located between Sounding Creek and the Neutral Hills. These whimsically patterned badlands are not tall—they rise about fifty metres above the surrounding prairie—but offer distant vistas from their tops. As Ki oo cus indicated, they support groves of poplar, but also chert pebbles.

27. *Chis seeks* — little poplar = possibly the Misty Hills, Alberta (Photo 14)
Perhaps the name comes from *a'síítsik* ('poplar'). The Misty Hills are located between the Mud Buttes and Sounding Creek. These hills, almost 280 feet high, are prominent. They would have been an easy landmark for people travelling to the Buffalo Nose (Nose Hill) in the Neutral Hills. They contain a creek and spring, wood, plenty of berry shrubs and game animals, chert and quartzite outcroppings, as well as major archaeological sites.[49]

28. *A qun is que* — plenty of berries = unidentified place on Sounding Creek near Esther, Alberta
{*A qun is que*} seems to combine *aká* ('many'), *iin* ('berry') and *ssko* ('place'). The dotted line that crosses Sounding Creek five days' journey south of Buffalo Nose (and about halfway to Chesterfield House) implies a location near where Sounding Creek changes course from generally eastward to northward flowing (not far from where Highway 41 crosses the creek). However, it is impossible to be precise because the Ki oo cus map, which shows the course of the creek as a broad arc, does not reveal that the route between Buffalo Nose and Chesterfield House roughly parallels Sounding Creek for some distance. The indication that there were "plenty of berries" at feature 28 offers no clue to the location because is not possible now to guess where berries might have been plentiful along Sounding Creek in 1801. However, there are many archaeological sites along a relatively straight line between the Nose and the confluence of the Red Deer and South Saskatchewan Rivers, including a newly found buffalo jump and an archaeological site containing horse bones in the upper layers.[50] Thus, this appears to have been a well-travelled route and camping location by First Nations people both before and after contact.

29. *Ocks as sax e kim me* — berries = unidentified wooded hills
This is a difficult feature to identify. The name appears to combine *ohksisís* ('nose') and *kimiko* ('hill'). This matches the name {kghx-yx} given by Nelson to the Neutral Hills.[51] However, its position on the Ki oo cus map suggests a location east of the route from Nose Hill to Chesterfield House on the right bank of Sounding Creek. The discrepancy may represent a transcription error by Fidler wherein Ki oo cus attached {ooks as sax e kim me} to feature 30 (Buffalo Nose), where no Blackfoot name is given. However, the rough draft of the map, on which the name appears beside feature 29 rather than in a legend, undermines this guess. It is also possible, as Nelson implied, that the Blackfoot name could apply to Nose Hill specifically, and to the long range of hills of which Nose Hill is a visually prominent but not particularly tall part. The possibilities, both of which are problematic, are discussed in turn.

Although Fidler wrote that "berries" could be found at feature 29, the markings on the Ki oo cus map suggest hills, perhaps more substantial than the Misty Hills and Mud Buttes. If feature 28 is near the location at which Highway 41 crosses Sounding Creek, feature 29 would likely be within a two-day journey of the crossing. There are no obvious or substantial hills in that region, although there are some hills between Salt Lake and Dragon Lake (at about N 51°39′ and W 110°13′). However, it is implausible that the Blackfoot would have associated these hills with Buffalo Nose, or the Neutral Hills more generally.

If we assume that Ki oo cus did attach the name {Ocks as sax e kim me} to feature 29, other possibilities should be considered. Substantial and well-wooded hills extend westward from the immediate right bank of Sounding Creek for about fifteen miles. These are part of a chain of hills about fifty miles long running roughly east-west, portions of which are now known as the Neutral Hills. If Ki oo cus was thinking of a portion of those hills, it is understandable that he would have used the name {Ocks as sax e kim me}, but it is odd that he would have placed feature 29 so far above Sounding Lake on both the rough and polished drafts of the map.

The Bodo Sand Hills, at the extreme east end of these hills, are too far east to be candidates for feature 29, but those hills illustrate how highly Indigenous people may have valued the resources of this entire chain of hills. The archaeological importance of the Bodo Sand Hills was unknown until 1995, when earth-moving machinery connected with pipeline development accidentally unearthed bison skulls there.[52] Since then archaeologists have described those hills as one of the largest archaeological sites on the Canadian prairies, leading the University of Alberta to establish an archaeological field school at the hamlet of Bodo and stimulating the formation of the Bodo Archaeological Society. Several studies have shown that Indigenous people—almost certainly including the ancestors of the Blackfoot—used the exceptionally archaeologically rich Bodo Sand Hills intermittently for about five thousand years, including and into the period shortly before and after the arrival of Europeans. The hills, consisting of stabilized sand dunes, were attractive as a bisoninsert hyphen: bison-procurement site, but also because of the accessible fresh water and abundant berries.[53] The recent and serendipitous discovery of this site suggests that countless archaeological sites still remain undiscovered in the soils of this region. Moreover, the fact that an archaeological site widely considered one of the most important on the Canadian prairies is not included on Ki oo cus's map reinforces this impression.

30. Buffalo Nose = Nose Hill/the Nose on the western edge of the Neutral Hills in central Alberta (Photo 10)

For the Blackfoot name, see note for landmark 29. "Buffalo Nose," "the Nose," or "Nose Hill" appears to have been one of the key features of this map, and a very important gathering place of the Siksika, the rest of the Blackfoot-speaking people, and other Indigenous communities including the Gros Ventre, Tsuut'ina, Cree, and Assiniboine. Both the Cree and Blackfoot referred to this singular, very prominent hill as Nose Hill in their own languages. The hill rises about four hundred feet above the surrounding plains, making it visible from a considerable distance, and allowing it to offer expansive vistas over the prairies, particularly to the south. The Neutral Hills generally, but especially the Nose specifically, located at the margins of the territories of several Indigenous people and well known to all of them, were an important gathering place particularly when trying to negotiate peace agreements (or sometimes agreements to mount raids together against common enemies). For example, in 1816, John Steward McFarlane, at the HBC's Paint River House (at the mouth of the Vermilion River) wrote to James Bird at Edmonton to inform him that Tsuut'ina, Piikani, Siksika, and Kainai "are all to assemble at the nose and smoke tobacco and after they intend to look out for the Stone Indians."[54] In February 1828, the Edmonton House journals noted that a party of Gros Ventre and Tsuut'ina visitors at Edmonton had informed the traders that "a rendezvous was fixed upon between the Stone Indians and themselves this summer (at the Nose) or at this Establishment [Edmonton] for the purpose of establishing a Peace amongst themselves."[55] Later in the same year, the journals noted that a band of Stoney had made peace with a band of Siksika and that the two people intended to meet at the Nose.[56] The fact that the hills had abundant animal, plant, water, and mineral (chert) resources enhanced its attractiveness as a gathering place of many people. There are dozens of archaeological sites on the top of Nose Hill, representing multiple camping episodes, and suggesting that Indigenous people have gathered there often over centuries. The draft penciled version of the Ki oo cus map includes three semi-circular icons, rather than the one on the inked version, suggesting that Ki oo cus may have intended to include the rest of the Neutral Hills extending about eighteen miles east of the Nose, and consisting of three sections divided by two noticeable valleys.

31. *Nā too o kee* — or Gods Lake = Manitou Lake, Saskatchewan (Photo 22)

The name comes from the Blackfoot words *naató'si* ('god/sun') and *aohkíí* ('lake'). Today's name of the lake is explained by the fact that "manitou" is the Cree equivalent to *naató'si*. On the map, Fidler indicated that it was a five days' march from Buffalo Nose to Gods Lake. Numerous archaeological sites including cairns, tipi rings, and rock alignments are located near the lake. This feature is discussed in more detail on pages 101–02.

32. *Now tok que* — a lake = Sounding Lake, Alberta
The name of this lake recalls the Blackfoot name, which comes from *ohtako* ('sound'). Nelson gave the name as {oghta-kway}.[57] The lake is prominent in Blackfoot and Cree mythology, according to which the lake received its name when an eagle with a snake in its claws flew out of the lake making a loud sound like thunder.[58] The lake is ephemeral, drying up completely during droughts, and somewhat saline when it fills. The lake was the site of the conclusion of a major adhesion to Treaty 6 in 1879.

33. Red Deers River = Yellowstone River, in Montana and Wyoming
On the rough draft, this river is clearly shown to flow into the Missouri. The omission of the line from the Rocky Mountains to the Missouri River on the more polished draft is clearly an error in transcription.

34. *Kee ow chee* — a hill = perhaps a hill overlooking Manitou Lake, or the sand hills south of Manitou Lake, in Saskatchewan
Ki oo cus may have been referring to any one of several hills on the east side of Manitou Lake, but he may also have been referring to the stabilized sand hills south of the lake. These hills, replete with fresh-water sloughs, must have supported bison herds, many kinds of berries, and thermal cover for animals and humans during the winter. The Blackfoot name may include the words for 'bear' and 'paw.'

Other Features

Woods edge = the edge of the parkland forests on the western and northern margins of the Great Plains
The significance of this line is discussed on pages 99–101.

Seven Persons Creek and Murray Lake, in Alberta (running from the Western Cypress Hills to the Bad River)
Nelson gave the name of this creek as 'Seven Persons' {ikitsíka-etapix}.[59] *Ihkitsik* is the Blackfoot word for 'seven.'

Swift Current Creek, in Saskatchewan (running from the Cypress Hills to the South Saskatchewan River)
According to Schultz, the Blackfoot called this the 'Swift-Flowing River' {iksikwoyi ituktai}.[60]

Chin Coulee and Chin Lake, in Alberta (running roughly parallel to and south of the Oldman River)

Nelson explained that the current English name is derived from the Blackfoot name {misto-amo} 'The beard.'[61] In contemporary Blackfoot, *mísstoan* means 'beard,' and *mohpsskína'* means 'chin.' George Mercer Dawson described the Chin Coulee in 1884 as "the most remarkable part of the valleys traversing this part of the plain, and from the Chin to its junction with Peigan Creek... has a length of nearly seventy miles. It is a trough-like valley from half a mile to a mile in width, and depressed from 150 to 250 feet below the prairie level. A number of small lakes lie in the valley and are connected by a little flowing water at seasons of flood, but during the summer some of them dry up completely."[62] There are apparently springs at various locations long the valley walls. The lip of the coulee has many tipi rings and a notable stone effigy.[63]

Day's marches indicated by circles

The length of apparent day's marches vary from about thirty miles per day between the Cypress Hills and Chesterfield House to about nine miles per day between Chesterfield House and the Neutral Hills. For further discussion of this feature of this map, see chapter 5.

Highwood, Oldman, Belly, Marias/Two Medicine, Teton, and Sun Rivers

Although not labelled on the map, these rivers appear to be depicted from north to south on this map between the Bad (Bow) and Mis sis sou ry (Missouri) Rivers.

Discussion

The Red Deer River, and a few features connected with it, are conspicuous on this map. The English name of this river can be attributed to the fact that the North American elk (*Cervus canadensis*), which was common in the Red Deer River region, reminded British traders of the European red deer (*Cervus elaphus*). However, the name appears to have been a translation of the Cree *Was-ka-sioo* and Blackfoot names for this river. That the Blackfoot (and Crow) also named the Yellowstone River, and another river west of the Rocky Mountains, as indicated by Ac ko mok ki's 1801 map, after the elk, would not have confused anyone. They also had the same name, {O mock at ti} ('Big River'), for the North Saskatchewan, Missouri, and Kootenay Rivers, merely differentiating them by adding "northern" or "southern" if the referent was ambiguous. Ki oo cus had to include the Red Deer and Bad (Bow) Rivers on his map to include the location of Chesterfield House, but the river valley was obviously important at the time, as it had been for many centuries before these maps were made. Ki oo cus included several remarkable places along the Red Deer River (see

2, 3, 4, and 25). Archaeologists have identified thousands of archaeological sites (including tipi rings, drive lanes for buffalo pounds and jumps, and medicine wheels) within a mile of either side of the river. During the 1970s, Gary Adams conducted an archaeological survey of the Red Deer River for approximately 35 to 50 miles between Blood Indian Creek and the Saskatchewan-Alberta border, and identified 693 sites within a mile of the river, approximately seven archaeological sites per mile![64] Since then, archaeologists have added to this number. Indigenous people must have started using the resources of the valley very soon after it became habitable with the retreat of the glaciers, 11,000 to 8,000 years ago, although the valley was used particularly intensively in the Late Precontact Period.[65]

Ki oo cus included only one tributary of the Red Deer River, Buffalo Tail Creek, a short creek that drains Buffalo Lake. Ki oo cus may have included it because Fidler was familiar with the creek and lake, but it was also a major destination for trading parties headed northward past the woods edge to HBC trading posts on the North Saskatchewan River. The lake, situated in knob and kettle topography, would be easiest to find by following Buffalo Tail Creek from the Red Deer River. It is interesting that Ki oo cus showed crossed lines at the mouth of the Buffalo Tail Creek, as if two creeks entered the Red Deer River from opposite sides. This may be a transcription error, where Fidler drew Tail Creek all the way to the Rocky Mountains rather than stopping at the Red Deer River. Alternatively, the lower line represents an effort to show that the Red Deer River changes direction exactly at the point where it receives the waters of Buffalo Lake. From its headwaters in the Rocky Mountains, the river flows generally northeast until it reaches the site of the present-day city of Red Deer, and then east to the mouth of Buffalo Tail Creek, before flowing almost due south for the next sixty miles. If so, Fidler may not have realized the fact, for he included both lines in his redrafted map.

As with the Red Deer River, Fidler used the English names for the Bow (then also known as the "Bad River") and "South Branch River." HBC traders referred to the North Branch and South Branch of the "Saskatchewan," "Saskatchewan" being derived from the Cree for "Swift Current." We can only guess about the origin of "Bad River." The river may have been difficult to ford both in the summer and winter because of its strong current in places. The fact that only the western portion of the river carried that name seems to support this guess, since upper sections of the river were more difficult to ford than lower portions. It has been speculated that another name for portions of the river, "Bow River," suggests that good wood for bows could be acquired there.[66]

The draft and final versions of this map include several tributaries of the Bad River/South Branch River. Only the more polished map shows the tributary originating in the Cypress Hills and entering the South Saskatchewan

River downstream from Chesterfield House. This is Swift Current Creek, which flows generally northeastward from Cypress Hills to the South Saskatchewan River through the present-day community of Swift Current, Saskatchewan. The mouth of that creek must have been near the eastern margins of Siksika territory where any Siskika could expect to encounter Gros Ventre bands, with whom the Siksika were generally at peace, or Plains Assiniboine bands, with whom the Siksika were increasingly at odds, during the early nineteenth century.

Both versions of the map also show Seven Persons Creek/Peigan Creek. Seven Persons Creek and Peigan Creek rise in low hills north of Pakowki Lake and in the Cypress Hills and accept the water of several tributaries draining the northwestern portion of the Cypress Hills before entering the South Saskatchewan River at Medicine Hat, Alberta. This valley provided an excellent north-south route through the otherwise arid prairies between the South Saskatchewan River and the Missouri River.

The line that crosses Seven Persons Creek at a right angle to it represents Chin Coulee, with Chin Lake apparently represented by a small circle. Chin Coulee is another underfit valley formed by glacial meltwaters. Today, this deep coulee has been dammed to create several reservoirs. Running more than sixty miles across otherwise exposed and arid prairies, it was an excellent route between the Cypress Hills and the Oldman River. Ki oo cus clearly understood that, on its western end, Peigan Creek flows into this underfit valley as it turned north as Seven Persons Creek. Chin Coulee and Forty Mile Coulee, a valley that runs northwest from the western portion of Chin Coulee towards the confluence of the Red Deer and Oldman Rivers, and the terraces above them, have a plethora of archaeological sites dating back thousands of years.[67] By including the Chin Coulee on this map (and implying, as we will argue, a travel route through Forty Mile Coulee), Ki oo cus was hinting at the significance of these oases on the otherwise dry prairies.

5

Tours and Trips on the Ac ko mok ki and Ki oo cus Maps

IN ADDITION TO INFORMATION ABOUT PLACES, Ac ko mok ki's 1801 map (Map 1A, 1B, and 1C) and Ki oo cus's map (Map 4A and 4B) contain clues about routes that Blackfoot people followed between landmarks and across their territory.

The War Track of 1801

The Blackfoot were acquainted with warfare. In 1854, James Doty noted that the Blackfoot "make frequent encursions into the territory of far distant Tribes, as the Snakes, Crows, Sioux & Flat Heads. These distant forays often consuming a year and sometimes two or three, are generally undertaken with the view of obtaining horses."[1] The dotted line in Ac ko mok ki's 1801 map, showing "the war track in 1801," offers a clue to the origins of the maps. The Chesterfield House journals show that a party of 175 Siksika men left Chesterfield House on 22 November 1800, and arrived back at Chesterfield House on 10 January 1801, after failing to find any enemy bands.[2] Peter Fidler may have been inspired by the knowledge that this party travelled far to the southwest of Chesterfield House to ask Ac ko mok ki for a map. Ac ko mok ki traced the route of the Blackfoot 41-day war excursion of 1800–01 on the 1801 map. It shows that the warriors travelled first south, to the western end of the Cypress Hills, then swung west until they skirted the western end of the West Butte of the Sweetgrass Hills. From there they travelled almost due southwest of the {ow wan nax} hills, crossed the Sun River near Sun River Crossing (near where Fort Shaw would later be built) and crossed the Missouri River just downstream from Beartooth Mountain (strengthening the argument that the {ow wan nax} hills are Square and Shaw Buttes). Once past the very rough country around Beartooth Mountain, they apparently travelled up the Missouri

Valley in search of enemies. On their return, they may have followed the Sixteenmile Creek (between the Big Belt and Bridger Mountains) up to the upper Smith River Valley, or travelled the Gallatin River/Bozeman Pass/Shields River route to find the Smith River. The Smith River Valley is broad and grassy. From there they travelled north to the Sweetgrass Hills, Cypress Hills, and back to Chesterfield House (Photo 15). Given that the expedition cannot have involved fewer than 800 miles of travel, the party covered well over 20 miles per day, something plausible for young male warriors travelling light, but not something that entire bands could achieve.

The fact that the 1801 map included the 1801 "war track" suggests that the return of the relevant war party prompted Fidler to acquire the first map, although an additional factor may have influenced him. Fidler indicated that, on 14 February 1793, during his winter with the Piikani, when at a pine grove along the Red Deer River, an old man said that they were about 30 miles from the confluence of the Red Deer and Bad (South Saskatchewan Rivers), when in fact they were more than three times as far.[3] Still holding to his mistaken belief on 3 February 1801, Fidler sent four men on horseback up the Red Deer River to collect pine pitch to seal bateaux then being constructed at Chesterfield House.[4] The men returned on 15 February 1801, "having not seen a single pine tree...although they say they went five successive days journey up the river." Fidler sceptically wrote, "I imagine they were very short ones."[5] While the men were away, Fidler had collected this first map from Ac ko mok ki, but Fidler obviously had not asked Ac ko mok ki about the location of the pine grove. One might hope that Fidler later apologized to these men, because Ki oo cus's 1802 map shows that the pines at {Kee Keep} (Wintering Hills) (where Fidler probably was in 1793) were located far up the Red Deer River.

Ac ko mok ki's Tour of the Old North Trail

Aside from the dotted line that shows the war track of 1801, Ac ko mok ki's map appears to shed significant light upon the Old North Trail, as described by Brings-Down-the-Sun, and other unnamed Indigenous trails that European settlers later also used, including the Bridger and Bozeman Trails. Blackfoot travels had been far more extensive by 1905 when Brings-Down-the-Sun described the route, but Ac ko mok ki's map appears to corroborate his description of the Old North Trail. The information is portrayed in different ways on the two versions of the map. The 1801 map indicates the number of "Days" required to get from one point to the other, while the 1802 map states, probably more consistent with what Fidler was told, that the numbers correspond to the "number of Nights the Inds Sleep in going from one place to the other." By "one place to the other," Ac ko mok ki did not mean to suggest that they travelled between each of those places per se, but that they travelled alongside them, using them as markers, while they themselves typically travelled outside of the forests, and east of the foothills. Since almost all of these landforms were also easily identifiable well onto the plains, it is difficult to gauge when a party was considered to be *at* one of the places on the map. Fidler recorded information that the Blackfoot slept ten nights travelling from Chief Mountain to Beartooth Mountain, about 160 miles. That included two nights between Chief Mountain and Heart Butte, five more nights to get to Haystack Butte, and three more to reach the Missouri River near Beartooth Mountain. While the Piikani must have travelled through that territory regularly with their entire bands in 1801, Ac ko mok ki's estimates seem to assume fast-moving Siksika parties of young men only. The Siksika in 1801 did not have enough horses to permit all members of a band to ride horses, so the distance a band could travel was limited by distance a person could walk. A party of young men on a war expedition might leave their horses behind, but they would travel light and quickly.

The war track of 1801 would have taken the warriors to the very shadows of Beartooth Mountain (Photo 5), but those whose destination was farther east, as those who aimed for Belt Butte, as Ac ko mok ki's map implied, could travel far onto the plains and still use landmarks such as Beartooth Mountain as navigational aids, Beartooth Mountain being discernible for more than 60 miles to the northeast. That would help explain why Ac ko mok ki indicated that the distance between Beartooth Mountain and Belt Butte could be traversed in only three days. In fact, someone destined from the vicinity of Haystack Butte to Belt Butte would probably cover the distance of about 70 miles in six days without getting within 30 miles of Beartooth Mountain. Similarly, whereas the crowns of Belt Butte and Wolf Butte are about 27 miles apart, if we assume that the traveller used those two landmarks as guides along the way, rather than as destinations, the 20 miles of undulating ground that might be traversed between the vicinity of Belt Butte and Wolf Butte is manageable. Understandably, given Fidler's indication that none of the Siksika had been as far south as landform N, the identity of some of the more remote landforms can probably never be known definitively, but the number of nights slept between landforms H and K does seem to suggest that K is a landform on the south side of the Musselshell River, L a landform on the upper Yellowstone, and N a landform near the Bighorn River.

Ki oo cus's Tours of the Northwestern Plains

One of the most remarkable, intriguing, and unique features of the Ki oo cus map is its inclusion of apparent travel routes through the plains. While other maps include some information about travel times and distances along the Rocky Mountains, information evidently related to the Old North

Trail, Ki oo cus includes what appear to be actual or hypothetical travel routes through the plains, with the dots between small circles probably indicating the distance that might be travelled in a day. This information is worth some careful examination. Deprived of any of the oral information that Ki oo cus must have included, we cannot know whether these are actual journeys, and we assume that, even if they were, the travellers would have stayed multiple nights in some of the locations. But, in some instances, we can determine how long, in days, it took to go between two geographical points that are known on the map, and hence determine the average distance that band travelled per day. So, while the traces appear to include about fifty days of travel, they may represent the movement of bands over several months. Part of this movement was also likely seasonal and many of the routes may have been travelled in the summer primarily, as some of the places depicted to the north would not have allowed horses to survive the winter without supplemental forage. Many of the unnamed stops are also in the middle of the plains at places having no significant landform or waterway. It is reasonable to assume that with a lack of water or wood, the band would not have lingered long there, whereas locations such as 26, 27, or 28 would have made it possible to stay longer because critical resources were readily available. Significantly, many of the lines appear to show real or possible travels in eastern portions of Siksika territory where the landmarks of the Rocky Mountains were too far away to assist with navigation.

Trip 1, from the Nose (30) to the Judith Mountains (24), via 26, 27, 28, Chesterfield House, Cypress Hills, and the Bears Paw Mountains (22)
Ki oo cus drew this route as a gently arcing route, although almost straight. When plotted on a modern map, it appears as a remarkably straight roughly north-south trip of about 360 miles. The distance between the Nose and Chesterfield House was almost exactly 100 miles as the crow flies, a distance shown to take about ten days. As Ki oo cus shows, the best and most direct route to the Judith Basin from Chesterfield House would have been directly south, between Many Island Lake[6] and the Great Sand Hills[7] and through the very distinct gap in the Cypress Hills,[8] crossing the Milk River somewhat west of present-day Havre, Montana, then skirting the western slopes of the Bears Paw Mountains, probably up Big Sandy Creek.[9] From there, the best route to avoid the broken country of the Missouri Breaks was to travel almost directly towards the outline of the North Moccasin Mountains/Judith Mountains (visible when the air is clear) to cross the Missouri River at the mouth of the Judith River, a very common gathering place for the Blackfoot-speaking people, and where they would conclude a treaty with the United States government in 1855.

With the information that the Siksika slept five nights when travelling from God's Lake (31) to the Nose (30), a distance of about 70 miles, this trip might be extended to a total of 430 miles, and about 25 days.

Trip 2, plausibly a continuation of Trip 1, from the Judith Mountains to a location on the Bad River

This trip of about 220 miles appears much straighter on a modern map than it does on Ki oo cus's map. A traveller departing the Judith or Big Snowy Mountains may have departed from the Judith Gap[10] and travelled north down the Judith River or one of its tributaries, perhaps stopping at the warm springs along the way. From there, by using the distinct Square Butte as a guide, the travellers could head towards where today's village of Square Butte stands. Then it is remarkably straight travelling to the eastern slopes of the Sweetgrass Hills. If water was scarce, the travellers could follow the Marias River and Willow Creek all the way to the hills. Past the Sweetgrass Hills, the route crossed the Milk River near Writing-on-Stone. It was normal to cross the Milk River at this point, which helps explain why the North-West Mounted Police established an outpost there near the boundary with the United States during the 1870s.[11]

Writing-on-Stone, a major archaeological location containing extensive rock art, was designated a World Heritage Cultural Landscape by UNESCO in 2019.[12] It was obviously incorporated into Blackfoot thinking. In 1855, when he travelled north from Fort Benton to visit the Blackfoot, James Doty mentioned crossing the "Milk River (Indian name *Ke-nock-sis-sah-ti*) at a place called 'the Writings,' which I had often heard spoken of by the Indians as a locality where white men [an apparent reference to Napi] had many years ago written upon the rocks."[13] His journals also imply that the location was a meeting place, although Blackfoot informants in the 1900s have indicated that the Blackfoot avoided immediate vicinity of the rock art because they regarded that location as a "sacred or ceremonial centre."[14]

After leaving the Milk River, the route of this trip passed west of Pakowki Lake. The brackish waters of Pakowki Lake are undrinkable, but the creek flowing into Pakowki Lake from the west through Etzikom Coulee (another underfit valley) was potable.[15] Ki oo cus shows the route from Etzikom Coulee running north to the fork of the Chin and Forty Mile Coulees (more underfit valleys).[16] The watered valley of Forty Mile Coulee would lead the travellers to a point downstream from the confluence of the Bow and Oldman Rivers. Ki oo cus shows no routes from this terminus, but from there a band could easily travel in any number of directions by following the valleys of the Bow, Oldman, or South Saskatchewan Rivers. What might be construed as a spur route from Trip 2 runs from the eastern Highwood Mountains to the Missouri, crossing the Missouri upstream from the Trip 2 trail, but still downstream from the confluence of the Marias, and then joining the main trail at a point about one and a half day's journey north of the Missouri River. This spur appears to be about forty miles long.

Trip 3, from the Highwood Mountains to the Yellowstone River

This journey appears to show travellers entering the "Rocky Mountains" after two days, suggesting that this route followed roughly the route that Montana Highway 89 now traverses between Monarch and Livingston, Montana, between the Crazy and Big Belt Mountains. This route is about 130 miles long. It is similar to Ac ko mok ki's return route on the 1801 war path.

Trip 4, Seven Persons Creek to the western end of the Highwood Mountains

Running nearly due north-south for about 140 miles, this route appears to begin at the headwaters of Seven Persons Creek, at Red Rock Coulee, where distinctive spherical red sandstone rocks (perhaps some of the "enormous boulders" of Napi's playgrounds) offer a haunting foreground to the Sweetgrass Hills (Photo 17A), normally prominent on the southern horizon, although they are about 55 miles away. The route goes south, first skirting east of Pakowki Lake and the Sweetgrass Hills (Photo 17) before crossing the Missouri and Teton Rivers at exactly the point (just east of present-day Fort Benton) where the Teton River flows to within a mile of the Missouri River before diverging again (Ki oo cus's rough draft seems to show the route slightly farther east than this), then to Belt Butte (Photo 6) and the Highwood Mountains (Photo 21), perhaps following Shonkin Creek. This route is about 150 miles long.

Discussion

The elastic scale on Siksika maps is effective. The Blackfoot clearly conceived of distance temporally. Distances on these maps are usually indicated according to the number of days required to cover a distance by normal mode of transport. This method was prevalent, perhaps universal, on Indigenous and early maps.[17] Since the distance covered in one day varied according to terrain, and distance between convenient camping places, the result is a different depiction of the landscape from what would be expected from a map in which distance is measured according to an absolute scale. Nevertheless, absolute distances, even if the informants had means to determine them, would have been less useful than these temporal distances. This concept of distance is particularly obvious in Ki oo cus's map. In some cases, the temporal distance is almost perfectly aligned with the absolute distance, most likely where the terrain was even. That is the case from the confluence of the Red and South Saskatchewan

Rivers to Sounding Creek and between Sounding Creek and the "Buffalo Nose." However, further south, between the Bears Paw Mountains and the Cypress Hills and from that point to the confluence of the Red and South Saskatchewan Rivers, the band appears to have covered much longer distances in one day.

Ac ko mok ki's 1801 map provides detailed information about the distances between points along the Rocky Mountains. This suggests that even the Siksika, the northeastern most group among the Blackfoot, were familiar with the region near the mountains. Indeed, the Siksika maps suggest that the woods edge/Rocky Mountains were key locations along an important travel route. Brings-Down-the-Sun's description of the Old North Trail, quoted earlier in this study, corresponds closely to the line representing the mountains south of the Bow River (Calgary), and the woods edge of Ki oo cus's map north of that river. Not actually a single trail, the Old North Trail was a series of trails that ran alongside the Rocky Mountains, and, like many Indigenous trails, was also used by European settlers and road builders. Perhaps the most significant archaeological study to date is Brian Reeves's reconstruction of the "inner" Old North Trail in the foothills of the Montana Rockies, based on local knowledge, aerial photographs, and archaeological survey.[18] Markers on the ground include cairns and travois tracks worn into the prairie by centuries (or millennia, as Reeves argued) of repeated use. The trail approximates portions of Highways 89, 287, and 464 in Montana, and Highways 6, 22, and 2 in Alberta.

Several routes documented on the maps (Ac ko mok ki's return trip on the 1801 war path, and Ki oo cus's trips 2 and 4) appear to follow at least in part the historic Whoop-Up Trail or Riplinger Trail from Fort Benton to Fort Macleod, maybe a part of an "outer" Old North Trail. According to George Bird Grinnell, the Whoop-Up Trail followed a Blackfoot route documented from oral tradition. Grinnell explained that "Old Man" (Napi), the creator/trickster of Blackfoot tradition,

> was travelling about, south of here, making the people. He came from the south, travelling north, making animals and birds as he passed along. He made the mountains, prairies, timber, and brush first. So he went along, travelling northward, making things as he went, putting rivers here and there and falls on them, putting red paint here and there in the ground,—fixing up the world as we see it to-day. He made the Milk River (the Teton) and crossed it, and, being tired, went up on a little hill and lay down to rest. As he lay on his back, stretched out on the ground, with arms extended, he marked himself out with stones,—the shape of his body, head, legs, arms, and everything.[19] There you can see those rocks to-day. After he had rested, he went on northward, and stumbled over a knoll and fell down on his knees. Then he said, "You are a bad

thing to be stumbling against"; so he raised up two large buttes there, and named them the Knees,[20] and they are called so to this day. He went on further north, and with some of the rocks he carried with him he built the Sweet Grass Hills.[21]

Napi's creative travel continued further north. The northern route varies depending on sources but seems to match historically known Indigenous trails.[22] Those route(s) are not drawn by either Ac ko mok ki or Ki oo cus, but go past several of the landmarks they (and Ak ko wee ak) depict. The route recorded by Grinnell in Alberta essentially matches the "outer" Old North Trail there, linking Fort Macleod, Calgary, and Edmonton, a route Highway 2 follows today. South of Calgary this route goes along the Foothills Erratic Train, a geological feature linked with the travels of Napi.[23] It is also associated with many archaeological sites.[24] The inner section of the trail in Alberta appears to have gone between the Porcupine Hills and the Front Range, from Brocket north to Big Hill, along what is now Highway 22:[25]

> After this, Old Man kept on, travelling north.[26] Many of the animals that he had made followed him as he went. These animals understood him when he spoke to them, and he used them as his servants. When he got to the north point of Porcupine Mountains, there he made some more mud images of people, and blew breath upon them, and they became people...After he had taught the people these things, he started off again, travelling north, until he came to where the Bow and Elbow rivers meet. There he made some more people, and taught them the same things. From here he again went on northward. When he had come nearly to the Red Deer's River,[27] he reached the hill where the Old Man sleeps.[28] There he lay down and rested himself. The form of his body is to be seen there yet.
>
> When he awoke from his sleep, he travelled further northward and came to a fine high hill. He climbed to the top of it, and there sat down to rest. He looked over the country below him, and it pleased him. Before him the hill was steep, and he said to himself, "Well, this is a fine place for sliding; I will have some fun," and he began to slide down the hill. The marks where he slid down are to be seen yet, and this place is known to all people as the "Old Man's Sliding Ground."[29]
>
> This is as far as the Blackfeet followed Old Man. The Crees know what he did further north.[30]

A variation of this story has Napi crossing the Bow at Blackfoot Crossing, near a prominent Napi effigy, and going north to another Napi effigy located near Rosebud.[31] The corresponding Indigenous route continues north past the {Hay now too can} recorded by Ki oo cus, then to Buffalo Lake and the Peace Hills.[32]

Scholars who study the acquisition of spatial knowledge distinguish between so-called route knowledge and configural knowledge. Route knowledge enables people to travel from one place to another because they recognize landmarks and locations along their way. Configural knowledge entails the ability to understand how locations relate to each other (ability to estimate distances and bearings between places). Configural knowledge enables people to imagine new routes through territory never previously traversed.[33] Most people can gain both types of knowledge (although there is a large variation among individuals in their ability to do so). The maps studied here present several routes, but the fact that these Blackfoot cartographers generated complex maps, rather than turn-by-turn instructions, show that they also possessed configural knowledge of the territory. The sophistication of this knowledge is evidenced by the fact that the distance between major landmarks and the network of bearings among landmarks must have enabled these men to imagine many more routes through this territory than are depicted on those maps. We believe, however, that anyone who seeks to accumulate the spatial knowledge of the territories covered by these maps by travelling through the territory, even with the assistance of an automobile or aircraft, will come away from the experience with a deep appreciation of the cognitive maps that Blackfoot people carried with them.[34]

Exploring the "Different Tribes" of Ac ko mok ki's Map and the Gros Ventre Map

TED BINNEMA, ANDREW COWELL, FRANÇOIS LANOË, AND HEINZ W. PYSZCZYK

ONE OF THE MORE REMARKABLE AND ENIGMATIC FEATURES of the maps Peter Fidler collected is the information about "different tribes" found on Ac ko mok ki's 1801 map (Map 1A, 1B, and 1C), and on the map he apparently obtained from the Gros Ventre (Map 5A).[1] Fidler considered the maps' information about Indigenous communities to be a very significant feature of the maps. Fidler must have hoped that the information would help him learn more about the Indigenous communities to the south and west of Chesterfield House, and must have been intrigued by the information, but he never wrote about the further use he may have made of the information.

Until now, scholars have used this feature of Ac ko mok ki's map narrowly towards trying to connect the different tribes on the map with known modern tribes. Linguistic knowledge and historical documents can assist in learning more about the communities shown on the maps. A historical document created almost fifty years before the maps were drawn offers some tantalizing evidence. In a long memorandum penned in 1757, the intelligent and curious French soldier Louis-Antoine, Comte de Bougainville (1729–1811), then stationed in New France during the Seven Years' War, summarized the information he gathered about New France. He included information about the Western Plains of North America that he must have obtained from French fur traders who had returned from the western interior during the war. Some of them, including La Corne, Sieur de St. Luc, served with Bougainville during the war. Some of his information must have been based on the explorations of Pierre Gaultier de Varennes et de La Vérendrye (1685–1749), who had visited the Mandan villages in 1738–39, and two of his sons, Louis-Joseph and François, who travelled a considerable distance into the Western Plains, certainly as far west as present-day South Dakota and the Black Hills, and likely within sight of the Bighorn Mountains, in 1742–43 in search of an inland sea, the Mer de l'Ouest.[2] The document is so significant because it is one of the few that can shed light upon the very dynamic situation on the Western Plains of North America in the mid-eighteenth century. By 1801, the Blackfoot and Gros Ventre were better armed with firearms and ammunition than their southern neighbours, and had acquired sufficient horses, that they could dominate those neighbours. Fifty years earlier, poorly armed and horseless Blackfoot and Gros Ventre bands were beleaguered by continual raids of their southern enemies. We have only fragmentary evidence about how the rapid expansion of the Numic-speaking people (Shoshone and Comanche) into the Western Plains was redrawing the tribal map of the region, but their expansion probably had victims aside from the Blackfoot and Gros Ventre. Moreover, the eventual spread of horses to the northeast, and the spread of European weaponry, must also have influenced the movement of unknown groups on the Western Plains as the ascendency of the Shoshone and Comanche was increasingly challenged. The situation was very different in the 1750s, when Blackfoot people were hard pressed by their enemies to the southwest who had acquired horses before they had. As a result, the Blackfoot-speaking people appear during the 1750s to have been pushed to the territory between the Red Deer and North Saskatchewan Rivers, and the Shoshone and their friends dominated the region to the south.[3] Bougainville described,

> La Mer d'Ouest [the Western Sea] post which includes forts Saint-Pierre, Saint-Charles, Bourbon, de la Reine, Dauphin, Poskoia, and des Prairies, all stockaded forts, *respectables* [formidable] only to the *sauvages*.
>
> Fort Saint Pierre is situated upon the left bank of the lake of Tekamamiouen or lac de la Pluie [Rainy Lake], 500 leagues [1,380 miles] from Michilimakinak and 300 [828 miles] from Kamanistiguoyia or the Trois Rivières to the northwest of Lake Superior.
>
> Fort Saint Charles is 60 leagues [165 miles] from that of Saint-Pierre, situated upon a prominent peninsula in the Lake of the Woods.
>
> Fort Bourbon [actually, Fort Maurepas] is 150 leagues [414 miles] from the preceding situated at the entry of Lake Ouimpeg [Lake Winnipeg].
>
> Fort la Reine [at today's Portage la Prairie, Manitoba] is upon the right bank of the river of the Assiniboels [Assiniboine River], 70 leagues [193 miles]

from Fort Bourbon [Maurepas]. These regions offer everywhere vast prairies; it is the route to the upper Missouri.

Fort Dauphin, 80 leagues [220 miles] from the preceding, is situated upon the river Minanghenachequeké or l'Eau Troublé [Dauphin Lake].

Fort Poskoia is on the river of this name [Saskatchewan River] 180 leagues [496 miles] from the preceding; from this fort you can go in 10 days to the Nelson river. Fort des Prairies [Prairie fort] is 80 leagues [220 miles] from Fort Poskoia in the upper part of the river of that name. This post has been *affermé* [leased] for 80,000 francs; the commandant is the *fermier* [lessee] and he has a fourth in the post. The *sauvages* who come to trade there are the Cristinaux [Cree] and the Assiniboels [Assiniboine]; these 2 nations form each 12 villages of 250 men taking one with the other; in an ordinary year there is made in this post from 300 to 400 packets of beavers, pékans [fishers], martins, otters, lynxes, carcajoux [wolverine], fouines [weasels?], foxes; there must also be counted 50 to 60 slaves red, or *panis de Jatihilinine*, a nation situated upon the Missouri which plays in America the role of the negroes in Europe. Only at this post is the trade in them carried on.

Le poste de la mer d'Ouest [the post of the Western Sea] deserves particular attention for two reasons, the first of which is that it is the nearest of all to the English establishments on Hudson Bay, whence their movements should be watched; the second is that it is from this post that the Sea of the West may be discovered; but to make this discovery it will be necessary for the voyageurs to abandon their interested views.

Voyage de la Véranderie.—The one who most forwarded this discovery is the Sieur de la Véranderie; from the Fort de la Reine he reached the Missouri, he met first [in 1738–39] of all upon this river the Mandannes or *Blancs Barbus* [Bearded Whites] to the number of 7 villages fortified by terraced stockades with a ditch, next the Kinongewiniris or les Brochets [Pike fish] to the number of 3 villages; in the upper part of the river, he found the Mahantas making also 3 villages, and along the Missouri, in descending it to the mouth of the river Wabiek or Shell [Coquille], 23 villages of *Panis*.[4]

To the south-west of this river and upon the two banks [of the?] Ouonaradeba or *à la Graisse* [Fat River] are the Hactannes or Gens du Serpent [Snake People]. They extend as far as the foot of a chain of very high mountains, which run north, east, and south, and to the south of which is the river Karoskiou or Cerise Pelée [Peeled Cherry], which is supposed to run towards California.

He continued his route, and found in those immense countries which are watered by the Missouri, opposite to and about 40 leagues [110 miles] from the Mahantas, the Owilinioek or Beaux Hommes [Handsome Men], four villages; opposite the Brochets, the Macateoualasites or Pieds-Noirs, 3 villages of about 100 cabins each; opposite the Mandannes are the Ospekakaerenousques or Gens du Plat Côté [People of the Flat Side], four villages; opposite the Panis are the Gens de l'Arc [People of the Bow] Atchapcivinioques in Cristinaux, and Utasibaoutchactas in Assiniboels, 3 villages; next were found the Makesch or Petits Renards, 2 villages; the Piwassa or Grand Parleurs [Great Talkers], 3 villages; the Kakakoschena or Gens de la Pie [Magpie People], 5 villages; the Kiskipisounouinini or Gens de la Jarretière [Garter People], 7 villages.

He could go no farther because of the war which was then raging between the Gens de la Jarretière and the next nation. However, I have somewhat improperly used the name *village* for all the nations who inhabit the prairies: they form, like the Tartars, but wandering hordes; they follow the animals whose hunting is their subsistence, their homes are cabins of skins.[5]

Although Bougainville's account betrays significant confusion and misinformation (he apparently conflated the various La Vérendrye explorations, and confused Fort Bourbon for Fort Maurepas), he was an intelligent officer who attempted to convey the state of knowledge as it existed among the French at the time. Moreover, some of his information seems to intersect with information from other sources. About some of the groups Bougainville mentions there is wide agreement; the {Mandannes} were the Mandan, the Beaux Hommes were the Crow, the Pied Noirs were the Blackfoot, for example.[6] The Fat River is probably the South Platte, which is called the 'Fat' or 'Tallow' or 'Grease' River in many Plains languages, including Arapaho, Cheyenne, Lakota, Kiowa, and Crow. It is appropriately southwest of the Shell River, which would correspond to the North Platte/Platte. Arapaho, Cheyenne, Lakota, and Kiowa all used this name for the North Platte/Platte, along which the Pawnee were located as described in the text. The Cerise Pelee might be either the Colorado (though it is not south of the South Platte) or the Arkansas or Rio Grande (though they do not run towards California). Bougainville did appear to admit uncertainty about this last river.

Other groups are mysterious. For example, it is difficult to identify the Brochet.[7] The account is particularly intriguing, however, for the fact that it, together with the maps, may offer some hints about the fluidity of Indigenous life on the Western Plains at the time. Three tribes on Ac ko mok ki's map may correspond with groups mentioned in Bougainville's 1757 memorandum: the Petit Renards, the {Kiskipisounouinini}, and the {Ospekakaerenousques}.

La Vérendrye encountered two villages of Petits Renards ('Small Foxes') in the fall of 1742.[8] These must be the two villages of "Makesch or Petits Renards" mentioned by Bougainville in 1757. Douglas R. Parks has connected these people with a people called by the Arikara, Tuhkiwáku ('Fox People'). A 1785 report by the Spanish governor of Louisiana, Esteban

Rodríguez Miró, described these people as once having been among the most numerous nations in North America, but thanks to warfare, primarily with the Comanche, they had even then been reduced to a few nomadic groups around the Little Missouri River.[9] In 1795, Jean-Baptiste Truteau described the {Tokiwaco} as a nomadic people allied with the Cheyenne, although he did not meet them.[10] Meriwether Lewis and William Clark also mentioned the {To-che-wah-Coo} ('Fox Indians') who inhabited the prairies west of the Arikara villages.[11] The placement of Ac ko mok ki's "Grey Fox Indians" suggests that these may be the same people. They may have been, as DeMallie, Parks, and Vézina have suggested in their edited volume of Truteau's 1794–96 journal, the Plains Apache, or they may have been a division of the Plains Apache, or an entirely separate group that was absorbed into their neighbours in the early nineteenth century.[12] The Petits Renards led La Vérendrye to the {Pioya}, who, in turn led him to a village of Gens des Chevaux who "were in great distress, nothing but tears and groans, all their villages having been destroyed by the Gens du Serpent and very few having escaped."[13] La Vérendrye added that "This Serpent tribe is considered very brave. They do not content themselves in a campaign with destroying a village, according to the custom of all the savages; they keep up the war from spring to autumn. They are very numerous, and woe to those who cross their path! They are not friendly with any tribe. It is said that in 1741 they had entirely ruined seventeen villages, killed all the men and the old women, made slaves of the young women and sold them on the coast for horses and merchandise."[14] Bougainville's {Hactannes} suggests {Ietan}, a name applied to the Shoshone.[15] Although they seem far east, they were very dominant in those years. The Gens de Chevaux in turn conveyed La Vérendrye to the Gens de l'Arc. The La Vérendryes accompanied the Gens de l'Arc in 1742 and 1743 as they travelled west hoping to attack a band of Gens du Serpent.[16]

According to Douglas Parks, the name {Kiskipisounouinini} ('Gens de la Jarretière' or 'Garter People') was derived from the Swampy Cree language.[17] It is more than plausible that the Blackfoot and Cree, who had close associations in the years before Ac ko mok ki drew his map, both referred to the same people as "Garter People." It is impossible to associate them with any known people, but Ac ko mok ki's map appears to corroborate the existence of those people and to assist us with their location. If they are the same people, their numbers had dropped significantly in the time between the 1740s and 1801.

Finally, Ac ko mok ki's "Rib" people may correspond to Bougainville's {Ospekakaerenousques} or Gens du Plat Côté. According to Parks, "the Old Cree form is *ospike·kan·iriniwak*: 'Rib People.'"[18] While many have speculated that this may be a reference to the Bitterroot Salish, Bougainville's reference to their location makes this unlikely. Ac ko mok ki's map forces us to consider the possibility that Ac ko mok ki and Bougainville were referring to a people between the Northwestern Plains and the Missouri River.

We need not assume that the three groups on Ac ko mok ki's map that seem to correspond with groups mentioned by Bougainville, but appear not to be mentioned again in documents after the first decade of the nineteenth century, correspond with any group that exists today. We may never know for sure, of course, but the rapidly changing situation on the Western Plains after the arrival and spread of the horse and gun, and the spread of smallpox, may well have caused certain groups to disappear at the same time as the Shoshone, Crow, and Cheyenne bands emerged there.

An important additional source is a list of Gros Ventre words and phrases that Fidler compiled at the end of his rough draft of his 1800 journals, a list that includes the names of several Indigenous groups. For convenience, the list of groups is provided below.[19]

Blackfoots [Siksika]	Waw tan ne tatch[20]
Blood Inds	Know win nā hawn[21]
Pecon	Nee cow batch[22]
Snake Ind	Se se an nen[23]
Crow Mtn	Ow win nin nin[24]
Flatheads	Caw caw aytch[25]
Blue mud	Naw cotch is seen in nin nin[26]
Cottona	Woos nā sib be ootch[27]
Sussews	Nay aytch eet thot[28]
Southn Inds [Cree]	Natut chog gah[29]
Long Hair Ind	Caw caw yaw etch[30]
Stone Ind	Naut te nay in[31]
Fall Ind	Oyawn in in[32]
Engl Man	Cheese ne hawd thu[33]
French Mn	Nee e haud thu[34]
Fatt man's gang of Blackfeet	Ben ne thit te[35]
Feathers [Old Swan] the Blackfoot Chief[36]	Ow ah bess se he[37]

This list is useful to any researcher seeking to extract useful evidence from the two maps. If we use these maps solely, or even primarily, as sources for our maps of the location of Plains Indigenous tribes at the beginning of the nineteenth century, we will miss much of the valuable evidence they contain. The evidence is especially intriguing and tantalizing because little other documentary evidence exists from that period about the locations of many of these groups. However, the evidence in the maps will be far more significant if we inquire first into the cartographers' intentions and understandings rather than being driven by our own.

Unlike their rivals to the southwest, the Blackfoot at the beginning of the nineteenth century possessed both horse and gun. This allowed them to dominate their neighbours in that direction. They clearly patrolled the Missouri basin so effectively that their nearest enemies to the south were well south of the Missouri River. Ac ko mok ki's map shows that much of the upper Missouri basin was an extensive neutral/war zone that no Indigenous group inhabited permanently. Unfortunately, the maps do not also indicate Cree, Assiniboine, Tsuut'ina, or Blackfoot bands. Such information would not only have shed more light on what the symbols mean, but would have provided valuable information about groups that were central to the Saskatchewan River fur trade. However, Hudson's Bay Company (HBC) traders were very familiar with those groups and with the Northeastern Plains, and Fidler clearly saw no reason to have his informants draw maps of that region. Thus, these maps can give us no reliable information of the Blackfoot's knowledge or perceptions of the region east of present-day Alberta.

Small circles indicated the locations of mostly nomadic Indigenous communities. Those circles, and the inclusion of number of "tents" that comprises each group, must have been a common convention, for Ac ko mok ki's map and the Gros Ventre map use the same convention, and it certainly was not conventional for European maps at that time. Our best guess is that the circles represent the cartographers' indication of the places where they would expect to find those people at particular times of the year (perhaps during winter when they were most sedentary, or, for enemies, where they might try to find them during a raid). Alternatively, a circle might represent the centre of a group's territory. The idea of the "camp circle" is central to the ideology and worldview of several, and perhaps almost all or all, nomadic Plains tribes. The languages often have highly developed cultural metaphors around the idea of the circle generally, the camp circle in particular, the centre of this circle, and movement towards and away from this central point.[38]

It may initially seem surprising that Plains Indigenous people would have indicated the locations of nomadic hunting and gathering people, as well as the location of villagers, by a single location on a map. Except for the sedentary groups, the circles cannot represent either permanent settlements or entire territories, but even for sedentary groups, we cannot assume that the circles represent villages. These locations are likely best thought of as the product of oral cultures that placed a high value on both memory and highly memorable conceptual categories and arrangements. It was likely very important to establish a "prototypical location" for each group, both in relation to the landscape and in relation to the other groups, as a basic starting point for geospatial and ethnic relationships. This would also explain the highly patterned nature of the circles on this map—lined up like beads along the string of the Missouri River, or running down the eastern slope of the Rocky Mountains in a similar fashion, and then stretching out onto the plains in a perfect line (locations 22–26). It would be much easier to conceptualize different groups in such linear order, rather than as random dots spread across the landscape. In part this also reflects the geographic realities of the plains and Rockies, where rivers were key travel corridors and resource-gathering locations, and where the base of the mountains was similarly valuable for both wayfinding, winter shelter, and the multiple resources found at this ecosystem juncture. But it also reflects a deeper tendency to conceptualize the landscape in highly symbolic ways that were also easily memorized.[39]

   This is not to say that tribal individuals were not aware of the everyday reality of highly mobile communities, for both their own groups and others. They must have tried to keep track of where the surrounding groups were in real time, for reasons of trade and other friendly interation, warfare, or diplomacy. Indeed, the linguistic and cultural metaphor of the path is equally important as that of the camp circle among Plains cultures.[40] The symbolic locations were simply starting points against which to calculate and keep track of actual movements. Of course, the farther they were from their homeland, the less they could keep track of other people, or even have a good conception of the prototypical positions of other people. The maps seem to illustrate this reality. The Gros Ventre map suggests that, for peoples more familiar to the Gros Ventre, the cartographer(s) carefully included different linear distances between circles, or placed the circles carefully in relation to landscape features. But distant groups far down the Missouri River and far to the south were simply placed along the most salient geographical reference points, with no differential linear distancing between the groups. Thus, these distant points on the map seem to represent more abstract and symbolic/conceptual views of the landscape, in comparison to the more localized sites and groups—which are even presented at a different, larger scale than the more distant points.

   The Gros Ventre map thus suggests that the Gros Ventre may have had only second-hand knowledge of the more distant areas. Still, it is very impressive that someone living in what is now northern Montana had knowledge of towns and tribes in present-day New Mexico and Arizona. Documents show that Gros Ventre bands spent extended periods (perhaps up to two years at a time) far to the south as early as the 1780s.[41] We also know that an Arapaho band was visiting Gros Ventre bands near

Chesterfield House even as this map was drawn. The map hints at Gros Ventre knowledge of present-day southern Colorado, northern New Mexico, and the Arkansas River Valley. While the Gros Ventre were pushed south by hostile Cree and Assiniboine, they were pulled south by their friendly relations with Cheyenne and Arapaho, and by access to European trade items that flowed out of Santa Fe throughout the seventeenth and eighteenth centuries long before the establishment of the Santa Fe Trail. It is possible that Gros Ventre individuals might have visited Spanish settlements before 1801, but it is more likely that they knew of the settlements second-hand and acquired Spanish trade goods through intermediaries such as the Comanche and Shoshone.[42]

The fact that there are more than thirty "different tribes" on each of the maps must immediately alert us to the probability that we will not find a one-to-one correlation between those different tribes and known present-day Indigenous "tribes"—Blackfoot, Tsuut'ina, Gros Ventre, Snake (Shoshone), Crow, Bitterroot Salish, Arapaho, Cheyenne, or Kiowa—as they are widely understood today. The degree to which we can find a correlation between the names of "tribes" on these maps and the names that ethnographers collected a century later shows that the Siksika and Gros Ventre understood such ethnolinguistic categories too. But it would be rash to assume that these are one-to-one correlations. While we might be able to associate a certain label on a map with a certain ethnonym recorded in the late nineteenth or early twentieth century, there are many examples in which the referents have changed. The most obvious illustration can be found among the Blackfoot-speaking people themselves. When Fidler compiled a list of Gros Ventre names for Indigenous tribes, he listed separate names for the three Blackfoot-speaking groups, but no name for the whole collectivity, either because the Gros Ventre did not have such a name, or because it was not commonly used. The word list suggests that, had the Gros Ventre cartographer included the Blackfoot-speaking people on his map, he would have included the Siksika, Kainai, and Piikani separately. In that case, the {Waw tan ne tatch} (Blackfoot) would refer to only a minority of the "Blackfoot" as presented in the maps and chapters of the highly regarded *Handbook of North American Indians*.[43] This is in fact the way this word is used in current Gros Ventre. The language maintains separate names for the Peigan and Blood, just as in the list presented above. In the case of the Siksika ("Blackfoot"), Kainai, and Piikani, the name "Blackfoot" has been applied by Europeans to all three divisions because Europeans encountered the Siksika before the others. In a partially parallel development, the Gros Ventre have applied the general name "enemies" (cɔɔtɔh) to the entirety of the Blackfoot Confederation.

In other cases, formerly autonomous but related communities coalesced in response to the effects of warfare and depopulation. For example, when these maps were drawn, no Awatixa or Aswxawi villagers would have considered themselves Hirá·ca (Hidatsa). Sixty years later, after the entire population of the three villages had coalesced, their descendants did. Similar dynamics affected many other communities on the plains. Rather than be disappointed that it proves impossible to use these maps to draw an authoritative map of tribal territories as of the beginning of the nineteenth century, we should be pleased that we have documents that offer tantalizing insights into the minds of Indigenous people who were alive at the time.

Ac ko mok ki's map and the unattributed map both show that the Siksika and Gros Ventre thought of themselves and their neighbours at least as much in terms of smaller units than ethnolinguistic units. On the other hand, some also thought of themselves in terms of larger groups. For example, anthropologists and historians have consistently considered the Gros Ventre and Arapaho to be separate "tribes." So did HBC traders. Fidler differentiated between the "Gros Ventre" and "Tattood" (Arapaho) "Indians." Ac ko mok ki's map reinforces the impression that the Blackfoot likewise thought of them as separate groups. The unattributed map, however, seems to corroborate other evidence that, in the early nineteenth century, the Gros Ventre and Arapaho thought of themselves as being ethnically especially closely related, as well as being more closely related to the three other "Arapahoan" groups documented by A.L. Kroeber and other early ethnographers, since the label "Falls" (more narrowly referring to the Gros Ventre) is added to the names of the other groups.

In many cases, the maps show the location of a particular band, not what we think of today as a tribe. While the evidence suggests that such bands or villages could persist as units for many decades, for various reasons their histories are very difficult to reconstruct. Names attached to bands differed among different people and changed over time, and bands were more likely than whole tribes to be absorbed into other bands if their fortunes declined. In many cases, it will probably be impossible to determine what "tribe" a particular name refers to, but the evidence about some of the groups whose identity can more confidently be determined gives us a valuable glimpse into Ac ko mok ki's world.

On one hand, the first group, identified as "Cho.que—Mud House Indians," seems straightforward. This must be a reference to Mandan, Hidatsa, or Arikara. In fact, although the Blackfoot may have had terms to differentiate those three people, in this case, it appears that Ac ko mok ki used a general term to refer to "earthlodge villagers." The Blackfoot, Cree, and other groups are known to have done so. For example, the Blackfoot used the name *ksáókò·yi·wa* ('one who has an earthlodge') to refer to the Arikara, Mandan, and Hidatsa.[44]

More intriguing is the fact that Ac ko mok ki placed these earthlodge villagers near the mouth of the Judith River. We could easily conclude, as D.W. Moodie and Barry Kaye did, that Ac ko mok ki placed the circle "much too far west."[45] However, if we come to that conclusion about a circle so close to Blackfoot territory, it would be difficult to escape the conclusion that Ac ko mok ki's map is an unreliable guide to the location of Indigenous communities at the beginning of the nineteenth century. But if we approach the map critically but with an open mind, rather than rejecting evidence in the Ac ko mok ki map that does not seem to corroborate what we think we already know, we must entertain the possibility that it offers tantalizing evidence regarding the history of the spread of Hidatsa people up the Missouri and the resulting Crow-Hidatsa schism. Fidler, at least, would not have been surprised by the map. As he travelled up the South Saskatchewan River to establish Chesterfield House, on 21 September 1800 (four days before arriving at the Chesterfield House site), Fidler noted, "*3 Mud Houses* on this side amongst a few poplars, they are of a circular form about 9 feet diameter & 4½ high, they appear to be nearly 20 years old, they are said to have been built by a small war party from the Miss sis soury river, who live in these kinds of habitations."[46] These houses were located at the place Fidler described as a particularly fine place for buffalo. Given that we know that Hidatsa travelled considerable distances up the Missouri River both to hunt and raid their enemies, perhaps Ac ko mok ki was not showing the location of the permanent Hidatsa and Mandan villages, but a location where Hidatsa or Crow hunting or raiding parties (and mud houses) could be encountered.[47] It does appear that it was a Hidatsa attack on Chesterfield House that led traders to abandon that location in 1805.[48]

Archaeologists have reported an earthlodge village built around 1740 as far northwest as Cluny, Alberta, and what appears to have been a combined tipi and earthlodge village, the Hagen Site, along the Yellowstone River just south of Glendive, Montana, probably used in the late seventeenth and early eighteenth centuries.[49] It seems unlikely that Ac ko mok ki meant to indicate that there was the equivalent of 150 tents at the one location, but he may have been indicating that the Hidatsa were a substantial presence as far west as the Judith River at the turn of the nineteenth century. The other mud house village, near the confluence of the Missouri and Yellowstone Rivers, is also more than plausible. Aside from its location essentially identical to the Hagen Site proper, it mirrors observations in 1805 by François-Antoine Larocque, who observed, in a coulee near the confluence of the Yellowstone and Missouri Rivers, "a lodge made in the form of those of the Mandan & Big Belly's [Hidatsa] (I suppose made by them) surrounded by a small Fort. The Lodge appears to have been made 3 or 4 years ago but was inhabitted [sic] last winter. Outside of the fort was a kind of stable in which the[y] kept their horses."[50]

The {Mak que a tuppee} (15) also seems easier than most to interpret. We can be almost certain that, given that {Mak que a tuppee} clearly means 'Wolf Persons,' that Ac ko mok ki was referring to the Pawnee-Loups, also known as the Skiri or Wolf Pawnee, the northernmost band of Pawnee. Many Plains people, including the Wolf Pawnee themselves, referred to these villagers, located on the Loup ('Wolf') River in what is Nebraska today, as Wolf People.[51] But it would be a mistake to assume that Ac ko mok ki referred to the Pawnee generally. On 12 April 1833, the German Prince Maximilian of Wied-Neuwied identified the Pawnee-Loups as one of four major divisions of the Pawnee.[52] However, it appears that the four divisions had no collective name for themselves in the early nineteenth century.[53] Neither, given what we have seen about the {Cho.que}, would it be safe to assume that Ac ko mok ki intended to show the location of the permanent earthlodge village of the Pawnee-Loups. Especially after they acquired horses, the Pawnee travelled extensively towards the west to hunt buffalo both in summer and winter when they were not busy with planting or harvesting their crops. It is likely that the Blackfoot-speaking people and the Pawnee-Loups were unaware of one another before the 1750s, but the vastly increased mobility that horses afforded meant that, even if they had not actually encountered one another directly, they were aware of each other by the beginning of the nineteenth century.

Many of the "tribes" included on Ac ko mok ki's map were what we would think of today as subunits of the Crow, Shoshone, Cheyenne, and other groups. Perhaps the greatest value in Ac ko mok ki's list of "tribes" is that it reinforces other evidence that the Indigenous people of the plains did not think of themselves or their neighbours wholly, or even primarily, in terms of the "tribes" familiar to most people today, and around which members of Plains Indigenous communities have come to identify more recently. Substantial ethnogenesis as well as disappearance of ethnic groups has occurred over the last 200 to 250 years. Evidence from the Gros Ventre further reinforces this impression. Fidler noted that the Gros Ventre had words for the Siksika, Kainai, and Piikani, but he also recorded the Gros Ventre names for Ac ko mok ki's and O mok api's Siksika bands.[54] This is unsurprising, since the Gros Ventre were closely affiliated with the "Blackfeet Confederacy," but had very different relations with its constituent bands (mostly cordial with Ac ko mok ki's band, but tense with O mok api's band). Still, this fact highlights the difficulty in distinguishing between a large and significant "band" and a "tribe"—for historians today trying to use these sources, but also perhaps for Gros Ventre people at the time.

Certainly, the evidence on Ac ko mok ki's map should cause us to question the recent tendency of historians to portray the "Blackfoot," "Lakota," or "Comanche" in the early nineteenth century as unified polities or even "empires."[55] There is abundant evidence that we will distort the history of Plains Indigenous "tribes" unless we acknowledge that they were composed of autonomous bands and villages that were not subject to any larger political authorities, or alternately, shifted their ethnic affiliations and allegiances over time.

Careful examination of Map 1C will reveal that we have placed "tribes" 2 to 5 between the Musselshell and the Yellowstone and tribes 7 to 11 between the Yellowstone and Bighorn despite their location on Ac ko mok ki's 1801 map. We do so because the historical documents of the late 1700s and early 1800s strongly suggest that the relevant groups were in those locations. We acknowledge that this interpretation assumed that the placement of those peoples on the Ac ko mok ki map was erroneous.

With the caveats noted above, we offer our best guess as to the identity of each of the "tribes" of Ac ko mok ki's map.

Ac ko mok ki's "Different Tribes"

Table 6.1 The "Different Tribes" of Ac ko mok ki's 1801 Map

Explanation	Tents	Possible Identity
1. Cho. que—Mud House Indians	150	Crow or Hidatsa[56]
2. Is sap poo—Crow Mountain Indians	200	Crow[57]
3. Ams cope sox sue—Sessew's Inds	70	unidentified[58]
4. Sip pe tā ke—The wrinkled Indians	90	unidentified[59]
5. Kix tā ka tap pee—Beaver Indians	90	possibly Cheyenne[60]
6. Cho.que. They go to war with No. 1	160	Hidatsa or Arikara?[61]
7. Nee Koo chis ak kā—Tattoo'd Inds	80	Arapaho[62]
8. Sin ne po tup pe—Grey Fox Inds	40	Tuhkiwaku (Petits Renards)?[63]
9. Ke ta kap sum—Garter Inds	30	Kiskipisounouinini?[64]
10. So hoo is too ye—Hairy or Beard Inds	50	Hevhaitaneo Cheyenne[65]
11. Ak ken nix sa tuppee—Thigh Inds	40	Perhaps Arapaho or Cheyenne[66]
12. Pik et a tuppe—Rib Inds	100	unidentified[67]
13. Oo aps six sa tuppe—Thigh Inds	20	Perhaps Arapaho or Cheyenne[68]
14. Oc sa tup pee—Scabby Inds	100	Northern Cheyenne[69]
15. Mak que a tuppee—Wolf Inds	200	Skiri or Wolf Pawnee[70]
16. Mut tā you que—Grass Tent Inds	180	A Bannock or Shoshone band[71]
17. Mem me ow you—fish eating Inds	20	Lemhi Shoshone[72]
18. Ne chick a pā soy—a particular root	60	Yamparika Comanche[73]
19. Nis che tap pe—Wood Indians	100	Jupe Comanche[74]
20. Sox sue chicks sin na tappee—Sussew Snake Inds	50	Shoshone[75]
21. Poo can nam a tappee—Pearl shell Inds.	70	a Shoshone band?[76]
22. Six too k tappee—Black	200	Bannock or Ute[77]
23. Cut tux pee too pin—Flatt heads	50	Bitterroot Salish[78]
24. Cum mun na tappee—Blue Mud Inds	60	Nez Perce[79]
25. Ap pa tuppee—Ermin or White Inds.	80	unidentified[80]
26. To kee pee tup pee—Those that collect shells		Pend d'Oreilles or Kalispel[81]
27. Ac cōōk sa tappee—Padling Inds.	30	Pend d'Oreilles or Kalispel[82]
28. At cha tappee—Snair Indians	18	(Snare) Shuswap[83]
29. Cut tux in nā mi—Weak Bow Inds.	18	Lower Kootenai[84]
30. Patch now	10	unidentified[85]
31. Cotton nā	22	Upper Kootenai[86]
32. Pun nus pee tup pin—Long hair Inds.	100	An interior Salish group[87]

The Tribes of the Gros Ventre Map

Table 6.2 The Locations of Tribes

Explanation		Tents	[Possible Identity]
1. Cock kaw etch —	Flatheads	50	Bitterroot Salish[88]
2. Cock kaw yaw etch	D° [Ditto]	40	Interior Salish[89]
3. See see an nen	Snake Inds	130	Northern Shoshone[90]
4. ow win nen	Crow Mount	100	Crow[91]
5. Ee thā chee nā		30	unidentified[92]
6. See see an nen		10	Northern Shoshone[93]
7. Nay aytch eet choh		20	"woods enemy"[94]
8. Nun ni en		100 Fall	Arapaho[95]
9. E tā seen		100	Cheyenne[96]
10. Tot teen		30	unidentified[97]
11. Neet chay in in		100	Kiowa[98]
12. Chow win in		20	unidentified[99]
13. E chaugh ā nin		10	Crow?[100]
14. On now win		10 Fall	Hanahawunena[101]
15. Naw wā ben nin nach		10	unidentified[102]
16. Wā tan nitch		200	Bannock or Ute[103]
17. Now wā se se an nen		300	Shoshone or Comanche[104]
18. See See an nen ne haud thue—			Spanish Settlements[105]
19. Oth thay in in		100	Navajo[106]
20. The he nin		100	Jicarilla Apache[107]
21. Now watch e ni in		20 Fall	Nawathinehena[108]
22. Nay aytch e chot		10	unidentified[109]
23. Chow win nin		8	Crow or Pawnee?[110]
24. Thot thok ki in in		13	Plains Apache[111]
25. Beth thow in in		20	Besawunena[112]
26. Ben eet chaw batch		40	possibly the Awaxawi division of Hidatsa[113]
27. Wan nuk ki an		40	Hidatsa[114]
28. A. k. thi a wootch		20	unidentified[115]
29. Ā beth thoo		15	unidentified[116]
30. Been nen in		100	unidentified[117]
31. Meen nā nin nā		300	Omaha and Ponca?[118]
32. Naw te nane Stone Inds		100	Dakota or Assiniboine[119]

Table 6.2 The Locations of Tribes (cont.)

Explanation	Tents	[Possible Identity]
33. Ne haud thoo—	French or English—	Europeans[120]
34. Con nan nin	20	Arikara[121]
35. Wat taw ben in in	10	unidentified[122]
36. Nawch e nen ne ah	30	Siouan people[123]

This Gros Ventre map depicts five "Fall" groups, revealing that in 1801, the Gros Ventre saw the five divisions of the Gros Ventre and Arapaho as related peoples, of which the Gros Ventre were the northernmost, just as Kroeber, in 1908, noted that "the Arapaho regard the Gros Ventre as the northernmost one of a group of five closely affiliated or related tribes of which they themselves form the largest."[124] The ethnonyms of the two groups are very similar. By 1908, the connections had become more attenuated, because of the distance between them, and the limitations on mobility of the late nineteenth century, but when Fidler obtained this map, and for several decades afterwards, members of the Gros Ventre and Arapaho visited one another for extended periods.

7

Contributions of Indigenous Cartography to Western Cartography

TED BINNEMA

IN MAY 1819, Peter Fidler drafted a nine-thousand-word annual report for the Hudson's Bay Company's (HBC) Red River District. On the first page of that report, he drew a map of the Red River District.[1] The map conformed nicely to Western cartographic conventions, complete with lines of latitude and longitude, except that Fidler put north at the bottom of the map (Map 6). A year later, Fidler prepared another annual report, this time for the "Manetoba [sic] District."[2] He once again included a map, the last that he is known to have submitted to the company (Map 7). The Governor and Committee must have found that map odd. Granted, when they explained the new requirement of the "annual district report" in 1814, the Committee had asked its officers to submit maps of their districts if possible. The Committee did assure its traders that "we are well aware that many of the Officers are not Draughtsmen, or capable of making out a distinct & accurate plan; but we shall think it an object to obtain from persons of Local Knowledge even the rudest Indian Sketch of the interior posts of a district, where no accurate Surveys have been made."[3] The maps drawn by HBC servants as a result of these requirements, including many obviously based upon Indigenous knowledge, continue to be valuable assets in the HBC Archives. Fidler, of course, was not only a draughtsman, but a surveyor fully capable of drawing a map in the Western style. Moreover, in 1795–96 and in 1808 he had conducted surveys of many of the places depicted on his map of 1820.

But with this 1820 map Fidler seemed deliberately to flout the cartographic conventions of the Western world. Fidler titled the map "A Sketch a la Savage of the Manetoba District."[4] The scale and directionality of the

145

map are inconsistent. The prose in the annual report was cogent, and a close examination of the map reveals that the cartographer was very familiar with the land that he portrayed on the map—so it seems that Fidler was lucid when he drew the map. Although Fidler did not explain why he submitted such unusual maps, they do aptly reflect some of Fidler's interests in cartography. With Europe's precise instruments, Fidler surveyed, measured, and charted an immense area of the interior of North America, but one of his greatest and most enduring geographical and cartographical contributions arose because he took Indigenous cartography seriously. Fidler was one of the earliest westerners to take a systematic approach to the collection, study, and preservation of Indigenous mapping in North America, and among the first to approach and collect them as artifacts.

Fidler's collection of maps continues to be valuable for anyone interested in Indigenous cartography and Western cartography. The first part of this book was devoted primarily to the study of Indigenous cartography in its own right. Indigenous maps are probably most valuable for what they can tell us about the Indigenous people and societies who created them. Maps are the oldest surviving documents created by many Indigenous people in North America and around the world. Fidler's collection of Blackfoot maps tells us much about the Blackfoot people at the turn of the nineteenth century. The fact that Fidler collected and documented five Indigenous maps of overlapping regions permits us today to gain insights from them that would not have been possible if he had collected one anonymously made Indigenous map.

Indigenous maps are also important, however, because they contributed significantly to European mapping. But those contributions have not been adequately recognized. Often, historians of cartography emphasize how developments in European technology and methodology have improved European mapping over the years, but the historian of cartography J.B. Harley once invited scholars to consider whether "an overemphasis on the scientific frontiers and the revolutions of mapping, on landmarks and innovations, or on the saga of how the unmappable was finally mapped has distorted the history of cartography."[5] Fidler's collection of maps reveals how complex and difficult it could be to transmit geographical and cartographical knowledge between non-Western and Western people. The actual contributions of Indigenous maps to Western cartography fell short of the potential because so much of the geographical information embedded in Indigenous maps was lost in translation.

The HBC was a commercial enterprise. The company's London Governor and Committee always wanted maps, but often reminded its servants that exploration and mapping were "to be made Subservient to promote the Company's Interest and increase Their Trade."[6] This helps explain why the company's geographical knowledge was remarkably limited until the

1750s, and why that knowledge increased dramatically in the 1750s as the company was forced to respond to growing competition from rivals operating in the interior.

If exploration and mapping were subservient to other concerns, HBC servants had to acquire geographical knowledge without incurring great expense. Obtaining knowledge from Indigenous people was the most diplomatic and cost-effective approach. Every HBC inland explorer or emissary before 1772 had used the services of Indigenous guides. As early as the 1710s, the company also relied on maps drawn by Indigenous people. In this, the HBC was not unique. Many explorers relied directly on Indigenous maps. For example, in 1541 after Jacques Cartier decided to travel no farther up the St. Lawrence River than the Cascades Rapids, he asked some St. Lawrence Iroquois for more information. The Iroquois responded "with certaine little stickes, which they layd upon the ground in a certaine distance, and afterward layde other small branches between both representing the Saults [rapids]."[7] In his reliance on Indigenous maps, Cartier was preceded by Christopher Columbus, and would be followed by Samuel de Champlain, John Smith, Robert Cavelier, Sieur de La Salle, Alexander Mackenzie, Lewis and Clark, and many others.[8]

The value of Indigenous maps was also well known and publicized in Europe well before Fidler's day. The French Recollet priest Chrestien Le Clercq explained of the Mi'kmaq in his *Nouvelle relation de la Gaspésie* (1691) that "they have much ingenuity in drawing upon bark a kind of map which marks exactly all the rivers and streams of a country of which they wish to make a representation. They mark all the places thereon exactly and so well that they make use of them successfully, and an Indian who possesses one makes long voyages without going astray."[9] Similarly, in his *New Voyage to Carolina* (1709) John Lawson, the surveyor general of North Carolina, noted that although the Indigenous people of North Carolina did not use letters,

> they will draw Maps very exactly of all the Rivers, Towns, Mountains and Roads, or what you shall enquire of them, which you may draw by their directions, and come to a small matter of latitude, reckoning by their day's journeys. These Maps they will draw in the Ashes of the Fire, and sometimes upon a Mat or Piece of Bark. I have put a Pen and Ink into a savage's Hand, and as he has drawn me the Rivers, Bays, and other Parts of a Country, afterwards I have found to agree with a great deal of Nicety.[10]

And Baron de Lahontan, a military man familiar with Indigenous people along the St. Lawrence and the Mississippi, in his *New Voyages to North America* (1703), generalized about "savages" that they were "as ignorant of *Geography* as of other *Sciences*, and yet they draw the most exact Maps imaginable of the Countries they're acquainted with, for there's nothing wanting in them but the Longitude and Latitude of Places: They set down the True *North* according to the *Pole Star*; the Ports, Harbours, River, Creeks and Coasts, of the Lakes; the Roads, Mountains, Woods, Marshes, Meadows, &c. counting the distances by Journey and Half-journeys of the Warriors, and allowing to every Journey Five Leagues."[11] Joseph François Lafitau, whose knowledge of Indigenous people was gained from his time at Saint-Louis du Sault (near Montreal) from 1712 to 1717, published a similar comment about the accuracy of Indigenous maps in his *Moeurs des sauvages ameriquains* (1724), even noting that they sometimes kept copies of maps for future reference.[12] The influence of Indigenous geographical knowledge on European mapping during the eighteenth century is nowhere better illustrated than in a well-known map drawn by the influential French cartographer Philippe Buache in 1754. In his *Carte physique des terrains les plus élevés de la partie occidentale du Canada*, Buache attempted to incorporate information from Indigenous informants into his Western-style main map, but in an inset map above this map he also transcribed a "*carte tracée par le Sauvage Ochagach et autres*."[13] Thus, not only did many European fur traders, explorers, cartographers, and military men rely upon Indigenous cartography since the earliest years of contact, but by the middle of the eighteenth century, commentary regarding these maps had been published in some of the most respected and widely read books on North American Indigenous people. And in 1791, in a book dedicated to Sir Joseph Banks, president of the Royal Society, and subscribed to by Banks, Samuel Wegg, and Alexander Dalrymple, former fur trader John Long noted that "the Indians are very expert in delineating countries on bark, with wood coal mixed with bear's grease, and which even the women do with great precision."[14]

Outside the realm of geographers and cartographers, there is no evidence that any European savants showed any interest in studying Indigenous mapping before the nineteenth century, but this is not because insufficient information had been published to pique their interest.[15] Some knowledge of mapping among the Indigenous people of Rupert's Land had also been published before Fidler joined the HBC. In his *History of the Voyages and Discoveries Made in the North* (1786), John Reinhold Forster noted the fact that two Chipewyan had drawn a map "on parchment with charcoal" in 1722.[16] Forster's comments hint at the fact that maps collected by HBC servants directly affected the actions of the HBC and some of its men.

It is not certain what map Forster referred to, but in and around 1716, James Knight, intelligent and ambitious overseas Governor of the HBC, asked several Indigenous people to draw maps for him—maps that contributed to his belief that the Northwest Passage could be found via Hudson Bay.[17] That conviction led him to organize an expedition to search for the

Northwest Passage—an expedition during which Knight and his entire party perished. Unfortunately, it appears that none of the maps that Knight collected still exists, but the HBC's reliance on Indigenous maps continued. In 1760, Moses Norton drafted a map, based on Indigenous maps, or at least on detailed information from Cree informants, that gave him hope that Chesterfield Inlet might lead to a Northwest Passage. That information inspired the expeditions of William Christopher and Moses Norton, in 1761 and 1762. Norton also collected the oldest extant map in the HBC collection that is explicitly attributed to named Indigenous cartographers. In 1762, he asked Idotlyazee, a Chipewyan man, to draw him a map of the Hudson Bay coast to the north of Churchill, and in 1767 he secured a map, drawn on leather, by Idotlyazee and Matonabbee, the Chipewyan who would guide Samuel Hearne on his third journey. Norton transcribed this map and submitted it to the company, and it influenced the instructions given to Hearne (Map 8).[18] It is also clear that portions of Andrew Graham's map of 1774 (Map 9) are based on maps or information supplied by Indigenous people. And in 1776, Thomas Hutchins drew a sketch of the area between Hudson Bay and Lake Winnipeg based in part on information supplied by Assiniboine informants.[19]

Even after the HBC hired Philip Turnor to apply Western methods of scientific surveying to the HBC territories, Indigenous knowledge remained important in HBC cartography. Many HBC maps that do not acknowledge a reliance on Indigenous maps or information nevertheless offer telltale evidence of their Indigenous sources. For example, a 1791 map by surgeon Edward Jarvis and Donald McKay (who had been in the region since 1779 and defected from a Canadian partnership in 1790) does not acknowledge its dependence on Indigenous informants, but shows abundant evidence of Indigenous influence (Map 10).[20] The waterways, depicted as beads on a string (see especially the area northwest of Lake Superior), and the depiction of small watercourses crucial for navigation (see especially the interior waterways that parallel the coast of Hudson Bay) between the Hayes, Severn, and Ekwan Rivers, betray not only a debt to Cree informants but a borrowing of Cree cartographic conventions.[21] This approach to mapping is typical of Cree maps of the region, and reflects the travel routes of the Cree, who avoided the open water of Hudson and James Bay, preferring to travel on these interior routes.[22] Turnor sought a map from a Chipewyan informant in 1791.[23] And, in 1792, at the end of his surveying career, Turnor himself drew a "Chart of Lakes and Rivers in North America by Philip Turnor Those Shaded Are from Actual Survey's the Others from Canadian and Indigenous Information."[24] Turnor obviously finished a fourteen-year career in Rupert's Land with a respect for Indigenous geographical knowledge.

So, by the time Fidler joined the HBC in 1788, information about the skill and significance of Indigenous cartographers had already been published in Europe. Furthermore, men—such as Andrew Graham, Thomas Hutchins, and John Reinhold Forster—who straddled the gap between the HBC's territories and the world of British science, had firsthand knowledge of the quality and importance of Indigenous mapping. It is impossible to know how the HBC's Committee might have responded had any such well-placed men asked the company, during the 1770s or 1780s, to collect Indigenous maps for the purposes of systematic study. Richard Ruggles correctly argued that, until the late 1770s, the HBC's "information about the interior of the country, its hydrographic patterns, and all else considered vital the trade was sacrosanct and lay locked in the records at Hudson's Bay House...not even the geographer of His Majesty the King was given access."[25] But by the early 1790s the Committee would have raised no objections to such a proposal. Unfortunately, British intellectuals, even cartographers such as Aaron Arrowsmith, were evidently poorly placed intellectually to appreciate the complexities of Indigenous mapping. The prominent historian of cartography J.B. Harley argued that intellectual trends made it more difficult for Europeans to appreciate Indigenous maps: "From at least the seventeenth century onward, European mapmakers and map users have increasingly promoted a standard scientific model of knowledge and cognition...This mimetic bondage has led to a tendency... to regard the maps of other non-Western or early cultures (where the rules of mapmaking were different) as inferior to European maps."[26] The fact that Fidler collected Indigenous maps, and even mimicked them in his own 1820 map, suggests that he did not consider Indigenous maps to be inferior, but Fidler's example nevertheless shows how difficult it was for those immersed in Western cartographic traditions actually to understand the cartographic languages in which Indigenous people communicated.

It seems most Europeans before the second half of the nineteenth century who took North American Indigenous maps seriously were men with direct experience with Indigenous people and the North American environments. But few of them collected and preserved maps. Malcolm Lewis, the foremost historian of North American Indigenous cartography, has explained that "there are relatively few extant examples of Indian maps because Indians and most whites have tended to treat them as ephemera."[27] The relatively few people who did collect such maps exhibited an unusual intellectual curiosity and appreciation for Indigenous knowledge. Perhaps the earliest among them was Francis Nicholson. Nicholson, who was elected a fellow of the Royal Society in 1706, and served as governor of Maryland, Virginia, South Carolina, New York, and Nova Scotia between 1690 and 1725, preserved four Indigenous maps.[28] Lewis and Clark were also notable. They, in the assessment of Lewis, acquired about thirty Indigenous "cartographic devices," on their expedition.[29] According to James P. Ronda, "more important than the quest for Indian maps was the effort by the Corps of Discovery, and especially William Clark, to understand both the structure and substance of those documents. They knew Indigenous maps represented a vital part of a broader encounter, an attempt to communicate important ideas and experiences across the cultural divide."[30] Probably at least seventeen of the thirty maps were preserved.[31] But Fidler was the most serious and systematic collector and student of Indigenous mapping. Well trained in Western surveying and cartography *and* appreciative and curious about Indigenous mapping, he became a thoughtful student of cartographic traditions on both sides of the Atlantic.

Scholars have already examined the history of mapping in the HBC and Fidler's role in that history. In his excellent and beautifully illustrated history of two centuries of cartography in the HBC, Ruggles emphasized Fidler's significance as a surveyor and mapper in the Western tradition. He found Fidler remarkable not only for the volume of his output but for its quality. The careful measurements, which provided an expanding network of more precise locations for the map of British America, were testimony that he was an apt pupil of Turnor. His maps were explicit in the conformation of rivers and lakes. His influence is seen in the work of several company mapmakers, most notably George Taylor Jr., who emulated his field and drafting technique.[32]

But Ruggles recognized that Fidler's methods were not merely conventional. His 1819 and 1820 maps were not his first imaginative maps. Ruggles argued that Fidler was "as far as originality is concerned, the most important innovator in the history of company cartography."[33] Although Ruggles was not referring to his 1819 and 1820 maps, Fidler's cartographic records simultaneously testify to his attachment to the values and standards ideas of post-Enlightenment Europe, and his openness to alternative ways of understanding and mapping landscape. Fidler was the most prolific surveyor and mapper in the history of the HBC, but he was also one of the most assiduous collectors of maps drawn by Indigenous people and untrained Canadians and Europeans. And his collection of Indigenous maps may well be his most significant cartographic legacy.

Fidler's career amply reflects the HBC Committee's belief that exploration and mapping were always to be subservient to the company's commercial interests. Still, although Fidler's trading often took precedence over those other activities, he was one of the relatively few HBC servants who was paid to conduct surveys. And Fidler was with the company at a time when his surveys and maps contributed significantly to European knowledge of the interior of North America. Fidler's contributions to some fields of science, including natural history and meteorology, might have been more significant if his efforts coincided better with surges of interest in Europe. But in his field of greatest interest, Fidler was particularly well placed to contribute to the mapping of the North American continent. Fidler served the company at a time when the company cooperated with the pre-eminent geographers and cartographers in London, particularly with Aaron and John Arrowsmith, the pre-eminent cartographers in London, whose firm produced frequently updated and oft-copied maps of North America—the most respected maps of North America for about fifty years beginning in 1795.[34] Aaron Arrowsmith's cooperation with the company appears to have begun shortly before he published his first great map of northern North America in 1795, although the very first version of that map, issued in January of that year, did not include material based on Hearne's journey to the Arctic Ocean.[35] An updated map, issued the same year, did include it.[36] Still, this does suggest that Ruggles was correct when he argued that it was only in 1795, after Fidler had begun his surveying, that "geographical information was regularly transferred from company sources to the Arrowsmith drafting tables and hence to other cartographers and the public."[37] Thus, Fidler was the first HBC servant who had the pleasure of witnessing the results of his surveys and his maps quickly incorporated into the regularly updated maps of Arrowsmith.[38]

 The content of David Thompson's maps was influenced by the fact that it was drawn by a fur trader, with the help of Indigenous informants, primarily for the benefit of Euro-Canadian fur traders. Thompson's maps show the fur trader's preoccupation with water systems navigable by canoes that form convenient fur trade routes, and with obstacles along these routes. Interestingly, there are aspects of Thompson's maps (showing rivers flowing into the Bow River that actually flow into another tributary of the Bow) that are erroneous by Western cartographic standards that conform well to cartographic conventions of the Blackfoot. These clues show that, although he did not acknowledge the fact, Thompson integrated Indigenous maps into his own.

 Thompson's explorations and surveys were more extensive than Fidler's, but for most of his career he conducted those explorations, surveys, and maps for the North West Company (NWC). Not only were the NWC's Montreal headquarters poorly located to facilitate cooperation with European cartographers, the NWC was understandably far more secretive with its surveys and maps than was the HBC. Some of Thompson's surveys appear to have been included in the map published in 1801 with Alexander Mackenzie's journals (and were thereafter incorporated into Arrowsmith's maps), and it appears that the HBC took at least one of Thompson's maps when it seized Fort William in 1816–17, and conveyed that map to Aaron Arrowsmith, who included its information in the 1817 edition of his map.[39] Thus, although Thompson is justly renowned for his remarkable map of the northwest—certainly a more impressive map than any map Fidler could have drawn of the same area—when Fidler died in 1822, his impact on the British cartography of British North America was considerably greater than Thompson's.[40]

If Fidler's contributions to the mapping of North America are significant, they are so in part because of his reliance on Indigenous people and upon non-Indigenous people untrained in cartography. Many Western maps of North America, including many HBC maps, bear clear but unacknowledged debts to Indigenous North Americans.[41] In other cases, explorers and mappers acknowledged their debt to Indigenous people explicitly, and sometimes in publication. Alexander Mackenzie did not hesitate to admit that he relied on maps drawn by Indigenous people. For example, Mackenzie noted that on 10 June 1793, a Sekani man on the Parsnip River told him about people on the other side of the divide, who lived in houses. He wrote, "I desired him to describe the road to the other river, by delineating it with a piece of coal, on a strip of bark, which he accomplished to my satisfaction. The opinion that the river did not discharge itself into the sea, I very confidently imputed to his ignorance of the country."[42] He explained that eleven days later, when on the Fraser River, he obtained another map from a Carrier (Dakelh) informant who obviously was familiar with the drawing of maps: "My first application to the native whom I have already particularly mentioned, was to obtain from him such a plan of the river as he should be enable to give me; and he complied with this request with a degree of readiness and intelligence that evidence proved it was by no means a new business to him."[43] Two days later, Mackenzie sought another map from villagers along the Fraser River. He wrote that among the villagers he met was an elderly man who "appeared to possess the character of a chief" and who "declared his wish to see me return to his land, and that his two young daughters should then be at my disposal."[44] Mackenzie explained that he

> proceeded to request the native, whom I had particularly selected, to commence his information, by drawing a sketch of the country upon a large piece of bark, and he immediately entered on the work, frequently appealing to, and sometimes asking the advice of, those around him. He described the river as running to the East of South, receiving many rivers, and every six or eight leagues encumbered with falls and rapids, some of which were very dangerous, and six of them impracticable. The carrying-places he represented as of great length, and passing over hills and mountains. He depicted the lands of three other tribes, in succession, who spoke different languages. Beyond them he knew nothing either of the river or country, only that it was still a long way to the sea; and that, as he had heard, there was a lake, before they reached the water, which the natives did not drink.[45]

Simon Fraser, who followed up Mackenzie's explorations on North Americas Pacific slope, also often sought Indigenous maps as he reconnoitered the Fraser River in 1808.[46] If many explorers obscured the fact that they often relied upon maps drawn by Indigenous people, Mackenzie and Fraser were exceptions. Had the European explorers of North America all preserved Indigenous maps the way Fidler did, it would now be possible to compile a comprehensive atlas of Indigenous maps of the entire continent. Unfortunately for us, Mackenzie and Fraser, like most European explorers, appear to have treated the Indigenous maps they received as disposable.

James Swain was another trader who did not hesitate to acknowledge his reliance on Indigenous informants. In 1815, when Swain drew a map of the Severn District, he prominently wrote in the centre of the map that it had been "laid down from Indian information" (Map 11). In 1833, Simon McGillivray Jr. obtained a map (now lost) of the Babine and Skeena Rivers from a young Babine (Natoot'en) chief named Tenewill, which he sent to the HBC's Governor and Committee.[47] In 1834, John M. McLeod collected an "Indian Chart" showing the Liard/Dease River system and a portion of the Stikine River (Map 12). And when he was on the northwest coast in 1841 and 1842, George Simpson, the North American Governor of the HBC, reported that "one man, known as the Arrowsmith of the north-east [north-west] coast, had gone far beyond his compeers, having prepared very accurate charts of most parts of the adjacent shores."[48] Simpson was probably referring to a Tongass Tlingit leader named Ebbits, who, in 1842 at Fort Simpson (near the mouth of the Skeena River) "gave Mr Work a chart of the Coast made by himself from this place as far as Stikine."[49] During the mid-nineteenth century, Arctic explorers such as William E. Parry, Charles Francis Hall, and F.W. Beechey frankly noted that they were indebted to the "astonishing precision" of Inuit maps.[50] And in 1869, Tlingit Chief Kohklux drew two maps of today's southern Yukon Territory that contributed to George Davidson's knowledge of that region.[51] In 1866, Frank L. Pope, assistant engineer for the Western Union Telegraph, while attempting to determine the best route for a telegraph line from North America to Europe via Bering Strait, admitted that Indigenous maps had been instrumental to his success:

> Much geographical information was obtained from the natives at various points some of which is extremely valuable and interesting and its general features will be found correct. It has been taken from charts roughly drawn by the natives themselves and afterwards explained by them through the medium of one of the Indians accompanying me, named "Alexis"; whose intelligence and knowledge of the different native dialects rendered him invaluable in the capacity of our interpreter. By this means a large amount of information has been obtained which would otherwise have been inaccessible.

> I am also under great obligations to Mr [George] Blenkinsop for the interest he has taken in procuring geographical information from the natives which will be found incorporated in the report.[52]

Pope explained that the maps he obtained

> may be fully relied on as far as regards the connections of different lakes, rivers, trails &, as well as the relative locations of falls, rapids, and portages but in the matters of proportion, and relative bearings and distances must taken with a great degree of allowance. The natives measure a trail or river not by its actual length but by the number of days required to pass over it which of course varies with the difficulties of the country. Fractions of a day are represented by "pipes." A "pipe" is the distance a man travels from the time he has finished his "smoke" until he wants to smoke again. Under this system of measurement, it is somewhat difficult to arrive at the actual distance between two given points.[53]

Pope acknowledged that he incorporated the Indigenous maps into his own maps—even using red ink on a now-lost map to signify information drawn from Indigenous maps—but he did not preserve any of the Indigenous maps he obtained.[54] From the eastern seaboard in the 1600s, to the Pacific northwest in the nineteenth century, Europeans benefitted from the geographical knowledge of Indigenous people who already had sophisticated cartographic traditions of their own. They learned how to interpret these maps, and clearly respected the sophisticated geographical knowledge they contained.

Still, no HBC trader (and few other people until the twentieth century) apart from Fidler ever showed any interest in Indigenous maps as things to be collected, catalogued, and preserved. Others saw these maps as practical instruments for the transfer of cartographical knowledge from Indigenous people to Europeans, not as worth preserving once that purpose had been accomplished.

Tellingly, the foremost authority on the history of cartography in the HBC found explicit evidence in the HBC Archives for the existence of only sixteen maps actually drawn by Indigenous people for HBC servants, apart from those collected by Fidler.[55] Of these, only three appear to be still extant, and one of those, although not explicitly attributed to Fidler, seems to have been directly connected to Fidler's efforts.[56] By contrast, Ruggles found evidence that Fidler collected approximately twenty-two Indigenous maps drawn by nineteen different cartographers.[57] These maps were drawn by members of at least six different ethnic groups, including Inuit, Chipewyan, Cree, Ojibwe, Blackfoot, and Gros Ventre. At least one copy of each of these maps is still preserved in the HBC Archives.

Fidler typically carefully recorded the provenance of the maps he collected. For example, one is listed as an "Iskemo sketch Drawn by Nay hek til lok an Iskemo 40 years of age 8th July 1809," and another "Drawn by Cot.aw.ney.yaz.zah a young man Jepewyan Feby 17th 1810."[58] In some cases, he also noted the acquisition of such maps in his journals. For example, in March of 1807, Fidler wrote in his rough version of the Cumberland House journals that "Cha cha pay tat te drawed a sketch of the Lower Country."[59] During those years, Fidler also collected at least sixteen maps drawn by HBC and Canadian traders untrained in surveying or cartography. These too he preserved.[60] Some of these Indigenous and Canadian maps depicted areas that Fidler had already surveyed himself. He used these maps when, during his furlough in England in 1811–12, he drafted a series of regional maps which he submitted to the HBC's Committee in March of 1812.[61] Unfortunately, these regional maps— perhaps the closest Fidler came to Thompson's magisterial map of the northwest—no longer exist. Ruggles has suggested that "the company likely turned them over to Aaron Arrowsmith for his use, as was its custom at the time."[62] If Arrowsmith kept them, they were probably destroyed when Arrowsmith's papers fell victim to the bombing of London during World War II.[63] The paper trail allows us to see how significantly the maps drawn by Indigenous people (and untrained non-Indigenous people) contributed to European maps of North America. More tantalizingly, it hints at how Indigenous maps may have contributed to the European mapping of the Americas more generally.

In the case of the Blackfoot maps of 1801 and 1802, Fidler made Indigenous contributions to the European mapping of the continent particularly transparent. Those maps, however, are also interesting for what they say about Fidler's systematic approach to the study of Indigenous mapping.

Fidler undoubtedly knew instantly that Ac ko mok ki's 1801 map (Map 1A) contained geographic information that would be highly valued by British cartographers at the time. Still, he did not convey the map to the London Committee that spring. Instead, he waited more than a year, at which time he submitted an only slightly revised copy of the map (Map 1B) to London. Of all the Indigenous maps collected by HBC servants, this revised map has attracted the greatest scholarly interest, because of its role in European/American exploration and British cartography of the upper Missouri River region, and because, as geographer D.W. Moodie has argued, this map is "one of the most impressive surviving examples of a general or area map constructed by North American Indians."[64]

Why did Fidler hold on to Ac ko mok ki's map for a whole year before deciding to redraft it and send it to London? Perhaps Fidler realized that the map contained a great deal of invaluable information that he simply could not interpret because of its unfamiliar cartographic style. Indigenous maps typically had a significant oral component, and Fidler may have been unsure whether he understood the graphic and oral messages clearly.[65] Perhaps though, Fidler doubted Ac ko mok ki's accuracy or truthfulness. Relations between the HBC servants and Ac ko mok ki had been very friendly, but Fidler must have been acutely aware that it was risky for the Siksika to convey accurate knowledge of the hotly contested Missouri River territory to any outsiders. He probably did not need to be told what Lawson in 1709 had noted, that "I have put a Pen and Ink into a savage's Hand, and as he has drawn me the Rivers, Bays, and other Parts of a Country, afterwards I have found to agree with a great deal of Nicety: But you must be very much in their Favour, otherwise they will never make these Discoveries to you; especially if it be in their own Quarters."[66] And Ac ko mok ki made it clear that the names of all of the rivers south of the Missouri were given in the Gros Ventre language. How familiar were the Blackfoot with that region?

Possibly then, Fidler's decision to hold back the map was rooted in his desire to collect more maps of the region. Additional maps would go a long way to confirming or falsifying information contained in Ac ko mok ki's map of 1801. Fidler would not have been the first to use such a technique. Champlain, on one occasion, collected two maps of the same place evidently to test the reliability of the information.[67] Gabriel Archer, an early explorer in Virginia, also tested the reliability of Indigenous maps. He wrote, "I caused now our kynde consort that described the River to us to draw it againe before kyng Arahatec, who in everything consented to his draught, and it agreed with his first relation. This we found a faythfull fellow, he was one that was appointed guyed for us."[68] The fact that Fidler supplemented Ac ko mok ki's map of 1801 with several more Indigenous maps of the same territory in 1802 before he conveyed a draft of Ac ko mok ki's map to London suggests that Fidler wanted to try to confirm the information contained in the first map, by acquiring other maps in 1802.

Fidler's approach suggests a system. On one hand, Fidler turned to Ac ko mok ki again. In February 1802 Ac ko mok ki drew his second map. Then, at about the same time, Fidler obtained maps from Ak ko wee ak, Ki oo cus, and the unidentified Gros Ventre cartographer(s).

One other relevant map exists in Fidler's collection. This map, barely discernable as a map, is scrawled in a book in which Fidler kept a rough journal of part of the 1800–01 trading season, and a number of other rough records. There, on folios 29d and 30, is an account of the trading goods at Cumberland House in 1799. Across the lines and numbers on folio 30 that are obviously part of the accounts are a number of other lines, some of which may or may not be part of a map, but many of which definitely constitute a map reminiscent of Ac ko mok ki's map of 1802, but depicting a region from the North Saskatchewan River to the Milk River.[69]

The ambiguous lines and the map are found in Map 13. It may have been drawn by an Indigenous person (in which case it was probably Ac ko mok ki), but may also represent Fidler's attempt to experiment with the cartographic style.

Possibly then, with some system, Fidler tried to collect geographical information about the territory south of Chesterfield House by seeking two maps drawn by one Siksika person, plus two other maps drawn by two other Siksika men, including one that apparently attempts to employ a Western cartographic style, and a map drawn by the Gros Ventre or Arapaho. After collecting those maps, he decided to redraft Ac ko mok ki's 1801 map, adding some graphic and verbal information, and sent it to the company's London Committee.

The Governor and Committee were obviously impressed with the content of the maps and letter, for soon after they arrived in London in late October they were sent to Arrowsmith, who incorporated this new information into his updated map of 1802 (Map 14).[70] The Committee also soon wrote to Alexander Dalrymple, hydrographer to the Admiralty, that "Mr. Peter Fidler having sent home some Maps & Papers which appear to convey much curious Information respecting the North Western Geography I am directed by the Governor & Committee of the Hudson's Bay Company to inform you that these Maps & papers are deposited with Mr. Arrowsmith & that it will be highly satisfactory to them, if his Discoveries should be of sufficient Importance to attract your Attention."[71] And the Committee also wrote to Sir Joseph Banks, president of the Royal Society, that Arrowsmith "considers them as important in ascertaining with some degree of certainty, the sources of the Missisoury, they also convey much curious information respecting the face of many Countries hitherto unknown to Europeans."[72]

Arrowsmith's interpretation of Ac ko mok ki's map is interesting. In an obvious effort to make his depiction plausible to a Western reader, Arrowsmith invented sinuous river courses and confluences even though he had no evidence for them. Indeed, he was particularly creative with the rivers north of the Missouri. Apparently impressed with Fidler's warning that the Siksika were less familiar with the region south of the Missouri, Arrowsmith depicted those rivers only near their apparent sources. But Arrowsmith ignored Fidler's twice-iterated descriptions about the Rocky Mountains south of the Missouri River. Arrowsmith gave his Rocky Mountains the same slight bend that appears on Ac ko mok ki's map, rather than showing the mountains swing eastward as he should have if he wanted to translate the totality (including the oral dimension) of Ac ko mok ki's map available to him into Western cartographic language. There is little doubt that Fidler would have been more successful in drawing a map in the

Western style, based on Ac ko mok ki's map, than Arrowsmith was. Indeed, despite the problems with Ki oo cus's map, Arrowsmith's map would almost certainly have been more useful had Fidler sent Arrowsmith Ki oo cus's map, rather than Ac ko mok ki's. European cartographers had long attempted to incorporate Indigenous maps into their own, and Arrowsmith was not the first to do so unsuccessfully.[73]

The history of Arrowsmith's depiction of the upper Missouri took an interesting turn when the United States president, Thomas Jefferson, sent Meriwether Lewis and William Clark on their expedition up the Missouri in 1804. Not surprisingly, he dispatched the Corps of Discovery with a copy of the latest edition of Arrowsmith's map, and Lewis and Clark considered it to be their most accurate map. However, Jefferson assumed that Arrowsmith's map incorporated information from actual explorations of Fidler, not poorly understood Blackfoot maps. On 15 July 1803, Jefferson wrote Lewis about a description he had just received of information about a point on the lower Columbia: "from this point Mount Hood is seen 20 leagues distant, which is probably a dependence of the Stony mountains, of which mr. Fiedler [Fidler] saw the beginning at about lat 40° and the source of the Missouri river is probably in the Stony mountains."[74] Jefferson was undoubtedly referring to the portions of Arrowsmith's map of 1802 drawn from Ac ko mok ki's information, and his letter reveals that Jefferson (and thus the Corps of Discovery) believed that Fidler had actually travelled as far south as the 40th parallel. Jefferson probably quite logically assumed that the solid lines along the eastern slope of the Rocky Mountains on Arrowsmith's map indicated that Fidler had seen and surveyed the upper reaches of each of those rivers, and that the dotted lines represented guesswork. That explains why Lewis and Clark were so dismayed by the inaccuracies of Arrowsmith's map. In his journal entry for 8 June 1805, Lewis wrote, "I now began more than ever to suspect the veracity of Mr. Fidler or the correctness of his instruments. For I see that Arrasmith in his late map of N. America has laid down a remarkable mountain in the chain of the Rocky Mountains called the tooth nearly as far South as Latitude 45°, and this is said to be from the discoveries of Mr. Fidler."[75] Despite its potential, Ac ko mok ki's (and Arrowsmith's) map contributed nothing to the success of the Corps of Discovery.

The Indigenous maps Fidler collected at Chesterfield House were among the first that he collected. Almost two decades later, when Fidler drafted his "A Sketch a la Savage of the Manetoba District," he showed that his respect for Indigenous cartographic conventions had survived a career that included the surveying of extensive regions of the western interior, as well as the laying out of river lots for the Selkirk settlers. In the meantime, Fidler's substantial contributions to British maps of North America had been based on a combination of scientific surveys conducted by sextant and compass, and geographical information gathered from Indigenous and non-Indigenous people.

Fidler, when he understood that Indigenous knowledge was based on significant experience, took such knowledge very seriously. His was an era in which, despite much published evidence attesting to the sophistication of Indigenous cartography, no European intellectual appears to have shown any interest in gathering and studying Indigenous maps. Indeed, while many traders, explorers, surveyors, and military men had benefitted from Indigenous maps, Fidler was unique in his systematic efforts to preserve and document Indigenous cartographic conventions. His approach to Indigenous cartography, then, sets him apart in the history of cartography during the late eighteenth and early nineteenth centuries.

Notes

A Note on Indigenous Names

1. Donald G. Frantz and Norma Jean Russell, *Blackfoot Dictionary of Stems, Roots, and Affixes* (Toronto: University of Toronto Press, 2017); Donald G. Frantz and Inge Genee, eds., *Blackfoot Dictionary* (2015–2024, ongoing), https://dictionary.blackfoot.algonquianlanguages.ca/.

Preface

1. Alice M. Johnson, *Saskatchewan Journals and Correspondence* (London: Hudson's Bay Record Society, 1967), 283.
2. *Kiááyo* (bear) and *oko'si* ('his child').
3. Lindsay Amundsen-Meyer and Jeremy J. Leyden, "Set in Stone: Re-examining Stone Feature Distribution and Form on the Northwestern Plains," *Plains Anthropologist* 65, no. 255 (2020): 195.

1 | Learning from Early Nineteenth-Century Blackfoot Maps

1. Rosalyn LaPier, "Land as Text: Reading the Land," *Environmental History* 28, no. 1 (2023): 45.
2. Ted (Theodore) Binnema, "How Does a Map Mean?: Old Swan's Map of 1801 and the Blackfoot World," in *From Rupert's Land to Canada: Essays in Honour of John E. Foster*, ed. Theodore Binnema, Gerhard Ens, and Roderick C. Macleod (Edmonton: University of Alberta Press, 2001), 201–24.
3. Rosalyn R. LaPier, *Invisible Reality: Storytellers, Storytakers, and the Supernatural World of the Blackfeet* (Lincoln: University of Nebraska Press, 2017).
4. James Doty to Isaac I. Stevens, 20 December 1854, Glenbow Archives, M-1100-145, 3.
5. For example, Lesley Cormack has argued that the belief that medieval cartographers assumed the world was flat stems from a misinterpretation of medieval T–O maps. Lesley B. Cormack, "Flat Earth or Round Sphere: Misconceptions of the Shape of the Earth and the Fifteenth-Century Transformation of the World," *Ecumene* 1, no. 4 (1994): 364–85. For a discussion of the subjectivity of maps, see J.B. Harley, "Maps, Knowledge, and Power," in *The Iconography of Landscape: Essays on the Symbolic Representation, Design and Use of Past Environments*, ed. Denis Cosgrove and Stephen Daniels (Cambridge: Cambridge University Press, 1988), 277–312; and J.B. Harley "Deconstructing the Map," *Cartographica* 26, no. 2 (1989): 1–20. Also see Harley's article, published posthumously, "Rereading the Maps of the Columbian Encounter," *Annals of the Association of American Geographers* 82 (1992): 522–42.

6. Barbara Belyea, "Amerindian Maps: The Explorer as Translator," *Journal of Historical Geography* 18, no. 3 (1992): 267, 268, 269. Also see Barbara Belyea, "Inland Journeys, Native Maps," in *Cartographic Encounters: Perspectives on Native American Mapmaking and Map Use*, ed. G. Malcolm Lewis (Chicago: University of Chicago Press, 1998), 135–55. That maps must be translated is also discussed in J.B. Harley and David Woodward, eds., *Cartography in Prehistoric, Ancient, and Medieval Europe and the Mediterranean*, vol. 1 of *The History of Cartography* (Chicago: University of Chicago Press, 1987), 3. Also see G. Malcom Lewis, "Maps, Mapmaking, and Map Use by Native North Americans," in *Cartography in the Traditional African, American, Arctic, Australian, and Pacific Societies*, ed. David Woodward and G. Malcolm Lewis, vol. 2, bk. 3 of *The History of Cartography* (Chicago: University of Chicago Press, 1998), 51–182; and Malcolm Lewis, ed., *Cartographic Encounters: Perspectives on Native American Mapmaking and Map Use* (Chicago: University of Chicago Press, 1998).

7. Mark Monmonier, *How to Lie with Maps* (Chicago: University of Chicago Press, 1991), 2. Therefore, as Monmonier argued *all* maps "must distort reality," "must offer a selective, incomplete view of reality"; all maps must lie (1). For a discussion of the necessity of "translating" Indigenous maps, see Michael T. Bravo, *The Accuracy of Ethnoscience: A Study of Inuit Cartography and Cross-Cultural Commensurability* (Manchester: Manchester Papers in Social Anthropology no. 2, 1996).

8. F.W. Beechey, *Voyage to the Pacific and Beering's Strait*, vol. 2 (London: Henry Colburn and Richard Bentley, 1831), 398–400; David Turnbull, "Maps and Mapmaking of the Australian Aboriginal People," in *Encyclopedia of the History of Science, Technology and Medicine in Non-Western Cultures*, ed. Helaine Selin (Dordrecht: Springer, 1997), 560; Robert A. Rundstrom, "A Cultural Interpretation of Inuit Map Accuracy," *Geographical Review* 80, no. 2 (1990): 157; Robert F. Spencer, "Map Making of the North Alaskan Eskimo," *Journal of the Minnesota Academy of Science* 23, no. 1 (1955): 46.

9. The only detailed study of any of these maps is contained in D.W. Moodie and Barry Kaye, "The Ac Ko Mok Ki Map," *The Beaver* 307, no. 4 (Spring 1977): 4–15. This article's analysis is limited to the "Ac Ko Mok Ki map," which is a version of the map of 1801 that Peter Fidler redrafted for the Governor and Committee of the HBC. It is more appropriate for present purposes to consider the Ac ko mok ki map. Moodie and Kaye were impressed by the quality of the Ac ko mok ki map, but their interpretation suggests that it was useless as a navigational tool for the region south of the Missouri River. The Ac ko mok ki map is also discussed in D.W. Moodie, "Indian Map-Making: Two Examples from the Fur Trade West," in *People Places Patterns Processes: Geographical Perspectives on the Canadian Past*, ed. Graeme Wynn (Toronto: Copp Clark Pitman, 1990), 56–67. A brief study of this map is found in three pages of Alice B. Kehoe, "How the Ancient Peigans Lived," *Research in Economic Anthropology*, no. 14 (1993): 94–97. All of the maps being discussed in this study have been described in Judith Beattie, "Indian Maps in the Hudson's Bay Company Archives: A Comparison of Five Area Maps Recorded by Peter Fidler, 1801–1802," *Archivaria*, no. 21 (1985–86): 166–75; and "The Indian Maps Recorded by Peter Fidler, 1801–1810," paper presented at the International Conference on the History of Cartography, Ottawa, 8–12 July 1985. Belyea criticizes Moodie and Kaye's approach directly but does not specifically question their identifications. The Ak ko wee ak and Ki oo cus maps are briefly studied alongside David Thompson's records by Randolph Freeman in *Geographic Naming in Western British North America: 1780–1820* (Edmonton: Alberta Culture, 1985).

10. Hudson's Bay Company Archives (HBCA) E.3/2, fos. 106d–107. The HBC traders tended to call Ac ko mok ki "Feathers," and the North West Company traders called him "Painted

Feathers." See Theodore Binnema, "Old Swan, Big Man, and the Siksika Bands, 1794–1815," *Canadian Historical Review* 77, no. 1 (1996): 1–32.

11. The rough copy of this map is found in HBCA B.39/a/2, fo. 93. A redrafted version can be found in HBCA E.3/2, fo. 104.
12. The rough copy is found at HBCA B.39/a/2, fo. 92d and Fidler's redrafted version in HBCA E.3/2, fo. 103d.
13. HBCA E.3/2, fos. 104d–105. A rough copy is in HBCA B.39/a/2, fos. 85d–86.
14. HBCA E.3/2, fos. 105d–106.
15. Moodie, "Indian Map-Making," 56.
16. Moodie, "Indian Map-Making," 56; Beattie, "Indian Maps," 173.
17. We must consider, however, the possibility that the cartographers may have been very reluctant to use paper and writing instruments. In 1841, George Simpson, the North American Governor of the HBC, wrote that "the savage stands...in awe of paper, pen, and ink...To him the very look of black and white is a powerful 'medicine.'" George Simpson, *Narrative of a Journey Round the World, during the Years 1841 and 1842*, 2 vols. (London: Henry Colburn, 1847), 242.
18. Samuel Hearne and Philip Turnor, *Journals of Samuel Hearne and Philip Turnor*, ed. J.B. Tyrrell (Toronto: Champlain Society, 1934), 443.
19. HBCA B.239/b/52, fo. 23, Philip Turnor to Joseph Colen, 24 July 1792.
20. Hearne and Turnor, *Journals of Samuel Hearne and Philip Turnor*, 555. For a scholarly discussion of Fidler's winter, see June Helm, "'Always with Them Either a Feast or a Famine': Living off the Land with Chipewyan Indians, 1791–1792," *Arctic Anthropology* 30, no. 2 (1993): 46–60.
21. HBCA B.24/a/1, 6 November 1792.
22. The leader is identified as {Sak e too} in HBCA B.24/a/1, fo. 42, William Tomison (Buckingham House) to James Tate (Manchester House), 11 November 1792. Fidler sent to London a map of the region he saw on this trip. The original map has not survived, although it was incorporated into Aaron Arrowsmith's map of North America, 1795 (a copy is found in HBCA G.4/26). Fidler's journals for the winter of 1792–93 are found at HBCA E.3/2, "Journal of a Journey," and have been published in Barbara Belyea, ed., *Peter Fidler: From York Factory to the Rocky Mountains* (Louisville: University Press of Colorado, 2020), 95–150.
23. For information on Fidler, see James G. MacGregor, *Peter Fidler: Canada's Forgotten Surveyor: 1769–1822* (Toronto: McClelland and Stewart, 1966); and Robert S. Allen, "Fidler, Peter," in *Dictionary of Canadian Biography*, vol. 6 (University of Toronto/Université Laval, 2003–), accessed September 23, 2024, http://www.biographi.ca/en/bio/fidler_peter_6E.html.
24. For a list, see Richard Ruggles, *A Country So Interesting: The Hudson's Bay Company and Two Centuries of Mapping, 1670–1870* (Montreal and Kingston: McGill-Queen's University Press, 1991), 266 (Appendix 9), and 199–204.
25. HBCA E.3/4, fos. 16 and 14d.
26. HBCA B.49/a/32b, 25 March 1807. This is either a map that has since disappeared, or a reference to HBCA E.3/4, fo. 13d, which is dated 1806.
27. Ruggles, *Country So Interesting*, 266 (Appendix 8).
28. The only combined general history of the Blackfoot and Gros Ventre peoples is John C. Ewers, *Blackfeet Indians: Ethnological Report on the Blackfeet and Gros Ventre Tribes of Indians* (New York: Garland, 1974). For a general history of the Northwestern Plains, see Theodore Binnema, *Common and Contested Ground: A Human and Environmental History of the Northwestern Plains* (Norman: University of Oklahoma Press, 2001). There are several general histories of the Blackfoot. Ewers relied on extensive documentary research and

interviews with Blackfoot informants in his excellent *The Blackfeet: Raiders on the Northwestern Plains* (Norman: University of Oklahoma Press, 1958). However, because Ewers did not have access to the Hudson's Bay Company Archives, that history is strongest for the period after 1806. Hugh A. Dempsey has published many books, primarily biographies, on Blackfoot history based on documentary records and oral evidence. His general surveys of Blackfoot history include "The Blackfoot," in *Plains*, ed. Raymond J. DeMallie, vol. 13 of *Handbook of North American Indians*, gen. ed. William C. Sturtevant (Washington, DC: Smithsonian Institute, 1990), 604–28; and "The Blackfoot Indians," in *Native Peoples: The Canadian Experience*, ed. R. Bruce Morrison and C. Roderick Wilson (Toronto: McClelland and Stewart, 1986), 404–35. The most recent general history is Ryan Hall, *Beneath the Backbone of the World: Blackfoot People and the North American Borderlands, 1720–1877* (Chapel Hill: University of North Carolina Press, 2020). Loretta Fowler and Regina Flannery have published the most important studies of Gros Ventre history before the 1870s. They collaborated on a brief history in Loretta Fowler and Regina Flannery, "Gros Ventre," in DeMallie, *Plains*, 677–94. For a book-length history, see Fowler's *Shared Symbols, Contested Meanings: Gros Ventre Culture and History, 1778–1984* (Ithaca, NY: Cornell University Press, 1987).

29. Unfortunately, a myth persists that fur traders established Chesterfield House in defiance of the wishes of the Blackfoot. R. Grace Morgan, *Beaver, Bison, Horse: The Traditional Knowledge and Ecology of the Northern Great Plains* (Regina, SK: University of Regina Press, 2020), 159–60.

30. Johnson, *Saskatchewan Journals*, 253.

31. HBCA B.34/a/3, "Chesterfield House Post Journals," 4 December 1801.

32. Information about all the known authors of these maps is summarized from Binnema, "Old Swan." Also see Theodore Binnema, "Conflict or Cooperation?: Blackfoot Trade Strategies, 1794–1815" (MA thesis, University of Alberta, 1992). Ac ko mok ki is discussed throughout this thesis; Ki oo cus on pp. 65–69, 71; and Ak ko wee ak on pp. 67–68, 71. Also see Binnema, *Common and Contested Ground*, 190–91; Hugh A. Dempsey, "A ca oo mah ca ye," in *Dictionary of Canadian Biography*, vol. 8 (University of Toronto/Université Laval, 2003–), accessed September 23, 2024, http://biographi.ca/en/bio/a_ca_oo_mah_ca_ye_8E.html.

33. See David A. Waller, "An Assessment of Individual Differences in Spatial Knowledge of Real and Virtual Environments" (PHD diss., University of Washington, 1999), 1.

34. Waller, "Assessment of Individual Differences," 17.

35. Walter McClintock, *The Old North Trail* (London: Macmillan, 1910), 434–35. Alice B. Kehoe discusses the connection between the "Rocky Mountains" and Old North Trail in "How the Ancient Peigans Lived," 96–97.

36. Jack Holterman, *Place Names of Glacier National Park* ([Helena, MT]: Riverbend Publishing, 2006).

37. Monmonier, *How to Lie with Maps*, 1.

38. Denis Wood, *The Power of Maps* (New York: Guilford Press, 1992), 1, emphasis original.

39. Warburton Pike, *The Barren Ground of Northern Canada* (London: Macmillan and Co., 1892), 280.

40. H. Somers Somerset, *The Land of Muskeg* (London: William Heineman, 1895), 201.

41. G.R. Crone, *Maps and Their Makers: An Introduction to the History of Cartography* (London: Hutchinson University Library, 1966), xi. For similar comments on non-Western maps, see Clara Egli Le Gear, "Map Making by Primitive Peoples," *Special Libraries* 35, no. 3 (1944): 82; and B.F. Adler, "Maps of Primitive Peoples," trans. H. de Hutorowicz, *Bulletin of the American Geographical Society*, no. 43 (1911): 672, 673. For an example of a map that uses a

coastline the same way, see June Helm, "Matonabee's Map," *Arctic Anthropology* 26, no. 2 (1989): 28–47.

42. David H. Pentland, "Cartographic Concepts of the Northern Algonquians," *Canadian Cartographer* 12, no. 2 (1975): 149, 157.

43. See Brian Reeves, "Ninaistákis—the Nitsitapii's Sacred Mountain: Traditional Native Religious Activities and Land Use/Tourism Conflicts," in *Sacred Sites, Sacred Places*, ed. David L. Carmichael et al. (New York: Routledge, 1994), 265; James Willard Schultz, *Blackfeet and Buffalo: Memories of Life among the Indians* (Norman: University of Oklahoma Press, 1962), 34; and Nelson, "Blackfoot Names," 159C (where the word is rendered {mis-tokis}). *Miisták* can also be interpreted to mean 'mountain' or 'The Mountains' in the case of the Rockies. Schultz identifies a specific area of the Lewis Range (Summit Mountain Ridge) as being the "backbone of the world" ({Makakin'si Ístúkí}, from *mamio'kakiikin* ['backbone'] and *miisták* ['mountains']), owing to its shape.

44. HBCA E.3/2, "Journal of a Journey," 30 December 1792. A similar passage appears in Fidler's note to the company published in Moodie and Kaye, "Ac Ko Mok Ki Map," 14.

45. In 1792, Fidler noted that the length of a day's journey was dependent on the distance between water sources, HBCA E.3/2, "Journal of a Journey," 4 December 1792.

46. Barb Tilander-Mack, ed. and comp., *Native Mapping Project: Treaty Seven Maps and Names* (n.p.: Friends of Geographical Names of Alberta Society, n.d.), 14, found that the upper Highwood River had its own name. Schultz gave different names for the Milk River, and for its north and south forks (*Blackfeet and Buffalo*, 374).

47. A fascinating account of Cree naming conventions is given in Pentland, "Cartographic Concepts," 157–58.

48. Moodie and Kaye, "Ac Ko Mok Ki Map," 13.

49. "Report on the Survey of the 3rd Base Line, Weste of the 4th Initial Meridian, and of the 2nd Base Line, from Range 25, Eastward, across the 4th Initial Meridian, to the 3rd initial Meridian, by Otto J. Klotz, Dominion Topographical Surveyor," in *Annual Report, Department of the Interior* (Ottawa: Maclean, Roger, & Co. 1883), 85.

50. Annora Brown, quoted in Molly P. Rozum, *Grasslands Grown: Creating Place on the U.S. Northern Plains and Canadian Prairies* (Winnipeg: University of Manitoba Press, 2021), 44.

51. James Doty, "A Visit to the Blackfoot Camp," ed. Hugh A. Dempsey, *Alberta Historical Review* 14, no. 3 (1966): 19. A fine study of the Sweetgrass Hills can be found in Johan F. Dormar, *Sweetgrass Hills: A Natural and Cultural History* (Lethbridge, AB: Lethbridge Historical Society, 2003).

52. HBCA E.3/2, "Journal of a Journey," 8 December 1792.

53. For short biographies of L'Heureux and Dawson, see Hugh A. Dempsey, "L'Heureux, Jean," in *Dictionary of Canadian Biography*, vol. 14 (University of Toronto/Université Laval, 2003–), accessed September 23, 2024, http://www.biographi.ca/en/bio/l_heureux_jean_14E.html; and Suzanne Zeller and Gale Avrith-Wakeam, "Dawson, George Mercer," in *Dictionary of Canadian Biography*, vol. 13 (University of Toronto/Université Laval, 2003–), accessed September 23, 2024, http://biographi.ca/en/bio/dawson_george_mercer_13E.html. Schultz wrote his own story in James Willard Schultz, *My Life as an Indian: The Story of a Red Woman and a White Man in the Lodges of the Blackfeet* (New York: Doubleday, Page & Company, 1907).

54. Harley, "Maps, Knowledge, and Power," 278.

55. Dawson, "Report," 17C.

56. No physical feature has been more significant among the Blackfoot than Chief Mountain. See Reeves, "Ninaistákis," 265–96. On the cultural importance of the Sweetgrass Hills to the Blackfoot, see Gerald A. Oetelaar, "Places on the Blackfoot Homeland: Markers of Cosmology, Social Relationships and History," in *Marking the Land: Hunter-Gatherer*

Creation of Meaning in their Environment, ed. William A. Lovis and Robert Whallon (New York: Taylor and Francis, 2016), 45–66; and J.F. Dormaar, "Sweetgrass Hills, Montana, USA," *Alberta Archaeological Review* Supplement (April 1997): 1–28.

57. Dawson, "Report," 28C.
58. Daniel J. Utting and Nigel Atkinson, "Proglacial Lakes and the Retreat Pattern of the Southwest Laurentide Ice Sheet across Alberta, Canada," *Quaternary Science Reviews* 225, no. 1 (2019): 106034; Chester B. Beaty, "Milk River in Southern Alberta: A Classic Underfit Stream," *Canadian Geographer / Géographie canadien* 34, no. 2 (1990): 171–74.
59. Brian Reeves and Margaret Kennedy, "Stone Feature Types as Observed at Ceremonial Site Complexes on the Lower Red Deer and the Forks of the Red Deer and South Saskatchewan Rivers with Ethnohistorical Discussion," *Archaeology in Montana* 58, no. 1 (2017): 1–44.
60. Reeves and Kennedy, "Stone Feature Types," 5. Although they acknowledge that some of these features may have been built by Gros Ventre (rather than Blackfoot speakers), Lindsay Amundsen-Meyer and Jeremy J. Leyden take issue with the grounds on which Reeves and Kennedy argue that some were. On the other hand, they argue that they have also found that anthropogenic stone features are often found at locations that afford good views of significant landforms such as Swan's Bill (Devil's Head Mountain), Chief Mountain, the Milk River Ridge, and the Sweet Grass Hills. See Amundsen-Meyer and Leyden, "Set in Stone," 175–202, esp. 194.
61. Pentland, "Cartographic Concepts," 158–59.
62. Pentland, "Cartographic Concepts," 159.
63. Jean L'Heureux, *Three-Persons and the Chokitapix: Jean L'Heureux's Blackfoot Geography of 1871*, trans. and ed. Allen Ronaghan (Red Deer: Central Alberta Historical Society Press, 2011).

2 | The Ac ko mok ki Map of 1801

1. See Binnema, "How Does a Map Mean?," and Binnema, *Common and Contested Ground*, 145–48.
2. Frantz and Russell, "stream" and "river," *Blackfoot Dictionary*.
3. Translations for Gros Ventre/Arapaho place names are taken from Andrew Cowell, Allan Taylor, and Terry Brockie, "Gros Ventre Ethnogeography and Place Names: A Diachronic Perspective," *Anthropological Linguistics* 58, no. 2 (2016): 132–70, and Andrew Cowell, personal communication (email) with Ted Binnema, 21 June 2022.
4. L'Heureux, *Three-Persons*, 73.
5. HBCA E.3/2, "Journal of a Journey," 10 December 1792.
6. L'Heureux, *Three-Persons*, 37, 87. But also see {Omak-etook-tey}, L'Heureux, *Three-Persons*, 72.
7. Doty, "Visit," 19.
8. Alan Rayburn, "Hot and Bothered by 'Disgusting Names,'" *Canadian Geographic* 113, no. 6 (November/December 1993): 80, 82.
9. Schultz, *Blackfeet and Buffalo*, 376, and C.C. Uhlenbeck and R.H. van Gulik, *A Blackfoot-English Vocabulary* (Amsterdam: Noord-Hollandsche Uitgevers Maatschappij, 1934), 245. Moodie and Kaye (9) suggest that this river is either the Marias River or its tributary, the Two Medicine Creek.
10. McClintock, *Old North Trail*, 438.
11. Schultz, *Blackfeet and Buffalo*, 376.
12. Moodie and Kaye (9) agreed that this is the Teton River.
13. Schultz, *Blackfeet and Buffalo*, 371.
14. See Thomas P. Roberts, "The Upper Missouri River from a Reconnaissance Made in 1872," *Contributions to the Historical Society of Montana*, no. 1 (1876): 259.

15. Schultz, *Blackfeet and Buffalo*, 371.
16. Schultz, *Blackfeet and Buffalo*, 377.
17. J.C. Nelson, "Blackfoot Names of a Number of Places in the North-West Territory, for the Most Part in the Vicinity of the Rocky Mountains," Appendix II to George Dawson, "Report on the Region in the Vicinity of the Bow and Belly Rivers, North-West Territory," *Geological and Natural History Survey and Museum of Canada Report of Progress, 1882-83-84*, 164C.
18. Montana Historical Society Archives, James H. Bradley Papers, MC 49, box 2, folder 10, book A, 81.
19. George Bird Grinnell, "Some Indian Stream Names," *American Anthropologist* 15, no. 2 (1913): 328. For a discussion, see Cowell, Taylor, and Brockie, "Gros Ventre Ethnogeography," 137.
20. Moodie and Kaye, "Ac Ko Mok Ki Map," 9.
21. Schultz, *Blackfeet and Buffalo*, 369.
22. Cowell, Taylor, and Brockie, "Gros Ventre Ethnogeography," 138.
23. Moodie and Kaye, "Ac Ko Mok Ki Map," 9.
24. Cowell, Taylor, and Brockie, "Gros Ventre Ethnogeography," 148. This agrees with Moodie and Kaye, "Ac Ko Mok Ki Map," 9.
25. Schultz, *Blackfeet and Buffalo*, 374.
26. Grinnell, "Some Indian Stream Names," 329.
27. Schultz, *Blackfeet and Buffalo*, 377. This agrees with Moodie and Kaye, "Ac Ko Mok Ki Map," 9.
28. Grinnell, "Some Indian Stream Names," 330.
29. Schultz, *Blackfeet and Buffalo*, 369. Moodie and Kaye (9) suggest that the river depicted by Fidler is either the Bighorn or Little Missouri. Also see Cowell, Taylor, and Brockie, "Gros Ventre Ethnogeography," 138.
30. Moodie and Kaye, "Ac Ko Mok Ki Map," 9.
31. Moodie and Kaye, "Ac Ko Mok Ki Map," 9.
32. HBCA E.3/2, "Journal of a Journey," 29 November 1792.
33. John Palliser, *Papers Relative to the Exploration by Captain Palliser of that Portion of British North America which lies between the Northern Branch of the River Saskatchewan and the Frontier of the United States; and between the Red River and Rocky Mountains* (London: George Edward Eyre and William Spottiswoode, 1859), 32. This mountain is the subject of Reeves's "Ninaistákis."
34. Schultz, *Blackfeet and Buffalo*, 373.
35. Meriwether Lewis and William Clark, *The Journals of the Lewis and Clark Expedition*, 13 vols., ed. Gary E. Moulton (Lincoln: University of Nebraska Press, 1983–2001), 8:103. Moodie and Kaye's conclusion that this is Teton Peak would assume a cartographic error on the part of Ac ko mok ki. Ac ko mok ki's estimate of the number of days' travel between points C and D and D and F would also seem inaccurate if this is Teton Peak. Moodie and Kaye, "Ac Ko Mok Ki Map," 9.
36. Moodie and Kaye, "Ac Ko Mok Ki Map," 9.
37. Schultz, *Blackfeet and Buffalo*, 369.
38. According to Moodie and Kaye, "most probably Rattlesnake Mountain" (9) near Cody, Wyoming, despite the incongruencies that interpretation assumes.
39. Moodie and Kaye (9) suggest Heart Mountain, Wyoming.
40. Moodie and Kaye (9) suggest the Big and Little Snowy Mountains.
41. Schultz, *Blackfeet and Buffalo*, 371.
42. Moodie and Kaye, "Ac Ko Mok Ki Map," 9.
43. Schultz, *Blackfeet and Buffalo*, 370.
44. Schultz, *Blackfeet and Buffalo*, 375.

45. Moodie and Kaye, "Ac Ko Mok Ki Map," 9.
46. Nelson, "Blackfoot Names," 167C.
47. Dawson, "Report," 48C.
48. Nelson, "Blackfoot Names," 163C; L'Heureux, *Three-Persons*, 73; Schultz, *Blackfeet and Buffalo*, 285.
49. Schultz, *Blackfeet and Buffalo*, 376; Nelson, "Blackfoot Names," 161C; L'Heureux, *Three-Persons*, 73.
50. Moodie and Kaye argue that "in view of their location as well as the types of features shown on the maps along the Rocky Mountain Front, these hills may well be the Judith Mountains in central Montana" (9). On the contrary, the location of these hills north of the Missouri River and between the Sun and Dearborn Rivers rules out the Judith Mountains.
51. Moodie and Kaye did not identify these hills.
52. Cowell, Taylor, and Brockie, "Gros Ventre Ethnogeography," 138. Moodie and Kaye (9) suggest the Crazy Mountains.
53. Cowell, Taylor, and Brockie, "Gros Ventre Ethnogeography," 138.
54. See Heinz W. Pyszczyk and Gabriella Prager, "Peter Fidler's Long Lost Chesterfield House: Have We Finally Found It?" *Saskatchewan Archaeology* 7, no. 2 (2021): 58–67.

3 | Three Indigenous Maps Drawn in 1802

1. Schultz, *Blackfeet and Buffalo*, 371.
2. Schultz, *Blackfeet and Buffalo*, 374; Nelson, "Blackfoot Names," 165C; L'Heureux, *Three-Persons*, 73.
3. Doty, "Visit," 17.
4. Schultz, *Blackfeet and Buffalo*, 374.
5. Nelson, "Blackfoot Names," 161C, 167C.
6. L'Heureux, *Three-Persons*, 73.
7. Nelson, "Blackfoot Names," 161C.
8. HBCA E.3/2, "Journal of a Journey," 31 December 1792.
9. James Doty to Isaac I. Stevens, 20 December 1854, Glenbow Archives, M-1100-145, 3.
10. Schultz, *Blackfeet and Buffalo*, 375; Dawson included his list in Nelson, "Blackfoot Names," 167C.
11. Nelson, "Blackfoot Names," 161C, 167C.
12. McConnell, quoted in Dawson, "Report," 93C.
13. Schultz, *Blackfeet and Buffalo*, 373.
14. Schultz, *Blackfeet and Buffalo*, 375.
15. Schultz, *Blackfeet and Buffalo*, 373.
16. Donald M. Lance, "The Origin and Meaning of 'Missouri,'" *Names: A Journal of Onomastics* 47, no. 3 (1999): 282.
17. Schultz, *Blackfeet and Buffalo*, 373; Nelson, "Blackfoot Names," 165C.
18. HBCA E.3/2, "Journal of a Journey," 28 February 1793.
19. Schultz, *Blackfeet and Buffalo*, 369; Nelson, "Blackfoot Names," 165C; L'Heureux, *Three-Persons*, 73.
20. Rich Aarstad et al., *Montana Place Names from Alzada to Zortman* (Helena: Montana Historical Society Press, 2009), 13.
21. Compare these identifications with those on Ac ko mok ki's 1801 map.
22. The location on the right bank of the Sun River suggests that Haystack Butte (see Photo 4) must be the landform. See discussion of Ac ko mok ki's 1801 map (page 70).
23. See Cowell, Taylor, and Brockie, "Gros Ventre Ethnogeography," 138.
24. See Barbara Belyea, "Mapping the Marias: The Interface of Native and Scientific Cartographies Cartographies," *Great Plains Quarterly* 17 (Summer/Fall 1997): 165–84.

25. HBCA B.34/a/3, "Chesterfield House Post Journals," 4 December 1801.
26. HBCA E.3/2, "Journal of a Journey," 5 December 1792.
27. HBCA E.3/2, "Journal of a Journey," 5 December 1792.
28. HBCA E.3/2, "Journal of a Journey," 25 December 1792.
29. HBCA E.3/2, "Journal from the mouth of the South Branch," 20 September 1800. Information of an event of 1801 is recorded in this entry dated 1800 because this copy of Fidler's journal was written later, with prefatory material in the 20 September 1800 entry.
30. See Binnema, "Conflict or Cooperation," 61; and Binnema, "Old Swan."
31. HBCA E.3/2. "Journal of a Journey," 16 December 1792
32. HBCA E.3/2. "Journal of a Journey," 14 December 1792.
33. Tilander-Mack, *Native Mapping Project*, 14.
34. HBCA E.3/2. "Journal of a Journey," 25 December 1792.
35. MacGregor, *Peter Fidler*, 74; Freeman, *Geographic Naming*, 51.
36. Michael C. Wilson, *Archaeological Studies in the Longview-Pekisko Area of Southern Alberta* (Edmonton: Archaeological Survey of Alberta, 1977).
37. Hugh Dempsey, *Napi: The Trickster* (Victoria, BC: Heritage House Publishing, 2018), 83.
38. Nelson, "Blackfoot Names," 162C.
39. HBCA E.3/2, "Journal of a Journey," 6 March 1793.
40. Nelson, "Blackfoot Names," 162C; L'Heureux, *Three-Persons*, 73.
41. Joachim Fromhold, *Alberta History, The Old North Trail (Cree Trail), 15,000 Years of Indian History, Prehistoric to 1750* ([Blackfalds, AB]: First Nations Publishing, 2012), 30.
42. Tilander-Mack, *Native Mapping Project*, 3.
43. Nelson, "Blackfoot Names," 160C.
44. Dawson, "Report," 27C; Nelson, "Blackfoot Names," 158C; L'Heureux, *Three-Persons*, 72.
45. Nelson, "Blackfoot Names," 158C; L'Heureux, *Three-Persons*, 43, 73.
46. Tilander-Mack, *Native Mapping Project*, 17; Nelson, "Blackfoot Names," 167C.
47. Jack W. Brink, *Imagining Head-Smashed-In: Aboriginal Buffalo Hunting on the Northern Plains* (Edmonton: Athabasca University Press, 2008), 25–26. Brink's *Imagining Head-Smashed-In* is an excellent introduction to Indigenous bison hunting, very accessible to a public audience, written by a foremost authority on the topic.
48. Tilander-Mack, *Native Mapping Project*, 14; Nelson, "Blackfoot Names," 162C.
49. Freeman, *Geographic Naming*, 43.
50. Lindsay M. Amundsen-Meyer, "Creating a Spatial Dialogue: A'kee Piskun and Attachment to Place on the Northwestern Plains," *Plains Anthropologist* 60, no. 234 (2015): 124–49.
51. McClintock, *Old North Trail*, 346–47.
52. Fromhold, *Alberta History*, 40.
53. Freeman, *Geographic Naming*, 48–49.
54. Nelson, "Blackfoot Names," 167C.
55. Schultz, *Blackfeet and Buffalo*, 72.
56. Nelson, "Blackfoot Names," 161C.
57. Nelson, "Blackfoot Names," 162C.
58. Gerald A. Oetelaar and David Meyer, "Movement and Native American Landscapes: A Comparative Approach," *Plains Anthropologist* 51, no. 199 (2006): 368.
59. Nelson, "Blackfoot Names," 162C.
60. Nelson, "Blackfoot Names," 158C.
61. Fromhold, *Alberta History*, 36.
62. HBCA E.3/2, "Journal of a Journey," Dec–Jan 1793.
63. See HBCA E.3/2, "Journal from the mouth of the South Branch of the Saskatchewan River to the confluence of the Bad & Red Deers Rivers where Chesterfield House is situated by Peter Fidler, 1800," 20 September 1800.

64. Herbert E. Bolton, "New Light on Manuel Lisa and the Spanish Fur Trade," *Southwestern Historical Quarterly* 17, no. 1 (1913): 61–66.
65. HBCA B.121/a/4, 12 May 1790.
66. Johnson, *Saskatchewan Journals*, 298.
67. Johnson, *Saskatchewan Journals*, 313.
68. James Andrew Cowell, personal correspondence (email) with Ted Binnema, 27 September 2022.
69. The Gros Ventre call themselves the *Aaniiih* ('white clay people'); see Barbara A. Latch, *A Concise Dictionary of Indian Tribes of North America* (Algonac, MI: Reference Publications, 1979), 166. {Nan ni en} appears to be the same term, which is used here to identify probably the Arapaho, close kin of the Gros Ventre. Some Arapaho spent the winter of 1801–02 with the Gros Ventre near Chesterfield House.

4 | The Ki oo cus Map of 1802

1. Assuming that Ki oo cus's exclusion of the North Saskatchewan River was intentional, it might be interpreted in any number of ways. Did Ki oo cus want to emphasize the fact that he and his band considered Chesterfield House to be the only post that was genuinely in their territory? Or did he want to downplay the importance of traders in the lives of the Blackfoot? We cannot know. However, for researchers of the Blackfoot, the map does remind us that the North Saskatchewan post journals can present only a fragmentary perspective on Blackfoot history. If the "woods edge" is to be interpreted as the edge of the territories of the Siksika at the time, the Siksika were nonetheless then familiar with the territory to the North Saskatchewan River, although, since the early 1790s, they were gravitating to the regions farther south.
2. HBCA E.3/2, "Journal of a Journey," 20 November 1792.
3. HBCA E.3/2, "Journal of a Journey," passim, but see especially, 28 February 1793.
4. HBCA E.3/2, "Journal of a Journey," 6 March 1793.
5. Nelson, "Blackfoot Names," 164C.
6. "Extract from Report on the Survey of Township Outlines, between the 3rd and 4th Initial meridians, by James F. Garden, D.L.S.," in *Annual Report, Department of the Interior* (Ottawa: Maclean, Roger, & Co. 1883), 83.
7. Several bison kill sites are located near Buffalo Lake. According to Captain John Palliser, "The Bull Lake, or as it is called by the Crees, 'Musloos Satikiegun,' is so styled from the resemblance of its outline to a buffalo hide stretched out for the purpose of being dressed; the small stream, La Queue, representing the tail of the animal." John Palliser, *The Journals, Detailed Reports, and Observations Relative to the Exploration by Captain Palliser…during the Years 1857, 1858, 1859, and 1860* (London: George Edward Eyre and William Spottiswoode, 1863), 88. Palliser's explanation of the origin of the lake's name should not be taken for granted. It is difficult to imagine a location from which the outline of the lake resembles an outstretched bison hide. It is at least as likely that the lake acquired its name because the vicinity of the lake was excellent bison hunting territory.
8. Nelson, "Blackfoot Names," 164C; L'Heureux, *Three-Persons*, 85.
9. Richard G. Forbis, "Field Notes on Sundial Hill and Buffalo Hill Cairns," 1958, Glenbow Archives, M-2105-24.
10. HBCA E.3/2, "Journal of a Journey," 28 February 1793.
11. L'Heureux, *Three-Persons*, 73; Nelson, "Blackfoot Names," 161C.
12. Eric J. Holmgren and Patricia M. Holmgren, *Over 2000 Place Names of Alberta*, 3rd ed. (Saskatoon: Western Producer Prairie Books, 1976), 122.
13. HBCA E.3/2, "Journal of a Journey," 28 February 1793.
14. L'Heureux, *Three-Persons*, 25.

15. MacGregor, *Peter Fidler*, 84. Also see Tracey Harrison, ed., *Central Alberta*, vol. 3 of *Place Names of Alberta* (Calgary: University of Calgary Press, 1994), 104.
16. Holmgren and Holmgren, *Over 2000 Place Names*, 113.
17. Richard G. Forbis, *Archaeological Site Inventory Data Form: ElPd-44* (Edmonton, AB: Historic Resources Management Branch, Alberta Culture, Arts and Status of Women, 1961), 1.
18. Nelson, "Blackfoot Names," 161C; L'Heureux, *Three-Persons*, 86; Holmgren and Holmgren, *Over 2000 Place Names*, 298.
19. McConnell, quoted in Dawson, "Report," 34C. Also see 92C.
20. L'Heureux, *Three-Persons*, 86; Margaret Kennedy, "A Map and Partial Manuscript of Blackfoot Country," *Alberta History* 62, no. 3 (2014): 10.
21. Holmgren and Holmgren, *Over 2000 Place Names*, 298.
22. L'Heureux, *Three-Persons*, 86.
23. Harrison, *Central Alberta*, 101.
24. Nelson, "Blackfoot Names," 164C.
25. David Thompson, *David Thompson's Narrative of His Explorations in Western America, 1784–1812*, ed. J.B. Tyrell (Toronto: Champlain Society, 1916), 324.
26. HBCA E.3/2, "Journal of a Journey," 30 November 1792.
27. L'Heureux, *Three-Persons*, 73; Nelson, "Blackfoot Names," 165C.
28. "Report on the Survey of the 11th Base Line, West of the 4th and 5th Initial Meridian, by C.A. Magrath, Dominion Topographical Surveyor," in *Annual Report, Department of the Interior* (Ottawa: Maclean, Roger, & Co. 1883), 102.
29. Maurice F.V. Doll, *The Boss Hill Site (FdPe 4) Locality 2: Pre-Archaic Manifestations in the Parkland of Central Alberta, Canada* (Edmonton: Alberta Culture, Historical Resources Division, Occasional Paper No. 2, 1982).
30. Nelson, "Blackfoot Names," 163C.
31. Nelson, "Blackfoot Names," 159C.
32. Nelson, "Blackfoot Names," 158C.
33. Nelson, "Blackfoot Names," 158C. Also see Dawson's {mo-ko-ons} in Nelson, "Blackfoot Names," 167C.
34. Joachim Fromhold, *Indian Place Names of the West* (Lulu, 2001), 69.
35. Dawson, "Report," 48C.
36. Nelson, "Blackfoot Names," 167C; Doty, "Visit," 19.
37. "Report on the Survey of the 3rd Base Line, West of the 4th Initial Meridian, and of the 2nd Base Line, from Range 25, Eastward, across the 4th Initial Meridian, to the 3rd initial Meridian, by Otto J. Klotz, Dominion Topographical Surveyor," in *Annual Report, Department of the Interior* (Ottawa: Maclean, Roger, & Co. 1883), 86.
38. Schultz, *Blackfeet and Buffalo*, 371.
39. Schultz, *Blackfeet and Buffalo*, 372.
40. Brian Reeves, "How Old Is the Old North Trail?" *Archaeology in Montana* 31, no. 2 (1990): 1–18.
41. Schultz, *Blackfeet and Buffalo*, 373.
42. Reeves and Kennedy, "Stone Feature Types," 5.
43. Nelson, "Blackfoot Names," 163C; L'Heureux, *Three-Persons*, 87.
44. Terry Beaulieu, "Place on the Plains: Modelling Past Movement along the Red Deer River" (PHD diss., University of Calgary, 2018), 243–45; Terry Beaulieu, "Decentring Archaeology: Indigenizing GIS Models of Movement on the Plains," *Plains Anthropologist* 67, no. 262 (2022): 157–59.
45. Nelson, "Blackfoot Names," 160C.
46. Nelson, "Blackfoot Names," 163C.
47. Frantz and Russell, "sáami," *Blackfoot Dictionary*; Nelson, "Blackfoot Names," 160C.

48. Nelson, "Blackfoot Names," 163C.
49. Don Hanna, *Historical Resources Impact Assessment, Hanna Region Transmission Development, Phase 1 Final Report, Permit 2010-182*, (Edmonton: Archaeological Survey of Alberta, 2011), 201.
50. Jeremy J. Leyden, *Historical Resources Impact Assessment, Keystone XL Pipeline Project, Alberta Segment. Final Report, Permit 2010-130*, (Edmonton: Historic Resources Management Branch, Alberta Culture and Community Services, 2011), 188–90.
51. Nelson, "Blackfoot Names," 164C.
52. See Terrance Gibson and Peggy McKeand, *Heritage Resources Impact Assessment of a Fletcher Challenge Petroleum Pipeline in the Eyehill Creek Locality, Bodo, Alberta, Permit 95–101*, report on file (Edmonton: Heritage Resource Management Branch, Alberta Community Development, 1996).
53. See Kurtis Alexander Blaikie, "Archaeological Investigations of FaOm-1: The Bodo Bison Skulls Site" (MA thesis, University of Alberta, 2005); Christie Peaches Grekul, "A Zooarchaeological Analysis of a Late Precontact Bison Kill Site in the Bodo Sand Hills of Alberta" (MA thesis, University of Alberta, 2007). The single best source can be found at Kennedy Munyikwa, et al., "Late Holocene Temporal Constraints for Human Occupation Levels at the Bodo Archaeological Locality, East-Central Alberta, Canada Using Radiocarbon and Luminescence Chronologies," *Plains Anthropologist* 59, no. 230 (2014): 109–43.
54. John S. McFarlane to James Bird, 24 February 1816, in Ted Binnema and Gerhard Ens, eds., *Hudson's Bay Company Edmonton House Journals, Correspondence, and Reports, 1806–1821* (Calgary: Historical Society of Alberta, 2012), 284.
55. Ted Binnema and Gerhard Ens, eds., *Hudson's Bay Company Edmonton House Journals: Including the Peigan Post, 1826–1834* (Calgary: Historical Society of Alberta, 2020), 208.
56. Binnema and Ens, *Hudson's Bay Company Edmonton House Journals, 1826–1834*, 220. For other references to encampments and meetings of various Indigenous groups at the Nose, see Binnema and Ens, *Hudson's Bay Company Edmonton House Journals, 1826–1834*, 301, 348.
57. Nelson, "Blackfoot Names," 160C.
58. Holmgren and Holmgren, *Over 2000 Place Names*, 257.
59. Nelson, "Blackfoot Names," 158C.
60. Schultz, *Blackfeet and Buffalo*, 86.
61. Nelson "Blackfoot Names," 158C.
62. Dawson, "Report," 19C. Also see Dawson, "Report," 150C.
63. J.M. Calder, *Stone Circles at Chin Coulee*, Archaeology in Southern Alberta, Occasional Paper No. 13 (Edmonton: Alberta Culture, Historical Resources Division,1979); Shawn Bubel, Gabriel Yanicki, and Jim McMurchy, "The Noble Point Effigy (DjPa-1)," *Alberta Archaeological Review*, no. 54 (2019): 9–17.
64. See Gary Adams, *Prehistoric Survey of the Lower Red Deer River, 1975*, Archaeological Survey of Alberta, Occasional Paper No. 3 (Edmonton: Archaeological Survey of Alberta, 1976).
65. Adams, *Prehistoric Survey*, 133.
66. See Ac ko mok ki's 1802 map.
67. John H. Brumley and Barry J. Dau, *Historical Resource Investigations within the Forty Mile Coulee Reservoir* (Edmonton: Archaeological Survey of Alberta, 1988).

5 | Tours and Trips on the Ac ko mok ki and Ki oo cus Maps

1. James Doty to Isaac I. Stevens, 20 December 1854, Glenbow Archives, M-1100-145, 4.
2. HBCA B.34/a/2, 22 November 1800 and 10 January 1801.

3. HBCA, E.3/2, 14 February 1793.
4. Johnson, *Saskatchewan Journals*, 284.
5. Johnson, *Saskatchewan Journals*, 285.
6. Recorded by Nelson, "Blackfoot Names," as {aka-naywass} ('many islands') and {aka-ámuskis} ('many lizards') (163C).
7. Recorded by Nelson, "Blackfoot Names," as {omaxi-spatchikway} ('big dunes') (163C). The Great Sand Hills are of major religious significance for the Blackfoot. It is the location where the dead go in the afterlife. This tradition has a deep antiquity. The Gray Site, located near the Great Sand Hills, contains evidence of communal burial dating as old as five thousand years. J.F.V. Millar, *The Gray Burial Site: An Early Plains Burial Ground* (Ottawa: Parks Canada Manuscript Report 30, 1978); J.F.V. Millar, "Mortuary Practices of the Oxbow Complex," *Canadian Journal of Archaeology*, no. 5 (1981): 103–17; William D. Wade, "Temporal and Biological Dimensions of the Gray Site Population," *Canadian Journal of Archaeology*, no. 5 (1981): 119–30.
8. Recorded by Nelson, "Blackfoot Names," as {á-ygh-kimi-kway} ('gap in the hills') (163C), it lent its name to the entire range of the Cypress Hills.
9. Recorded by Schultz, *Blackfeet and Buffalo*, as {áhmi saptsiko} ('sandy up') (369).
10. Recorded by Schultz, *Blackfeet and Buffalo*, as {Itsipótsi Stukwi} ('Where the Moutnains Come from Both Sides') (373).
11. Doty, "Visit," 19.
12. See James D. Keyser, "Writing-On-Stone: Rock Art on the Northwestern Plains," *Canadian Journal of Archaeology*, no. 1 (1977): 15–80; and Jack W. Brink, *Archaeological Investigations at Writing-On-Stone, Alberta*, Archaeology in Southern Alberta, Occasional Paper No. 12 (Edmonton: Alberta Culture, Historical Resources Division, 1978).
13. Doty, "Visit," 19.
14. Doty, "Visit," 22.
15. Recorded by Nelson, "Blackfoot Names," as {Etzi-kom} ('valley') (159C). The fresh-water creek entering the west arm of Pakowki Lake was an important camping place. Gerald A. Oetelaar and D. Joy Oetelaar, "People, Places and Paths: The Cypress Hills and the Niitsitapi Landscape of Southern Alberta," *Plains Anthropologist*, no. 51 (2006): 388.
16. Recorded by Nelson, "Blackfoot Names," as {Eno-kimi} ('long lake') (159C).
17. See Crone, *Maps and Their Makers*, xi; Le Gear, "Map Making," 79; and Adler, "Maps of Primitive Peoples," 671. North American fur traders and Indigenous people who travelled by canoe measured portages by "poses" (number of rests). Modern westerners continue to measure distance this way. Countless people think it normal to describe distance in terms of minutes or hours taken to walk, drive, or fly from one place to another.
18. Reeves, "How Old."
19. Stone effigies of trickster Napi are known throughout the Blackfoot territory, although this specific one is not documented in the Montana State archaeology database.
20. Recorded by Schultz, *Blackfeet and Buffalo*, as {Mutóksisiko} (373) and by Nelson, "Blackfoot Names," as {Motuksis} (165C) (both meaning 'knees'), these two buttes are located about thirty-two miles northwest of Fort Benton, and twenty-two miles due east of Brady, Montana. In contemporary Blackfoot, *mottoksís* refers to a knee.
21. George Bird Grinnell, *Blackfoot Lodge Tales* (New York: Charles Scribner's Sons, 1907), 137.
22. Fromhold, *Alberta History*.
23. Gerald A. Oetelaar and D. Joy Oetelaar, "The Structured World of the *Niitsitapi*: The Landscape as Historical Archive among Hunter-Gatherers of the Northern Plains," in *Structured Worlds: The Archaeology of Hunter-Gatherer Thought and Action*, ed. Aubrey Cannon (Oakville, CT: Equinox, 2011), 69–94; María N. Zedeño, Evelyn Pickering, and

François Lanoë, "Oral Tradition as Emplacement: Ancestral Blackfoot Memories of the Rocky Mountain Front," *Journal of Social Archaeology* 21, no. 3 (2021): 306–23.

24. Lindsay Amundsen-Meyer, "Nested Landscapes: Ecological and Spiritual Use of Plains Landscapes during the Late Prehistoric Period" (PHD diss., University of Calgary, 2014).
25. Fromhold, *Alberta History*, 9.
26. Past Rocky Spring Ridge and the Milk River Ridge, depicted on Ki oo cus's map.
27. Past Lone Pine, depicted on Ki oo cus's map.
28. Probably Antler Hill near Innisfail, Alberta. Recorded by Nelson, "Blackfoot Names," as {napia-okanes} (161C) and by L'Heureux, *Three-Persons*, as {nape-okan} (34), both meaning Old Man's Lodge. The same name appears to have been used for several Napi effigies in the Red Deer region.
29. Unidentified location. Dempsey, in *Napi*, puts it in the vicinity of the Wildcat Hills, but those are south of the Red Deer River, not north (11). It could be North Butte (recorded by Nelson, "Blackfoot Names," as 'Snake's Nose' (165C) {Piksisina-oksisis}) where, ironically, a downhill ski resort exists today.
30. Grinnell, *Blackfoot Lodge Tales*, 142–44.
31. Dempsey, *Napi*, 10.
32. Fromhold, *Alberta History*, 11.
33. See Stephen C. Hirtle and Judith Hudson, "Acquisition of Spatial Knowledge for Routes," *Journal of Environmental Psychology* 11, no. 4 (1991): 335–45.
34. For a fascinating study, see M.R. O'Connor, *Wayfinding: The Science and Mystery of How Humans Navigate the World* (New York: St. Martin's Press, 2019).

6 | Exploring the "Different Tribes" of Ac ko mok ki's Map and the Gros Ventre Map

1. Andrew Cowell is Professor of Linguistics at the University of Colorado. He has published *The Aaniiih (Gros Ventre) Language: A Revitalization Reference Grammar* (University of Nebraska Press, 2024) and, with Alonzo Moss Sr., *The Arapaho Language* (University Press of Colorado, 2008). He has also published lexical databases of the Arapaho (https://verbs.colorado.edu/arapaho/public/view_search) and Gros Ventre languages (the latter based heavily on the earlier work of Allan Taylor, and shared only with the Gros Ventre tribe at the moment). He is a (non-native) speaker of both Arapaho and Gros Ventre. Gros Ventre and Arapaho words cited in this chapter come from his personal knowledge and field notes, as well as lexical databases, unless otherwise noted.
2. Reuben Gold Thwaites, "The French Regime in Wisconsin," *Collections of the State Historical Society of Wisconsin*, no. 18 (1908): 185.
3. Archaeological evidence for the spread of the Shoshone people into what is now Montana and Alberta is limited, in part because of the short duration of this event (which does not translate well into the archaeological record), and in part because it is difficult to link archaeological materials with specific groups (based mostly on architecture, ceramic, and projectile point styles). It does appear, however, that the archaeological culture associated with ancestral Blackfoot (Old Women) contracts to the north at that time, coincidentally with the spread of archaeological cultures associated with the Great Basin (Highwood culture, possibly ancestral Shoshone) and the middle Missouri (One Gun culture, possibly ancestral Hidatsa/Crow; and Mortlach culture, possibly ancestral Assiniboine) regions. Trevor Peck, *Light from Ancient Campfires: Archaeological Evidence for Native Lifeways on the Northern Plains* (Edmonton: Athabasca University Press, 2011); J. Rod Vickers and Trevor Peck, "Identifying the Prehistoric Blackfoot: Approaches to Nitsitapii (Blackfoot) Culture History," in *Painting the Past with a Broad Brush*, ed. David L. Keenlyside and Jean-Luc Pilon (Ottawa: University of Ottawa Press, 2009), 473–97; Dale Walde, "Mortlach and One-Gun: Phase to Phase," in *Archaeology on the Edge: New Perspectives from the*

Northern Plains, ed. Jane Kelley and Brian Kooyman (Calgary: University of Calgary Press, 2004), 39–51.

4. In "French Regime in Wisconsin," Thwaites wrote, "This passage is difficult of interpretation. The Mahantas may have been the Maha, or Omaha, a Siouan tribe; but they are not known to have lived so far north. Neither does one descend the Missouri to reach the Riviere a la Coquille, which was the usual name given by French voyageurs to the Musselshell—a large northern affluent of the Missouri. Nor do the Panis (Pawnee) wander on the Musselshell, unless one accepts the conjecture that these were the Arikara, of the same linguistic stock as the Pawnee (Caddoan). The Arikara, however, were not known to have in historic times ascended so far to the north. The whole passage is confused, and doubtless interchanges the Musselshell and Platte Rivers, to the latter of which the description better applies" (188–89).

5. The memorandum was published in French in *Documents inédits sur l'histoire de la marine et des colonies Revue maritime et colonial: Mémoire de Bougainville sur l'état de la Nouvelle-France à l'époque de la guerre de Sept ans, (1757)* (N.p.: N.p., c. 1790), 578–79. An English translation was published in J.V. Brower, *The Missouri River and Its Utmost Source: Curtailed Narration of Geologic, Primitive and Geographic Distinctions Descriptive of the Evolution and Discovery of the River and Its Headwaters* (St. Paul, MN: Pioneer Press, 1897), 65–66. The version here—the authors' translation—retains more of the original French than Brower's version, but is influenced by it. Also see Thwaites, "French Regime in Wisconsin," 185–90.

6. Douglas R. Parks, "Enigmatic Groups," in *Plains*, ed. Raymond J. DeMallie, vol. 13 of *Handbook of North American Indians*, gen. ed. William C. Sturtevant (Washington, DC: Smithsonian Institute, 1990), 967.

7. Parks, "Enigmatic Groups," in DeMallie, *Plains*, 967.

8. Pierre Gaultier de Varennes de la Vérendrye, *Journals and Letters of Pierre Gaultier de Varennes de la Vérendrye and His Sons, with Correspondence between the Governors of Canada and the French Court, Touching the Search for the Western Sea*, ed. Lawrence J. Burpee (Toronto: Champlain Society, 1927), 410–11.

9. Parks, "Enigmatic Groups," in DeMallie, *Plains*, 967, 969–70.

10. Jean-Baptiste Truteau, *A Fur Trader on the Upper Missouri: The Journal and Description of Jean-Baptiste Truteau, 1794–1796*, trans. Mildred Mott Wedel, ed. Raymond J. DeMallie, Douglas R. Parks, and Robert Vézina (Lincoln: University of Nebraska Press, 2017), 253.

11. Lewis and Clark, *Journals of the Lewis and Clark Expedition*, 3:136.

12. Truteau, *A Fur Trader*, 605n3.

13. La Vérendrye, *Journals and Letters*, 412.

14. La Vérendrye, *Journals and Letters*, 412.

15. Both of these words are likely originally from Cheyenne, since *-etane* is the Cheyenne noun final for 'man' or more loosely for 'person,' and is used in ethnonyms. Louise Fisher et al., *Cheyenne Dictionary* (Lulu, 2017).

16. La Vérendrye, *Journals and Letters*, 414–22.

17. Parks, "Enigmatic Groups," in DeMallie, *Plains*, 969.

18. Parks, "Enigmatic Groups," in DeMallie, *Plains*, 969.

19. HBCA B.34/a/1, fo. 17b. The first fifteen folios comprise Fidler's rough journal for the period ending 20 November 1800. After that, Fidler collected a list of Gros Ventre words and phrases. Most of the content is clearly geared towards the words and phrases a trader would want to know. Only the list of Indigenous communities is transcribed here. On an earlier page (fo. 16d), Fidler noted that the Gros Ventre referred to William Tomison as "Nin nen ne—fat man" (*niinnen'i*). Note that in Gros Ventre standard orthography, the apostrophe represents a glottal stop, while /Θ/ indicates the sound 'th' as in 'three.' The

symbol /ɔ/ represents an open /o/, similar to in English 'pot.' The symbol /c/ represents the sound 'ts' as in 'pots.' Sounds written in superscript are devoiced or whispered.

20. wɔɔ'taanihtaach 'they have black feet.' A.L. Kroeber, "Ethnology of the Gros Ventre," *Anthropological Papers of the American Museum of Natural History*, vol. 1, part 4 (New York: American Museum of Natural History, 1908), recorded this as {Waotäⁿnixtääts} ('black-feet') (147).
21. kɔɔwunahaanɔh. Kroeber, "Ethnology," recorded this as {Kaⁿwinähääⁿ} (147).
22. niik'oubaach 'they wear grey blankets.' Kroeber, "Ethnology," recorded the Gros Ventre name for the Piikani as {Tsāⁿt'} (147). This is the word cɔɔtɔh meaning 'enemies' and also 'Blackfeet' generally (all groups).
23. siisiiyaanennɔh 'snake men.'
24. 'oounennɔh 'crows.'
25. kɔɔkɔɔ'aach 'they have frog-like/sloping heads.'
26. nɔɔkɔΘisiiniiinennɔh 'white mud men.'
27. wɔnɔɔsıbyouh(u)ch 'they smell bad.' The Gros Ventre form here is amply documented in the current language.
28. naayaaciicɔɔtɔh 'timber/woods/forest enemies' or 'timber/woods/forest Blackfoot' or 'timber/woods/forest Comanche' (since the word for 'enemy' was also applied to Blackfoot or Comanche groups by the Gros Ventre). The {...eet thot} is likely a misprint in the original source for {...eet chot} based on other renderings of this word in the early sources.
29. nɔɔcihɔh 'rabbits.' Kroeber, "Ethnology," recorded this as {Naⁿtsaⁿ} (147).
30. kɔɔkɔɔya'aach 'they have frog-like/sloping faces.'
31. nɔɔtinaahinɔh or nɔɔtineihinɔh. The first form is what would be expected etymologically and based on the modern Gros Ventre form, but the transcription actually suggests the second form (which is closer to Arapaho).
32. 'ɔ'ɔɔɔniinennɔh 'white clay men.' The word is now used for the Assiniboine.
33. ??? nih'ɔɔtoouh '??? tricksters, spiders.'
34. nih'ɔɔtoouh 'tricksters, spiders.'
35. No clear meaning can be determined for this form. A best-guess transcription would be biniiΘitiih, which appears to be an inanimate subject, intransitive verb in the plural (i.e., 'they are X', with root biiΘiti-), but no obvious meaning can be detected for such a verbal root, and it would be surprising to name a band of humans using an inanimate-subject verb.
36. Ac ko mok ki.
37. Hudson's Bay Company (HBC) traders knew Ac ko mok ki ('Old Swan') as Feathers, and the North West Company traders as Painted Feathers, because this man apparently took on the name Ac ko mok ki ('Old Swan') only upon his father's death in 1794. The Gros Ventre version of this name does not appear to mean either 'old swan' or 'feathers.' The first part most closely resembles 'ɔwuh- 'many,' while the second part is unclear, but appears to be most likely a noun ending in -iihiih, meaning 'one who is...'
38. See Andrew Cowell, *Naming the World: Language and Power among the Northern Arapaho* (Tucson: University of Arizona Press, 2018), 50–62, for discussion of this topic for the Arapaho, Lakota and Blackfoot.
39. See Cowell, *Naming the World* on Arapaho ethnogeography; Cowell, Taylor, and Brockie, "Gros Ventre Ethnogeography, 132–71, on Gros Ventre ethnogeography; and William C. Meadows, *Kiowa Ethnogeography* (Austin: University of Texas Press, 2008) on Kiowa ethnogeography.
40. See Cowell, *Naming the World*, 55–62.
41. Binnema, *Common and Contested Ground*, 153, 171.
42. Binnema, *Common and Contested Ground*, 181.

43. The introductory map shows as "Blackfoot" the territory of all three divisions, and the chapter on the "Blackfoot" does likewise. DeMallie, *Plains*, ix.
44. Douglas R. Parks, "Arikara," in DeMallie, *Plains*, 389.
45. Moodie and Kaye, "Ac Ko Mok Ki Map," 6.
46. Johnson, *Saskatchewan Journals*, 266n3. Discussion of other documentary evidence of earthlodge villages well west of the known Mandan and Hidatsa can be found in Binnema, *Common and Contested Ground*, 70, 77–81.
47. For some discussion of the evidence that scholars may have underestimated the presence of mobile Hidatsa bands, see Binnema, *Common and Contested Ground*, 77–78.
48. Binnema, *Common and Contested Ground*, 185–86.
49. Cluny and another site in the Porcupine Hills are grouped into the One Gun culture. William Byrne, *The Archaeology and Prehistory of Southern Alberta as Reflected by Ceramics* (Ottawa: Archaeological Survey of Canada Paper No. 14. National Museum of Man Mercury Series, National Museums of Canada, Ottawa, 1973); William Byrne, "A Demonstration of Migration on the Northern Great Plains," in *Archaeological Essays in Honor of Irving B. Rouse*, ed. Robert C. Dunnell and Edwin S. Hall Jr. (New York: Mouton, 1978), 247–73; R.G. Forbis, *Cluny, an Ancient Fortified Village in Alberta*, Occasional Paper No. 4 (Calgary: Department of Archaeology, University of Calgary, 1982); W. Jeffrey Kinney, "The Hagen Site, 24DW1: A Review of Historical Data and a Reassessment of Its Ceramic Assemblage and Position in Northern Plains Prehistory" (MA thesis, University of Montana, 1996); W. Raymond Wood and Alan Downer, "Notes on the Crow-Hidatsa Schism," *Plains Anthropologist* 22, no. 8 (1977): 83–100.
50. W. Raymond Wood and Thomas D. Thiessen, eds., *Early Fur Trade on the Northern Plains: Canadian Traders among the Mandan and Hidatsa Indians, 1738–1818* (Norman: University of Oklahoma Press, 1985), 197.
51. Douglas R. Parks, "Pawnee," in DeMallie, *Plains*, 544–45.
52. Prince Alexander Philipp Maximilian of Wied, *The North American Journals of Prince Maximilian of Wied*, 3 vols., ed. Stephen S. Witte and Marshal V. Gallagher, eds., trans. William J. Orr, Paul Schach, and Dieter Karch (Norman: University of Oklahoma Press, 2010), 2:8.
53. Parks, "Pawnee," in DeMallie, *Plains*, 544–45.
54. Fidler recorded the Gros Ventre names for the "Blackfoot" (Siksika) as {Waw tan ne tatch}, for the Kainai as {Kow win nā hawn}, and the Piikani as {Nee cow batch}. The Gros Ventre knew "Feathers" (Ac ko mok ki) as {Ow ah bess se he}, and "Fatt mans gang of Blackfeet" as {Ben ne thit te}. HBCA B.34/a/1, fo. 17b. The Blackfoot name for this man was {O mok api} ('Fat Man,' or 'Big Man'). He led a Siksika band distinct from Ac ko mok ki's. The Gros Ventre names for the Siksika and Kainai agree with the Gros Ventre and Arapaho names indicated by Hugh Dempsey in "Blackfoot," in DeMallie, *Plains*, 623, 624. The Gros Ventre name for the Piikani does not agree with the name noted by Dempsey, but agrees with the modern documented Gros Ventre name for this group. Dempsey noted that the Gros Ventre name for Piikani translated as "enemies" (627). In 1801, the Gros Ventre were still generally friendly with the Piikani. As noted earlier, the word "enemies" likely applied to some or all of the Blackfoot groups as a more general catch-all.
55. Hall, *Beneath the Backbone*; Pekka Hämäläinen, *Lakota America: A New History of Indigenous Power* (New Haven, CT: Yale University Press, 2019); Pekka Hämäläinen, *The Comanche Empire* (New Haven, CT: Yale University Press, 2008).
56. From *ksáá* ('earth') and *ookóówa* ('house').
57. *Issapowa* and *ssapo* have been recorded as Blackfoot names for Crow. Fred W. Voget, "Crow," in DeMallie, *Plains*, 715. This group may have referred specifically to the Ashalaho band or "Mountain Crow."

58. From *aamsskaap* ('south') and an unknown word. The location agrees with where {Sussews} appear to be placed on the Gros Ventre map (7). The HBC traders used the term {Sessew} to refer to the Tsuut'ina (Sarcee). However, the term {sessew} also appears to have been used for other tribes. In that case, the "south sessew" may have referred to a southern group, possibly Crow, in contrast to the "real sessew" (Tsuut'ina) to the north. Also see group 20.

59. Unknown etymology. Moodie and Kaye (6) proposed a reference to the Masikota division of the Cheyenne.

60. From *ksísskstaki* ('beaver') and *tapi* ('people')? This somewhat resembles the Blackfoot word for Cheyenne *ki.xtsipimi.tapi.wa.* (John H. Moore, Margot P. Liberty, and A. Terry Strauss, "Cheyenne," in DeMallie, *Plains*, 864, 881); and *kiihtsipimiitapi* (Frantz and Russell, *Blackfoot Dictionary*). One must wonder if Fidler assumed that he heard the word for beaver (*ksisskstaki*) embedded in the Blackfoot name for the Cheyenne.

61. Perhaps a reference to the dispute between Crow and Hidatsa as recorded in tradition. See Wood and Downer, "Notes."

62. Includes final *-otsisa'kaa* ('tattooed'). In this case, the English term makes the identity straightforward. Many groups referred to the Arapaho as "Tattooed People" in their own languages, and "Arapaho" is probably derived from the Hidatsa and Mandan term, which translates at "Tattooed People." It is also the term by which Fidler knew the Arapaho.

63. From *sinopáá* ('swift fox') and *tapi* ('people').

64. From *ki'takápssin* ('garter').

65. Includes final *-yisstoyi* ('beard'). Also see Moore, Liberty, and Strauss, "Cheyenne," in DeMallie, *Plains*, 882.

66. From *ikinaki* ('leg') and *tapi* ('people'). Probably an erroneous repetition of 13, as 11 is depicted on the map.

67. From *ohpikíístsi* ('ribs') and *tapi* ('people').

68. From *oápisakis* ('thigh') and *tapi* ('people').

69. From an unknown word and *tapi* ('people'). The Oevemana band of Northern Cheyenne were known as the "scabby" people.

70. From *makóyi* ('wolf') and *tapi* ('people').

71. From *matóyi* ('grass') and *ookóówa* ('house').

72. From *mamíí* ('fish') and *ooyi* ('eater').

73. See McClintock, *Old North Trail*, 525. {Nits-Ik-Opa} ('double root') is the Blackfoot name for Squaw Root or Yampah (*Perideridia gairdneri*). Also see Frantz and Russell, *Blackfoot Dictionary*, *niistsikápa's* ('double root'). Several groups, including the Shoshone and Crow, used the ethnonym "yampah eaters" to refer to the Yamparika Comanche, or to the Comanche more generally. Thomas W. Kavanaugh, "Comanche," in DeMallie, *Plains*, 902. The number of tents suggests a reference only to the Yamparika. The Yamparika were the northernmost division of the Comanche. It this identification is correct, Ac ko mok ki's understanding of the location of these distant people was vague. However, according to Kavanaugh, the name "root people" could also refer to Shoshone. Thomas W. Kavanaugh, *The Comanches: A History, 1706–1875* (Lincoln: University of Nebraska Press, 1966), 494n9.

74. From *miistsís* ('forest') and *tapi* ('people')? The Jupe Comanche ('wood people,' or 'timber people') were closely connected with the Yamparika. Kavanaugh, *The Comanches*, 494n9.

75. From *saahsi* (?), *piksííksiinaa* ('snake'), and *tapi* ('people'). See group 3 on the meaning of *sussew*. The reference to snake makes it likely that this was a Shoshone band.

76. From an unknown word and *tapi* ('people').

77. From *sik* ('black'), possibly *ootokísa* ('skin'), and *tapi* ('people'). The Bannock and Ute were known as the Black People to the Gros Ventre/Arapaho.

78. Unknown etymology, which could relate to 29. The Bitterroot Salish were familiar to the HBC traders, so the identity is obvious. However, the Blackfoot does not correspond to known Blackfoot ethnonyms.
79. From *komono* ('violet' or 'green') and *tapi* ('people'). As noted above, Fidler recorded the Gros Ventre name for the "Blue Mud Indians" as {Naw cotch is seen in nin nin} ('white mud men'). HBCA B.34/a/1, fo. 17b.
80. From *áápaiai* ('ermine') or *áápi* ('white'), and *tapi* ('people').
81. Unclear etymology, though ends with *tapi* ('people').
82. From *aahkioohsa'tsis* ('boat') and *tapi* ('people'). In sign language, paddling was used to refer to Pend d'Oreilles and Kalispel.
83. Probably from *okaa* ('snare') and *tapi* ('people'). The Snare Indians were a small band that appears to have inhabited the upper reaches of the North Thompson and Fraser Rivers. They were probably Shuswap people.
84. From an unknown word and *náámaa* ('bow').
85. Unknown etymology.
86. The Blackfoot name for the Kootenai is *kottonaa'*. Fidler elsewhere gave the Gros Ventre name for the {Cottona} as {Woon nā sil be ootch} (*wɔnɔɔsibyouhuch* 'they smell bad'). HBCA B.34/a/1, fo. 17b.
87. From *-inno* ('long'), *ssp* ('hair'), and *tapi* ('people'). On the Gros Ventre map, the {Caw kaw yaw etch} are identified as "Flathead," but in a list of Gros Ventre words and phrases, Fidler indicated that the {Caw caw yaw etch} were "Long Hair Indians." HBCA B.34/a/1, fo. 17b. That would suggest that an Interior Salish other than the Bitterroot Salish is intended here.
88. In a Gros Ventre list of words, Fidler rendered "Flat heads" as {Caw caw aytch} (HBCA B.34/a/1, fo. 17b). The current Gros Ventre name for the Flathead is *kɔɔkɔɔ'aach* 'they have sloped/frog-like heads.' Kroeber recorded the Gros Ventre name for the Bitterroot Salish as {kaakaäänin} (*kɔkɔɔ'aanen'i*) glossed as "flathead-man." Kroeber, "Ethnology," 147. The *-nen'I* means 'man.' All of these forms contain the Gros Ventre root for "flathead." The different endings might be attributable to the fact that Kroeber's word was applied to the entire people generally, but Fidler's renderings were to separate divisions of the Bitterroot Salish, but free variation between verbal forms means 'they are X' and nominal forms meanings 'X man' is common in both Arapaho and Gros Ventre ethnonyms. Ferdinand V. Hayden recorded the Arapaho ethnonym for the Bitterroot Salish as {ka-ka'-i-thi} (*kookoo'eiʒi*' 'they have sloped/frog-like heads'). Ferdinand V. Hayden, *On the Ethnography and Philology of the Indian Tribes of the Missouri Valley* (Philadelphia: C. Sherman & Son, 1862), 326.
89. In a word list, Fidler identified the {Caw caw yaw etch} as "Long Hair Inds." See HBCA B.34/a/1, fo. 17b. In current Gros Ventre *kookooya'aach* ('they have sloping/frog-like faces') refers to Interior Salish.
90. *siisiiyaanennoh* 'snake men.'
91. This corresponds well to the known Gros Ventre and Arapaho ethnonyms for the Crow (*'oounennɔh* and *houunenno*, respectively). Kroeber rendered the Gros Ventre name for the Crow as {hounen} (crow men). Kroeber, "Ethnology," 147. Hayden rendered it as {A-i-nun'}. Hayden, *On the Ethnography*, 326. When this map was made, the Gros Ventre and Arapaho were on better terms with the Crow than the Blackfoot-speaking groups were. HBC traders at this time often referred to the Crow as the "Crow Mountain Indians," but the Gros Ventre name denotes only "Crow people." In fact, it is likely that this was a reference to the River Crow. Current Gros Ventre has a specific name for the Mountain Crow, *nɔh'ɔhoounennɔh* 'Upland Crows.'
92. No clear etymology or transcription. Best guess transcription is *'iiθei'ciineih*.
93. *siisiiyaanennɔh* 'snake men.' See 3. This appears to refer to a small band of Shoshone. It may be a repetition of 3, as a "6" is not depicted on the map.

Notes   179

94. *naayaaciicɔɔtɔh* means "woods enemies." Fidler elsewhere indicated that the Gros Ventre referred to "Sussews" as {Nay aytch eet shot}. HBCA B.34/a/1, fo. 17b. The Stoney apparently referred to the Sarcee as "woods enemy." But this group is in the wrong place to be the Sarcee. It agrees with the location in which Ac ko mok ki put "Sessew's Inds." It might be a reference to a division of the Crow.

95. The Gros Ventre word is *'inɔn'aanɔh*. Also see Loretta Fowler, "Arapaho," in DeMallie, *Plains*, 840. Kroeber recorded the Gros Ventre name for the Arapaho as {hinan'än}. He recorded the Arapaho autonym as {hinanaei-naⁿ}. It is evident that the Gros Ventre applied the ethnoym/autonym to this largest division of the Arapaho. In 1908, Kroeber reported that the smaller divisions had been absorbed into the larger. Kroeber, "Ethnology," 145–46.

96. The Gros Ventre name for the Cheyenne is *'itasiinɔh*. The Arapaho use the same term, *hitesiino'*.

97. Analysis unclear. Best guess on the form is *tooutiinɔh* (a plural animate noun).

98. *niicaahiinẹnnɔh* 'river men.' Jerrold E. Levy, "Kiowa," in DeMallie, *Plains*, 924, gave the Arapaho ethnonym for the Kiowa as {ni·čci·héhi·nén} (River Person), and Hayden as {ni-ci'-he-nen-a}. Hayden, *On the Ethnography*, 326. The Arapaho form is *niiciihiinenno'* or archaic *niiciihehiinenno'* 'river men.'

99. This form clearly includes the final element *-inennɔh* 'men/people.' The initial element *cɔ(ɔ)w-* is unclear however, and no etymology or meaning is apparent for the overall form.

100. Jim Gibson has hypothesized that the {Chow win nin} and {E Chaugh a nin} were bands of Mountain Crow. The location of the groups supports this interpretation. The first Gros Ventre word may simply be a mishearing of *'oounenɔh* 'crow men.' It certainly contains the ending *-nennɔh* 'men.' The second word looks most plausibly like *'iicɔɔ(ɔ)-?-nennɔh* 'rib' or 'pipe'-?-men.' This could be the same group as the "Rib People" referred to by Bougainville. Jim Gibson, untitled paper, HBCA, PP1988-14.

101. Fidler's indication that these were "Fall" allows us to identify this as one of the small Arapaho bands that was later absorbed into other bands. These are almost certainly the {Hanahawunena} Arapahoan group. See Fowler, "Arapaho," in DeMallie, *Plains*, 861. Gros Ventre *'ɔɔ'nɔhwuunennɔh*, Arapaho *hoo'onohowuunenno'*.

102. The element *nɔɔba'eei-* means "southwards", so *nɔɔba'eei-biininaa-ch* is a reference to people from the south, or more specifically a southern component of the *biininaach*.

103. Gros Ventre called the Bannock *wɔɔ'taanihiinennɔh* 'black men,' while the Arapaho used the same term for the Ute, *woo'teenehi3i'* 'they are black.' Kroeber, "Ethnology," 147; Also see 22 on Ac ko mok ki's map.

104. The name combines the words "southward" (*nɔɔba'eei-*) with the name for Shoshone (*siisiiyaanennoh*). Thus, this may refer to a southern Shoshonean group or a northern division of the Comanche, or perhaps a division of the Utes. Hayden indicated that the Arapaho "formerly" called the Comanche "snakes" but that they latterly used the term {Ca'-tha} (*coo3o'* 'enemies'). Hayden, *On the Ethnography*, 326.

105. The name for the Spanish, *siisiiyaanennɔh nih'ɔɔtoouh*, is a compound of the name for Shoshone, followed by the name for French or English Europeans, thus 'Shoshone Whites.' Given that Fidler indicated that even the "Tattood Indians" had never seen a European before they met him, his informants must have reported on these people based on repute. Perhaps the Gros Ventre associated these Europeans with the Snake (Shoshone/Comanche/Ute) who had direct contact with the Spanish in New Mexico.

106. The word *'ɔteeinennɔh*, translates to 'sheep men,' which must certainly refer to the Navajo.

107. The Gros Ventre, *ti'iihiinennɔh* ('killdeer men') is likely a reference to the Jicarilla Apache. The same word is used by the Arapaho for this group.

108. *nɔɔwɔcinahaanɔh*. The Nawathinehena (South People) were the southernmost division of the Arapaho. At the time, their language was quite divergent from Arapaho, Gros Ventre, or

Besawunena, although they transitioned to the language of the Arapaho over the course of the nineteenth century when they merged with the latter and lost their distinctive identity. Andrew Cowell, "The Phonology of the NoowoΘineheeno? Language and Its Relation to Arapaho and Cheyenne," in *Papers of the Fifty-Second Algonquian Conference*, ed. Monica Macaulay and Margaret Noodin (East Lansing: Michigan State University Press, 2023), 1–17. For more on this group, see Fowler, "Arapaho," in DeMallie, *Plains*, 840, 861; Ives Goddard, "The Languages of the Plains: Introduction," in DeMallie, *Plains*, 76; A.L. Kroeber, "Arapaho Dialects," *University of California Publications in American Archaeology and Ethnology* 12, no. 3 (1916): 74. The Arapaho had not yet split into northern and southern bands in 1800, so while these people were a separate, southerly Arapahoan people, they were not directly ancestral to the eventual Southern Arapaho.

109. The similarity of the name of this tiny band with that of 7, despite what appears to be a great distance between them, is intriguing.

110. Again, the similarity of the name of this tiny band with that of 12 is intriguing.

111. No Gros Ventre name for the Plains Apache (Kiowa Apache) is known, but the Arapaho ethnonym for the Plains Apache is *ɜoxkoheinenno'* (dubiously translated as "people who play on bone instruments"), Morris W. Foster and Martha McCollough, "Plains Apache," in DeMallie, *Plains*, 940.

112. Fowler "Arapaho," in DeMallie, *Plains*, 840, 861, indicated that the Besawunena (Big Lodge People, or Wood Lodge People) were the northernmost Arapaho division, but in fact their language was transitional between Arapaho and Gros Ventre, so they must have been located between these two groups. Note that they are placed far to the south on this map. Also see Goddard, "Languages of the Plains," in DeMallie, *Plains*, 61, 62.

113. *biniicɔbaach* translates as 'they go on foot' (as opposed to riding) or more loosely 'they walk.' The Awaxawi were known as 'gens de soulier' in French and 'Shoe Indians' in English.

114. The recorded Arapaho and Gros Ventre ethnonyms for the Mandan and Hidatsa—{wa-nuk'-e-ye'-na} and {Wuhnókayan}, respectively—are very similar to each other and to Fidler's rendering, which corresponds to *wɔhnɔkɔyaanɔh* ('lodges in a row') (Arapaho *woohnokoyeinoo'* 'lodges in a row' or *woohnokoyeiɜi'* 'they have lodges in a row'). Both terms denoted earthlodge dwellers. The general term "Hidatsa" dates from the second half of the nineteenth century. Before that time, the term was used to refer only to one of the three divisions of these people. Frank Henderson Stewart, "Hidatsa," in DeMallie, *Plains*, 344. Note that another recorded Gros Ventre term for the Hidatsa specifically is 'lower Gros Ventres' (*nɔɔwɔɔɔ'ɔɔniiinennɔh*).

115. If Fidler confused the *s* sound and *th* sound, the cartographer may have intended *'aakisii'ouhuch* 'they are small.'

116. *'aabeΘoou'* means "Big Crow."

117. This could be *biniiinennoh* ('soldiers/club men') or perhaps *bih'ihiinennoh* ('deer men').

118. The Arapaho and Cheyenne apparently did not distinguish between the Omaha and Ponca, using their own pronunciation of the Omaha name (Arapaho *howohoono'*). Donald N. Brown and Lee Irwin, "Ponca," in DeMallie, *Plains*, 431.

119. *Nɔɔtineihinɔh*. In a word list, Fidler indicated that the Gros Ventre referred to the "Stone Inds" as {Naut te nay in}. HBCA B.34/a/1, fo. 17b. According to Kroeber, "Ethnology," 147, the Gros Ventre referred to the Assiniboine as {naⁿdjineihin}, and the Sioux as {naⁿwinaⁿdjinei} (*nɔɔwu-nɔɔtineihinɔh*, 'lower-Assiniboine') while the Arapaho referred to the Sioux as {naⁿtinei} (*nootinei*, pl. *nootineihino'*).

120. In his separate word list, Fidler indicated that the Gros Ventre referred to the French as {Nee e haud thu} (*nih'ɔɔtoouh*), but the English as {Cheese ne haud thu} (*?-nih'ɔɔtoouh*). HBCA B.34/a/1, fo. 17b. Kroeber recorded the Arapaho word for Europeans as {nih'āⁿθaⁿ}

(nih'oo3oo) and the Gros Ventre word as {nix'ãⁿt} (nih'ɔɔtɔh—singular). Kroeber, "Arapaho Dialects," 75. The words mean 'spider,' 'trickster,' and 'white person' in both languages.

121. kɔnɔɔniinɔh. The Arapaho word for the Arikara is koonoonii3i', dubiously glossed as 'they have broken jaws,' or alternately the noun konoonii(n), pl. konooniino'.

122. {wat taw} is a prefix, suggesting a connection with the {Been nen in} (30), but its Gros Ventre meaning is unclear. 35 is not depicted on the map.

123. This may be a reference to the Dakota. See 32. No Gros Ventre meaning is apparent for the form.

124. Kroeber, "Ethnology," 145.

7 | Contributions of Indigenous Cartography to Western Cartography

1. HBCA B.22/e/1.
2. HBCA B.51/e/1.
3. HBCA A.6/18, fo. 199–213, enclosure to letter from the Governor and Committee to Thomas Thomas, Governor of the Northern Department, Hudson Bay House, London, 9 April 1814, head 74.
4. HBCA B.22/e/1, fos. 1d–2.
5. J.B. Harley, "The Map and the Development of the History of Cartography," in *Cartography in Prehistoric, Ancient, and Medieval Europe and the Mediterranean*, ed. J.B. Harley and David Woodward, vol. 1 of *The History of Cartography* (Chicago: University of Chicago Press, 1987), 3–4. Also see Belyea, "Inland Journeys, Native Maps." For a fine study of Indigenous maps geared towards a popular and scholarly audience, see Mark Warhus, *Another America: Native American Maps and the History of Our Land* (New York: St. Martin's Press, 1997).
6. Quoted in Ruggles, *Country So Interesting*, 3.
7. Quoted in Lewis, "Maps, Mapmaking," 67–68.
8. Louis De Vorsey, "Amerindian Contributions to the Mapping of North America: A Preliminary View," *Imago Mundi* 30, no. 1 (1978): 71–78; Lewis, "Maps, Mapmaking"; James P. Ronda, "'A Chart in His Way': Indian Cartography and the Lewis and Clark Expedition," *Great Plains Quarterly* 4, no. 1 (1984): 43–53.
9. Chrestien Le Clercq, *New Relation of Gaspesia: With the Customs and Religion of the Gaspesian Indians*, trans. and ed. William F. Ganong (Toronto: Champlain Society, 1910), 136.
10. John Lawson, *A New Voyage to Carolina* (London: N.p., 1709), 205.
11. Louis Armand de Lom d'Arce, Baron de Lahontan, *New Voyages to North America* (London: Printed for H. Bonwicke, T. Goodwin, M. Wotton, B. Tooke; and S. Manship, 1703), 2:13.
12. Lewis, "Maps, Mapmaking," 81.
13. Reproductions of Buache's map have been published often. One of these, together with a helpful discussion can be found in Barbara Belyea, *Dark Storm Moving West* (Calgary: University of Calgary Press, 2007), 52–53. See also *Carte physique des terrains les plus élevés de la partie occidentale du Canada*, McGill University Libraries, Internet Archive, https://archive.org/details/McGillLibrary-123774-2150.
14. John Long, *Voyages and Travels of an Indian Interpreter and Trader* (London: Printed for the author, 1791), 83.
15. William Robertson cited Lafitau and Lahontan frequently in his *History of America*, but he showed no interest in their descriptions of Indigenous mapping. See William Robertson, *History of America*, 3rd ed., 3 vols. (London: Strahan, Cadell, and Balfour, 1780), passim. Examples can be found at 2:86, 96, 102, 104, 106, 109, 152, 156, 158–60, 163.
16. John Reinhold Forster, *History of the Voyages and Discoveries* (London: G.G.J. and J. Robinson, 1786), 388; Lewis, "Maps, Mapmaking," 136.

17. Ruggles, *Country So Interesting*, 30.
18. Ruggles, *Country So Interesting*, 42–43. For an analysis of the map drawn in 1716–17 (HBCA G.1/29), another drawn in 1760 (G.2/8), and the map by Matonabbee and Idotlyazee drawn in 1767 (G.2/27) see Helm, "Matonabee's Map."
19. Ruggles, *Country So Interesting*, 243.
20. The map by Edward Jarvis and Donald McKay (HBCA G.1/13) and a similar one by John Hodgson (HBCA G.2/28) are discussed in John Jackson, "Inland from the Bay: Mapping the Fur Trade," *The Beaver* 72, no. 1 (Feb.–Mar. 1992): 37–42; and in R. Raymond Wood, "The Earliest Map of the Mandan Heartland: Notes on the Jarvis and Mackay 1791 Map," *Plains Anthropologist* 55, no. 216 (2010): 155–76. This map was incorporated into Arrowsmith's 1795 map.
21. For a valuable study, see Pentland, "Cartographic Concepts," 149–60.
22. See Jennifer S.H. Brown, "Rupert's Land, *Nituskeenan*, Our Land: Cree and English Naming and Claiming around the Dirty Sea," in *New Histories for Old: Changing Perspectives on Canada's Native Pasts*, ed. Ted Binnema and Susan Neylan (Vancouver: UBC Press, 2007), 18–40. The beads-on-a-string cartographic style appears to have been typical of all Indigenous people in the Canadian Shield region. When John Long described the maps he received, he noted that "their drafts consist principally of lakes and rivers, as they seldom travel much by land; and when their track over land is described, it is perhaps only a short portage which they cross in order again to pursue their journey over their favourite element." Long, *Voyages and Travels*, 83.
23. The map drawn by Shew dithe da on 25 July 1791 of the region between Great Slave Lake and the Hudson Bay is printed in Hearne and Turnor, *Journals of Samuel Hearne and Philip Turnor*, 419. This is the only Indigenous map that Turnor is known to have collected.
24. HBCA G.2/13, discussed in Ruggles, *Country So Interesting*, 53–54, 197.
25. Ruggles, *Country So Interesting*, 4. For a further discussion, see Ted Binnema, *Enlightened Zeal: The Hudson's Bay Company and Scientific Networks, 1670–1870* (Toronto: University of Toronto Press, 2016), 47–74.
26. Harley, "Deconstructing the Map," 4.
27. G. Malcolm Lewis, "Indian Maps: Their Place in the History of Plains Cartography," *Great Plains Quarterly* 4, no. 2 (1984): 91.
28. Gregory A. Waselkov, "Indian Maps of the Colonial Southeast," in *Powhatan's Mantle: Indians in the Colonial Southeast*, ed. Peter H. Wood, Gregory A. Waselkov, and M. Thomas Hatley (Lincoln: University of Nebraska Press, 1989): 293–94.
29. G. Malcolm Lewis, "Indian Maps," in *Old Trails and New Directions: Papers of the Third North American Fur Trade Conference*, ed, Carol M. Judd and Arthur J. Ray (Toronto: University of Toronto Press, 1980), 11.
30. Ronda, "'A Chart in His Way,'" 43.
31. Ronda, "'A Chart in His Way,'" 51–52.
32. Ruggles, *Country So Interesting*, 61.
33. Ruggles, *Country So Interesting*, 9.
34. Coolie Verner, "The Arrowsmith Firm and the Cartography of Canada," in *Explorations in the History of Canadian Mapping: A Collection of Essays*, ed. Barbara Farrell and Aileen Desbarats (Ottawa: Association of Canadian Map Libraries and Archives, 1988), 53.
35. Verner, "Arrowsmith Firm," 53. Evidence that Arrowsmith cooperated with the company before 1794 can be found in the fact that the results of surveys by Turnor, Fidler, and Ross were published as *Result of Astronomical Observations Made in the Interior Parts of North America*, and *Observations Made at Slave Lake*, both of which were "printed for A. Arrowsmith" in 1794, and in the fact that Arrowsmith's first map incorporated the results of those surveys.

36. Verner, "Arrowsmith Firm," 53.
37. Ruggles, *Country So Interesting*, 60. Also see Binnema, *Enlightened Zeal*, 95–97, 104–23.
38. Ruggles, *Country So Interesting*, 61–67; Binnema, *Enlightened Zeal*, 123.
39. Victor G. Hopwood, "David Thompson and His Maps," in *Explorations in the History of Canadian Mapping: A Collection of Essays*, ed. Barbara Farrell and Aileen Desbarats (Ottawa: Association of Canadian Map Libraries and Archives, 1988), 207, 206, 209.
40. Binnema, *Enlightened Zeal*, 96–98, 111–18, 120–23.
41. De Vorsey, "Amerindian Contributions," 71–78.
42. Alexander Mackenzie, *Voyages from Montreal* (London: T. Cadell, Jr. and W. Davies, 1801), 204.
43. Mackenzie, *Voyages from Montreal*, 247.
44. Mackenzie, *Voyages from Montreal*, 253.
45. Mackenzie, *Voyages from Montreal*, 253
46. Simon Fraser, *The Letters and Journals of Simon Fraser: 1806–1808*, ed. W. Kaye Lamb (Toronto: Dundurn Press, 2007), 87, 97, 103, 154, 160, 163, 219, 229.
47. Simon McGillivray, "Voyage to Simpson's River by Land Summer 1833," HBCA B.188/a/18, fo. 2.
48. Simpson, *Narrative of a Journey*, 1:207.
49. HBCA B.201/a/6, 8 March 1842. Also see James R. Gibson, *Fort Simpson Post Journals, 1834–1843*, vol. 3 (pub. by author, 2022), 781.
50. Rundstrom, "Cultural Interpretation," 158–61; Beechey, *Voyage to the Pacific*, 2:398–400; John Spink, "Eskimo Maps from the Canadian Eastern Arctic" (MA thesis, University of Manitoba, 1969).
51. George Davidson, "Explanation of an Indian Map of the Rivers, Lakes, Trails and Mountains of the Chilkat to the Yukon Drawn by the Chilkat Chief, Kohklux, in 1869," *Mazama* (April 1901), 75–82; John Cloud, "The Tlingit Map of 1869: A Masterwork of Indigenous Cartography," *Expedition* 54, no. 2 (2012): 10–18.
52. Frank L. Pope, "Report" of the British Columbia and Stekine Exploring Expedition," Reports of Western Union Telegraph Company Explorations in western Canada, under Maj. Frank L. Pope, 1865–1866, National Anthropological Archive, Smithsonian Institution, Washington, DC, MS 1682, Pt. 3, 35.
53. Pope, "Report," Pt. 2, 4–5.
54. Pope, "Report," Pt. 2, 4.
55. Ruggles, *Country So Interesting*, 266 (Appendix 10).
56. This is because Fidler collected a map by the same Inuit cartographer in the same year. See Ruggles, *Country So Interesting*, 204 (see his entries 135A and 136A).
57. See Ruggles, *Country So Interesting*, 266 (Appendix 9), and 199–204.
58. HBCA E.3/4, fos. 16 and 14d.
59. HBCA B.49/a/32b, 25 March 1807. This is either a map that has since disappeared, or a reference to HBCA E.3/4, fo. 13d, which is dated 1806.
60. Ruggles, *Country So Interesting*, 266 (Appendix 8).
61. Ruggles, *Country So Interesting*, 66.
62. Ruggles, *Country So Interesting*, 66.
63. Verner, "The Arrowsmith Firm," 47.
64. Moodie, "Indian Map-Making," 65. The redrafted version of the map is found at HBCA G. 1/25.
65. De Vorsey, "Amerindian Contributions," 77.
66. Lawson, *New Voyage to Carolina*, 205.
67. Lewis, "Maps, Mapmaking" 72.
68. De Vorsey, "Amerindian Contributions," 74.

69. HBCA B.34/a/1, fo. 29d–30.
70. A copy of Arrowsmith's map can be found in HBCA G.3/672.
71. HBCA A.5/4, fol 103d, Alexander Lean to Alexander Dalrymple, 17 December 1802.
72. HBCA A.5/4, Alexander Lean to Sir Joseph Banks, 17 December 1802.
73. Barbara Belyea, "Inland Journeys, Native Maps," *Cartographica* 33, no. 2 (1996): 1–16.
74. Quoted in Herman R. Friss, "Cartographic and Geographic Activities of the Lewis and Clark Expedition," *Journal of the Washington Academy of Sciences* 44, no. 11 (1954): 346.
75. See Lewis and Clark, *Journals of the Lewis and Clark Expedition*, 4:268. Also see Belyea, "Mapping the Marias," 168–69; and Binnema, "How Does a Map Mean," 201–08.

Bibliography

Archival Sources

Glenbow Archives, Calgary, Alberta, Canada
M-1100-145 James Doty Report to Isaac I. Stevens, 20 December 1854.
M-2105-24 Richard G. Forbis. 1958. "Field Notes on Sundial Hill and Buffalo Hill Cairns."

Hudson's Bay Company Archives, Winnipeg, Manitoba, Canada (HBCA)

A. London Headquarters Records
A.5/4 Governor and Committee Official General Outward Correspondence, 1796–1808
A.6/18 Governor and Committee Official General Outward Correspondence, 1810–1816

B. Official Post Records
B.22 Brandon House Records
B.24 Buckingham House
B.34 Chesterfield House
B.39 Nottingham House
B.49 Cumberland House
B.51 Fort Dauphin
B.121 Manchester House
B.201 Fort Simpson
B.239 York Factory

E. Personal Papers
E.3/2 Peter Fidler, Journals of Exploration and Survey, 1790–1806.
E.3/4 Peter Fidler, Journal of Exploration and Survey, 1809.

G. Maps
G.1/13 "A Map of Hudsons Bay and Interior Westerly Particularly Above Albany 1791 J. Hodgson."
G.1/25 "An Indian Map of the Different Tribes That Inhabit on the East & West Side of the Rocky Mountains with All the Rivers & Other Remarkbl. Places, Also the Number of Tents etc. Drawn by the Feathers or Ac ko mok ki—a Black Foot Chief—7th Feby. 1801—Reduced 1/4 from the Original Size—by Peter Fidler."
G.2/13 "Chart of Lakes and Rivers in North America by Philip Turnor Those Shaded Are from Actual Survey's the Others from Canadian and Indian Information."
G.2/27 "Map of Land North of Churchill River by Captain Mea'to'na'bee & I'dot'ly'a'zees."

G.2/28 "An Accurate Map of the Territories of the Hudson's Bay Company in North America." J. Hodgson.

G.3/672 "A Map Exhibiting All the New Discoveries in the Interior Parts of North America, Inscribed by Permission to the Honorable Governor and Company of Adventurers of England Trading into Hudsons Bay in Testimony of Their Liberal Communications to Their Most Obedient and Very Humble Servant, A. Arrowsmith," 1802.

G.4/26 "A Map Exhibiting All the New Discoveries in the Interior Parts of North America, Inscribed by Permission to the Honorable Governor and Company of Adventurers of England Trading into Their Most Obedient and Very Humble Servant, A. Arrowsmith," 1795.

Montana Historical Society Archives, Helena, Montana, United States
MC 49 James H. Bradley Papers

Smithsonian Institution Archives, Washington, DC, United States
MS 1682 Reports of Western Union Telegraph Company Explorations in Western Canada, under Maj. Frank L. Pope, 1865–1866, National Anthropological Archive

Published Sources

Aarstad, Rich, Ellie Arguimbau, Ellen Baumler, Charlene Porsild, and Brian Shovers. *Montana Place Names from Alzada to Zortman.* Helena: Montana Historical Society Press, 2009.

Adams, Gary. *Prehistoric Survey of the Lower Red Deer River, 1975.* Archaeological Survey of Alberta Occasional Paper 3. Edmonton: Archaeological Survey of Alberta, 1976.

Adler, B.F. "Maps of Primitive Peoples." Translated by H. de Hutorowicz. *Bulletin of the American Geographical Society*, no. 43 (1911): 669–79. https://www.jstor.org/stable/199915?seq=2.

Amundsen-Meyer, Lindsay M. "Creating a Spatial Dialogue: *A'kee Piskun* and Attachment to Place on the Northwestern Plains." *Plains Anthropologist* 60, no. 234 (2015): 124–49. https://doi.org/10.1179/2052546X14Y.0000000018.

Amundsen-Meyer, Lindsay. "Nested Landscapes: Ecological and Spiritual Use of Plains Landscapes during the Late Prehistoric Period." PHD diss., University of Calgary, 2014. http://hdl.handle.net/11023/1585.

Amundsen-Meyer, Lindsay, and Jeremy J. Leyden. "Set in Stone: Re-examining Stone Feature Distribution and Form on the Northwestern Plains." *Plains Anthropologist* 65, no. 255 (2020): 175–202. https://doi.org/10.1080/00320447.2020.1716921.

Beattie, Judith. "Indian Maps in the Hudson's Bay Company Archives: A Comparison of Five Area Maps Recorded by Peter Fidler, 1801–1802." *Archivaria*, no. 21 (1985–86): 166–75. https://archivaria.ca/index.php/archivaria/article/view/11246.

Beaty, Chester B. "Milk River in Southern Alberta: A Classic Underfit Stream." *Canadian Geographer / Géographie canadien* 34, no. 2 (1990): 171–74. https://doi.org/10.1111/j.1541-0064.1990.tb01265.x.

Beaulieu, Terry. "Decentring Archaeology: Indigenizing GIS Models of Movement on the Plains." *Plains Anthropologist* 67, no. 262 (2022): 149–71. https://doi.org/10.1080/00320447.2022.2060685.

Beaulieu, Terry. "Place on the Plains: Modelling Past Movement along the Red Deer River." PHD diss., University of Calgary, 2018. http://hdl.handle.net/1880/107708.

Beechey, F.W. *Voyage to the Pacific and Beering's Strait.* Vol. 2. London: Henry Colburn and Richard Bentley, 1831.

Belyea, Barbara. "Amerindian Maps: The Explorer as Translator." *Journal of Historical Geography* 18, no. 3 (1992): 267–77. https://doi.org/10.1016/0305-7488(92)90203-L.

Belyea, Barbara. *Dark Storm Moving West.* Calgary: University of Calgary Press, 2007.

Belyea, Barbara. "Inland Journeys, Native Maps." In *Cartographic Encounters: Perspectives on Native American Mapmaking and Map Use*, edited by G. Malcolm Lewis, 135–55. Chicago: University of Chicago Press, 1998.

Belyea, Barbara. "Inland Journeys, Native Maps." *Cartographica* 33, no. 2 (1996): 1–16. https://doi.org/10.3138/X286-G041-2RP1-8057.

Belyea, Barbara. "Mapping the Marias: The Interface of Native and Scientific Cartographies." *Great Plains Quarterly*, no. 17 (1997): 165–84.

Belyea, Barbara, ed. *Peter Fidler: From York Factory to the Rocky Mountains*. Louisville: University Press of Colorado, 2020.

Binnema, Theodore. *Common and Contested Ground: A Human and Environmental History of the Northwestern Plains*. Norman: University of Oklahoma Press, 2001.

Binnema, Theodore. "Conflict or Cooperation?: Blackfoot Trade Strategies, 1794–1815." MA thesis, University of Alberta, 1992.

Binnema, Theodore. *Enlightened Zeal: The Hudson's Bay Company and Scientific Networks, 1670–1870*. Toronto: University of Toronto Press, 2016.

Binnema, Theodore. "How Does a Map Mean?: Old Swan's Map of 1801 and the Blackfoot World." In *From Rupert's Land to Canada: Essays in Honour of John E. Foster*, edited by Theodore Binnema, Gerhard Ens, and Roderick C. Macleod, 201–24. Edmonton: University of Alberta Press, 2001.

Binnema, Theodore. "Old Swan, Big Man, and the Siksika Bands, 1794–1815." *Canadian Historical Review* 77, no. 1 (1996): 1–32. https://doi.org/10.3138/CHR-077-01-01.

Binnema, Ted, and Gerhard Ens, eds. *Hudson's Bay Company Edmonton House Journals, Correspondence, and Reports, 1806–1821*. Calgary: Historical Society of Alberta, 2012.

Binnema, Ted, and Gerhard Ens, eds. *Hudson's Bay Company Edmonton House Journals: Including the Peigan Post, 1826–1834*. Calgary: Historical Society of Alberta, 2020.

Blaikie, Kurtis Alexander. "Archaeological Investigations of FaOm-1: The Bodo Bison Skulls Site." MA thesis, University of Alberta, 2005. https://doi.org/10.7939/r3-3hp5-z995.

Bolton, Herbert E. "New Light on Manuel Lisa and the Spanish Fur Trade." *Southwestern Historical Quarterly* 17, no. 1 (1913): 61–66. https://www.jstor.org/stable/30234587.

Bravo, Michael T. *The Accuracy of Ethnoscience: A Study of Inuit Cartography and Cross-Cultural Commensurability*. Manchester: Manchester Papers in Social Anthropology No. 2, 1996.

Brink, Jack W. *Archaeological Investigations at Writing-On-Stone, Alberta*. Archaeology in Southern Alberta, Occasional Paper No. 12. Edmonton: Alberta Culture, Historical Resources Division, 1978.

Brink, Jack W. *Imagining Head-Smashed-In: Aboriginal Buffalo Hunting on the Northern Plains*. Edmonton: Athabasca University Press, 2008.

Brower, J.V. *The Missouri River and Its Utmost Source: Curtailed Narration of Geologic, Primitive and Geographic Distinctions Descriptive of the Evolution and Discovery of the River and Its Headwaters*. St. Paul, MN: Pioneer Press, 1897.

Brown, Donald N., and Lee Irwin. "Ponca." In DeMallie, *Plains*, 416–31.

Brown, Jennifer S.H. "Rupert's Land, *Nituskeenan*, Our Land: Cree and English Naming and Claiming around the Dirty Sea." In *New Histories for Old: Changing Perspectives on Canada's Native Pasts*, edited by Theodore Binnema and Susan Neylan, 18–40. Vancouver: UBC Press, 2007.

Brumley, John H., and Barry J. Dau. *Historical Resource Investigations within the Forty Mile Coulee Reservoir*. Edmonton: Archaeological Survey of Alberta, 1988.

Bubel, Shawn, Gabriel Yanicki, and Jim McMurchy. "The Noble Point Effigy (DjPa-1)." *Alberta Archaeological Review*, no. 54 (2019): 9–17.

Byrne, William. *The Archaeology and Prehistory of Southern Alberta as Reflected by Ceramics.* Ottawa: Archaeological Survey of Canada Paper No. 14. National Museum of Man Mercury Series, National Museums of Canada, Ottawa, 1973.

Byrne, William. "A Demonstration of Migration on the Northern Great Plains." In *Archaeological Essays in Honor of Irving B. Rouse*, edited by Robert C. Dunnell and Edwin S. Hall Jr., 247–73. New York: Mouton, 1978.

Calder, J.M. *Stone Circles at Chin Coulee.* Archaeology in Southern Alberta, Occasional Paper No. 13. Edmonton: Alberta Culture, Historical Resources Division, 1979.

Canada. Department of the Interior. *Annual Report, Department of the Interior.* Ottawa: Maclean, Roger, & Co., 1883.

Cloud, John. "The Tlingit Map of 1869: A Masterwork of Indigenous Cartography." *Expedition* 54, no. 2 (2012): 10–18.

Cormack, Lesley B. "Flat Earth or Round Sphere: Misconceptions of the Shape of the Earth and the Fifteenth-Century Transformation of the World." *Ecumene* 1, no. 4 (1994): 364–85. https://doi.org/10.1177/147447409400100404.

Cowell, Andrew. *Naming the World: Language and Power among the Northern Arapaho.* Tucson: University of Arizona Press, 2018.

Cowell, Andrew. "The Phonology of the NoowoΘineheeno? Language and Its Relation to Arapaho and Cheyenne." In *Papers of the Fifty-Second Algonquian Conference*, edited by Monica Macaulay and Margaret Noodin (1–17). East Lansing: Michigan State University Press, 2023.

Cowell, Andrew, Allan Taylor, and Terry Brockie. "Gros Ventre Ethnogeography and Place Names: A Diachronic Perspestive." *Anthropological Linguistics* 58, no. 2 (2016): 132–70.

Dawson, George. "Report on the Region in the Vicinity of the Bow and Belly Rivers, North-West Territory." In *Geological and Natural History Survey and Museum of Canada Report of Progress, 1882-83-84.* Montreal: Dawson Brothers, 1885.

DeMallie, Raymond J., ed. *Plains*, Vol. 13 of *Handbook of North American Indians*, edited by William C. Sturtevant. Washington, DC: Smithsonian Institute, 1990.

Dempsey, Hugh A. "The Blackfoot." In DeMallie, *Plains*, 604–28.

Dempsey, Hugh A. "The Blackfoot Indians." In *Native Peoples: The Canadian Experience*, edited by R. Bruce Morrison and C. Roderick Wilson, 404–35. Toronto: McClelland and Stewart, 1986.

Dempsey, Hugh. *Napi: The Trickster.* Victoria, BC: Heritage House Publishing, 2018.

De Vorsey, Louis. "Amerindian Contributions to the Mapping of North America: A Preliminary View." *Imago Mundi* 30, no. 1 (1978): 71–78. https://doi.org/10.1080/03085697808592469.

Documents inédits sur l'histoire de la marine et des colonies Revue maritime et coloniale: Mémoire de Bougainville sur l'état de la Nouvelle-France à l'époque de la guerre de Sept ans, (1757). N.p.: N.p., c. 1790.

Doll, Maurice F.V. *The Boss Hill Site (FdPe 4) Locality 2: Pre-Archaic Manifestations in the Parkland of Central Alberta, Canada.* Edmonton: Alberta Culture, Historical Resources Division, Occasional Paper No. 2, 1982.

Dormar, Johan F. *Sweetgrass Hills: A Natural and Cultural History.* Lethbridge, AB: Lethbridge Historical Society, 2003.

Doty, James. "A Visit to the Blackfoot Camp." Edited by Hugh A. Dempsey. *Alberta Historical Review* 14, no. 3 (1966): 17–26.

Ewers, John C. *The Blackfeet: Raiders on the Northwestern Plains.* Norman: University of Oklahoma Press, 1958.

Ewers, John C. *Blackfeet Indians: Ethnological Report on the Blackfeet and Gros Ventre Tribes of Indians.* New York: Garland, 1974.

Fisher, Louise, Wayne Leman, Leroy Pine Sr., and Marie Sanchez. *Cheyenne Dictionary*. Lulu, 2017.

Forbis, Richard G. *Archaeological Site Inventory Data Form: ElPd-44*. Edmonton: Historic Resources Management Branch, Alberta Culture, Arts and Status of Women, 1961.

Forbis, Richard G. *Cluny, an Ancient Fortified Village in Alberta*. Occasional Paper No. 4. Calgary: Department of Archaeology, University of Calgary, 1982.

Forster, John Reinhold. *History of the Voyages and Discoveries Made in the North*. London: G.G.J. and J. Robinson, 1786.

Foster, Morris W., and Martha McCollough. "Plains Apache." In DeMallie, *Plains*, 926–40.

Fowler, Loretta. "Arapaho." In DeMallie, *Plains*, 840–62.

Fowler, Loretta. *Shared Symbols, Contested Meanings: Gros Ventre Culture and History, 1778–1984*. Ithaca, NY: Cornell University Press, 1987.

Fowler, Loretta, and Regina Flannery. "Gros Ventre." In DeMallie, *Plains*, 677–94.

Frantz, Donald G., and Inge Genee, eds. *Blackfoot Dictionary*. 2015–2024 (ongoing). https://dictionary.blackfoot.algonquianlanguages.ca/.

Frantz, Donald, and Norma Jean Russell. *Blackfoot Dictionary of Stems, Roots, and Affixes* Toronto: University of Toronto Press, 2017.

Fraser, Simon. *The Letters and Journals of Simon Fraser: 1806–1808*. Edited by W. Kaye Lamb. Toronto: Dundurn Press, 2007.

Freeman, Randolph. *Geographic Naming in Western British North America: 1780–1820*. Edmonton: Alberta Culture, 1985.

Friss, Herman R. "Cartographic and Geographic Activities of the Lewis and Clark Expedition." *Journal of the Washington Academy of Sciences* 44, no. 11 (1954): 338–51.

Fromhold, Joachim. *Alberta History: The Old North Trail (Cree Trail), 15,000 Years of Indian History, Prehistoric to 1750*. [Blackfalds, AB]: First Nations Publishing, 2012.

Fromhold, Joachim. *Indian Place Names of the West*. Lulu, 2001.

Gibson, James R. *Fort Simpson Post Journals, 1834–1843*. Vol. 3. Published by the author, 2022.

Gibson, Terrance, and Peggy McKeand. *Heritage Resources Impact Assessment of a Fletcher Challenge Petroleum Pipeline in the Eyehill Creek Locality, Bodo, Alberta*. Permit 95-101, report on file. Edmonton: Heritage Resource Management Branch, Alberta Community Development, 1996.

Goddard, Ives. "The Languages of the Plains: Introduction." In DeMallie, *Plains*, 61–70.

Grekul, Christie Peaches. "A Zooarchaeological Analysis of a Late Precontact Bison Kill Site in the Bodo Sand Hills of Alberta." MA thesis, University of Alberta, 2007.

Grinnell, George Bird. *Blackfeet Indian Stories*. New York: Charles Scribner's Sons, 1913.

Grinnell, George Bird. *Blackfoot Lodge Tales*. New York: Charles Scribner's Sons, 1907.

Grinnell, George Bird. "Some Indian Stream Names." *American Anthropologist* 15, no. 2 (1913): 327–31.

Hall, Ryan. *Beneath the Backbone of the World: Blackfoot People and the North American Borderlands, 1720–1877*. Chapel Hill: University of North Carolina Press, 2020.

Hämäläinen, Pekka. *The Comanche Empire*. New Haven, CT: Yale University Press, 2008.

Hämäläinen, Pekka. *Lakota America: A New History of Indigenous Power*. New Haven, CT: Yale University Press, 2019.

Hanna, Don. *Historical Resources Impact Assessment, Hanna Region Transmission Development, Phase 1 Final Report (Permit 2010-182)*. Edmonton: Archaeological Survey of Alberta, 2011.

Harley, J.B. "Deconstructing the Map." *Cartographica* 26, no. 2 (1989): 1–20. https://doi.org/10.3138/E635-7827-1757-9T53.

Harley, J.B. "The Map and the Development of the History of Cartography." In *Cartography in Prehistoric, Ancient, and Medieval Europe and the Mediterranean*, edited by J.B. Harley and David Woodward, 1–42. Vol. 1 of *The History of Cartography*. Chicago: University of Chicago Press, 1987.

Harley, J.B. "Maps, Knowledge, and Power." In *The Iconography of Landscape: Essays on the Symbolic Representation, Design and Use of Past Environments*, edited by Denis Cosgrove and Stephen Daniels, 277–312. Cambridge: Cambridge University Press, 1988.

Harley, J.B. "Rereading the Maps of the Columbian Encounter." *Annals of the Association of American Geographers*, no. 82 (1992): 522–42.

Harley, J.B., and David Woodward, eds. *Cartography in Prehistoric, Ancient, and Medieval Europe and the Mediterranean*. Vol. 1 of *The History of Cartography*. Chicago: University of Chicago Press, 1987.

Harrison, Tracey, ed. *Central Alberta*. Vol. 3 of *Place Names of Alberta*. Calgary: University of Calgary Press, 1994.

Hayden, Ferdinand V. *On the Ethnography and Philology of the Indian Tribes of the Missouri Valley*. Philadelphia: C. Sherman & Son, 1862.

Hearne, Samuel, and Philip Turnor. *Journals of Samuel Hearne and Philip Turnor*. Edited by J.B. Tyrell. Toronto: Champlain Society, 1934.

Helm, June. "'Always with Them Either a Feast or a Famine': Living off the Land with Chipewyan Indians, 1791–1792." *Arctic Anthropology* 30, no. 2 (1993): 46–60. https://www.jstor.org/stable/40316337.

Helm, June. "Matonabee's Map." *Arctic Anthropology* 26, no. 2 (1989): 28–47. https://www.jstor.org/stable/40316183.

Hirtle, Stephen C., and Judith Hudson. "Acquisition of Spatial Knowledge for Routes." *Journal of Environmental Psychology* 11, no. 4 (1991): 335–45. https://doi.org/10.1016/S0272-4944(05)80106-9.

Holmgren, Eric J., and Patricia M. Holmgren. *Over 2000 Place Names of Alberta*, 3rd ed. Saskatoon: Western Producer Prairie Books, 1976.

Holterman, Jack. *Place Names of Glacier National Park*. [Helena, MT]: Riverbend Publishing, 2006.

Hopwood, Victor G. "David Thompson and His Maps." In *Explorations in the History of Canadian Mapping: A Collection of Essays*, edited by Barbara Farrell and Aileen Desbarats, 205–10. Ottawa: Association of Canadian Map Libraries and Archives, 1988.

Jackson, John. "Inland from the Bay: Mapping the Fur Trade." *The Beaver* 72, no. 1 (February–March 1992): 37–42.

Johnson, Alice M. *Saskatchewan Journals and Correspondence*. London: Hudson's Bay Record Society, 1967.

Kavanaugh, Thomas W. "Comanche." In DeMallie, *Plains*, 886–906.

Kavanaugh, Thomas W. *The Comanches: A History, 1706–1875*. Lincoln: University of Nebraska Press, 1966.

Kehoe, Alice B. "How the Ancient Peigans Lived." *Research in Economic Anthropology*, no. 14 (1993): 87–105.

Kennedy, Margaret. "A Map and Partial Manuscript of Blackfoot Country." *Alberta History* 62, no. 3 (2014): 5–14.

Keyser, James D. "Writing-on-Stone: Rock Art on the Northwestern Plains." *Canadian Journal of Archaeology*, no. 1 (1977): 15–80. https://www.jstor.org/stable/41102181.

Kinney, W. Jeffrey. "The Hagen Site, 24DW1: A Review of Historical Data and a Reassessment of Its Ceramic Assemblage and Position in Northern Plains Prehistory." MA thesis, University of Montana, 1996.

Kroeber, A.L. "Arapaho Dialects." *University of California Publications in American Archaeology and Ethnology* 12, no. 3 (1916): 71–138.

Kroeber, A.L. "Ethnology of the Gros Ventre." *Anthropological Papers of the American Museum of Natural History.* Vol. 1, part 4. New York: American Museum of Natural History, 1908.

Lahontan, Louis Armand de Lom d'Arce, Baron de. *New Voyages to North America.* London: Printed for H. Bonwicke, T. Goodwin, M. Wotton, B. Tooke; and S. Manship, 1703.

Lance, Donald M. "The Origin and Meaning of 'Missouri.'" *Names: A Journal of Onomastics* 47, no. 3 (1999): 281–90. https://doi.org/10.1179/nam.1999.47.3.281.

LaPier, Rosalyn R. *Invisible Reality: Storytellers, Storytakers, and the Supernatural World of the Blackfeet.* Lincoln: University of Nebraska Press, 2017.

LaPier, Rosalyn. "Land as Text: Reading the Land." *Environmental History* 28, no. 1 (2023): 40–46. https://doi.org/10.1086/722618.

La Vérendrye, Pierre Gaultier de Varennes de. *Journals and Letters of Pierre Gaultier de Varennes de la Vérendrye and His Sons, with Correspondence between the Governors of Canada and the French Court, Touching the Search for the Western Sea.* Edited by Lawrence J. Burpee. Toronto: Champlain Society, 1927.

Lawson, John. *A New Voyage to Carolina.* London: N.p., 1709.

Le Clercq, Chrestien. *New Relation of Gaspesia: With the Customs and Religion of the Gaspesian Indians.* Translated and edited by William F. Ganong. Toronto: Champlain Society, 1910.

Le Gear, Clara Egli. "Map Making by Primitive Peoples." *Special Libraries* 35, no. 3 (1944): 79–83.

Levy, Jerrold E. "Kiowa." In DeMallie, *Plains*, 907–25.

Lewis, G. Malcolm. "Indian Maps." In *Old Trails and New Directions: Papers of the Third North American Fur Trade Conference*, edited by Carol M. Judd and Arthur J. Ray, 9–23. Toronto: University of Toronto Press, 1980.

Lewis, G. Malcolm. "Indian Maps: Their Place in the History of Plains Cartography." *Great Plains Quarterly* 4, no. 2 (1984): 91–108.

Lewis, G. Malcolm. "Maps, Mapmaking, and Map Use by Native North Americans." In *Cartography in the Traditional African, American, Arctic, Australian, and Pacific Societies*, edited by David Woodward and G. Malcolm Lewis, Vol. 2, bk. 3 of *The History of Cartography*, 51–182. Chicago: University of Chicago Press, 1998.

Lewis, G. Malcolm, ed. *Cartographic Encounters: Perspectives on Native American Mapmaking and Map Use.* Chicago: University of Chicago Press, 1998.

Lewis, Meriwether, and William Clark. *The Journals of the Lewis and Clark Expedition.* 13 vols. Edited by Gary E. Moulton. Lincoln: University of Nebraska Press, 1983–2001.

Leyden, Jeremy L. *Historical Resources Impact Assessment, Keystone XL Pipeline Project, Alberta Segment. Final Report, Permit 2010-130.* Edmonton: Historic Resources Management Branch, Alberta Culture and Community Services, 2011.

L'Heureux, Jean. *Three-Persons and the Chokitapix: Jean L'Heureux's Blackfoot Geography of 1871.* Translated and edited by Allen Ronaghan. Red Deer: Central Alberta Historical Society Press, 2011.

Long, John. *Voyages and Travels of an Indian Interpreter and Trader.* London: Printed for the author, 1791.

MacGregor, James G. *Peter Fidler: Canada's Forgotten Surveyor: 1769–1822.* Toronto: McClelland and Stewart, 1966.

Mackenzie, Alexander. *Voyages from Montreal.* London: T. Cadell, Jr. and W. Davies, 1801.

Maximilian, Prince Alexander Philipp of Wied. *The North American Journals of Prince Maximilian of Wied.* 3 vols. Edited by Stephen S. Witte and Marshal V. Gallagher. Translated by William J. Orr, Paul Schach, and Dieter Karch. Norman: University of Oklahoma Press, 2010.

McClintock, Walter. *The Old North Trail.* London: Macmillan, 1910.

Meadows, William C. *Kiowa Ethnogeography.* Austin: University of Texas Press, 2008.

Millar, J.F.V. *The Gray Burial Site: An Early Plains Burial Ground.* Ottawa: Parks Canada Manuscript Report 30, 1978.

Millar, J.F.V. "Mortuary Practices of the Oxbow Complex." *Canadian Journal of Archaeology*, no. 5 (1981): 103–17. https://www.jstor.org/stable/41058605.

Monmonier, Mark. *How to Lie with Maps*. Chicago: University of Chicago Press, 1991.

Moodie, D.W. "Indian Map-Making: Two Examples from the Fur Trade West." In *People Places Patterns Processes: Geographical Perspectives on the Canadian Past*, edited by Graeme Wynn, 56–67. Toronto: Copp Clark Pitman, 1990.

Moodie, D.W., and Barry Kaye. "The Ac Ko Mok Ki Map." *The Beaver* 307, no. 4 (Spring 1977): 4–15.

Moore, John H., Margot P. Liberty, and A. Terry Strauss. "Cheyenne." In DeMallie, *Plains*, 863–87.

Morgan, R. Grace. *Beaver, Bison, Horse: The Traditional Knowledge and Ecology of the Northern Great Plains*. Regina, SK: University of Regina Press, 2020.

Munyikwa, Kennedy, Krista Gilliland, Terrance Gibson, Elizabeth Mann, Tammy M. Rittenour, Christie Grekul, and Kurtis Blaikie-Birkigt. "Late Holocene Temporal Constraints for Human Occupation Levels at the Bodo Archaeological Locality, East-Central Alberta, Canada Using Radiocarbon and Luminescence Chronologies." *Plains Anthropologist* 59, no. 230 (2014): 109–43. https://doi.org/10.1179/2052546X14Y.0000000011.

Nelson, J.C. "Blackfoot Names of a Number of Places in the North-West Territory, for the Most Part in the Vicinity of the Rocky Mountains." Appendix II to George Dawson, "Report on the Region in the Vicinity of the Bow and Belly Rivers, North-West Territory." In *Geological and Natural History Survey and Museum of Canada Report of Progress, 1882-83-84*, 158C–167C. Montreal: Dawson Brothers, 1885.

O'Connor, M.R. *Wayfinding: The Science and Mystery of How Humans Navigate the World*. New York: St. Martin's Press, 2019.

Oetelaar, Gerald A. "Places on the Blackfoot Homeland: Markers of Cosmology, Social Relationships and History." In *Marking the Land: Hunter-Gatherer Creation of Meaning in their Environment*, edited by William A. Lovis and Robert Whallon, 45–66. New York: Taylor and Francis, 2016.

Oetelaar, Gerald A., and David Meyer. "Movement and Native American Landscapes: A Comparative Approach." *Plains Anthropologist* 51, no. 199 (2006): 355–74. https://www.jstor.org/stable/25670890.

Oetelaar, Gerald A., and D. Joy Oetelaar. "People, Places and Paths: The Cypress Hills and the Niitsitapi Landscape of Southern Alberta." *Plains Anthropologist*, no. 51 (2006): 375–97.

Oetelaar, Gerald A., and D. Joy Oetelaar. "The Structured World of the *Niitsitapi*: The Landscape as Historical Archive among Hunter-Gatherers of the Northern Plains." In *Structured Worlds: The Archaeology of Hunter-Gatherer Thought and Action*, edited by Aubrey Cannon, 69–94. Oakville, CT: Equinox, 2011.

Palliser, John. *The Journals, Detailed Reports, and Observations Relative to the Exploration by Captain Palliser...during the Years 1857, 1858, 1859, and 1860*. London: George Edward Eyre and William Spottiswoode, 1863.

Palliser, John. *Papers Relative to the Exploration by Captain Palliser of that Portion of British North America which lies between the Northern Branch of the River Saskatchewan and the Frontier of the United States; and between the Red River and Rocky Mountains*. London: George Edward Eyre and William Spottiswoode, 1859.

Parks, Douglas R. "Arikara." In DeMallie, *Plains*, 365–90.

Parks, Douglas R. "Enigmatic Groups." In DeMallie, *Plains*, 965–73.

Parks, Douglas R. "Pawnee." In DeMallie, *Plains*, 515–47.

Peck, Trevor. *Light from Ancient Campfires: Archaeological Evidence for Native Lifeways on the Northern Plains*. Edmonton: Athabasca University Press, 2011.

Pentland, David H. "Cartographic Concepts of the Northern Algonquians." *Canadian Cartographer* 12, no. 2 (1975): 149–60. https://doi.org/10.3138/R6N1-5H13-K455-760L.

Pike, Warburton. *The Barren Ground of Northern Canada*. London: Macmillan and Co., 1892.

Pyszczyk, Heinz W., and Gabriella Prager. "Peter Fidler's Long Lost Chesterfield House: Have We Finally Found It?" *Saskatchewan Archaeology* 7, no. 2 (2021): 58–67.

Rayburn, Alan. "Hot and Bothered by 'Disgusting Names.'" *Canadian Geographic* 113, no. 6 (November/December 1993): 80–82.

Reeves, Brian. "How Old Is the Old North Trail?" *Archaeology in Montana* 31, no. 2 (1990): 1–18.

Reeves, Brian. "Ninaistákis—the Nitsitapii's Sacred Mountain: Traditional Native Religious Activities and Land Use/Tourism Conflicts." In *Sacred Sites, Sacred Places*, edited by David L. Carmichael, Jane Hubert, Brian Reeves, and Audhild Schanche, 265–95. New York: Routledge, 1994.

Reeves, Brian, and Margaret Kennedy. "Stone Feature Types as Observed at Ceremonial Site Complexes on the Lower Red Deer and the Forks of the Red Deer and South Saskatchewan Rivers with Ethnohistorical Discussion." *Archaeology in Montana* 58, no. 1 (2017): 1–44.

Roberts, Thomas P. "The Upper Missouri River from a Reconnaissance Made in 1872." *Contributions to the Historical Society of Montana*, no. 1 (1876).

Robertson, William. *History of America*. 3rd ed. 3 vols. London: Strahan, Cadell, and Balfour, 1780.

Ronda, James P. "'A Chart in His Way': Indian Cartography and the Lewis and Clark Expedition." *Great Plains Quarterly* 4, no. 1 (1984): 43–53. https://www.jstor.org/stable/24467602.

Rozum, Molly P. *Grasslands Grown: Creating Place on the U.S. Northern Plains and Canadian Prairies*. Winnipeg: University of Manitoba Press, 2021.

Ruggles, Richard. *A Country So Interesting: The Hudson's Bay Company and Two Centuries of Mapping, 1670–1870*. Montreal and Kingston: McGill-Queen's University Press, 1991.

Rundstrom, Robert A. "A Cultural Interpretation of Inuit Map Accuracy." *Geographical Review* 80, no. 2 (1990): 155–68. https://www.jstor.org/stable/215479.

Schultz, James Willard. *Blackfeet and Buffalo: Memories of Life among the Indians*. Norman: University of Oklahoma Press, 1962.

Schultz, James Willard. *My Life as an Indian: The Story of a Red Woman and a White Man in the Lodges of the Blackfeet*. New York: Doubleday, Page & Company, 1907.

Simpson, George. *Narrative of a Journey Round the World, during the Years 1841 and 1842*. 2 vols. London: Henry Colburn, 1847.

Somerset, H. Somers. *The Land of Muskeg*. London: William Heineman, 1895.

Spencer, Robert F. "Map Making of the North Alaskan Eskimo." *Journal of the Minnesota Academy of Science* 23, no. 1 (1955): 46–49. https://digitalcommons.morris.umn.edu/jmas/vol23/iss1/7.

Spink, John. "Eskimo Maps from the Canadian Eastern Arctic." MA thesis, University of Manitoba, 1969.

Stewart, Frank Henderson. "Hidatsa." In DeMallie, *Plains*, 329–48.

Sturtevant, William C., gen. ed. *Handbook of North American Indians*. 15 vols. Washington, DC: Smithsonian Institute, 1978–2022.

Thompson, David. Tyrrell, J.B., ed. *David Thompson's Narrative of His Explorations in Western America, 1784–1812*. Edited by J.B. Tyrell. Toronto: Champlain Society, 1916.

Thwaites, Reuben Gold. *The French Regime in Wisconsin*. Madison: State Historical Society of Wisconsin, 1908.

Tilander-Mack, Barb, ed. and comp. *Native Mapping Project: Treaty Seven Maps and Names*. N.p.: Friends of Geographical Names of Alberta Society, n.d.

Truteau, Jean-Baptiste. *A Fur Trader on the Upper Missouri: The Journal and Description of Jean-Baptiste Truteau, 1794–1796*. Edited by Raymond J. DeMallie, Douglas R. Parks, and Robert Vézina. Lincoln: University of Nebraska Press, 2017.

Turnbull, David. "Maps and Mapmaking of the Australian Aboriginal People." In *Encyclopedia of the History of Science, Technology and Medicine in Non-Western Cultures*, edited by Helaine Selin, 1276–78. Dordrecht: Springer, 1997.

Uhlenbeck, C.C., and R.H. van Gulik. *A Blackfoot-English Vocabulary*. Amsterdam: Noord-Hollandsche Uitgevers Maatschappij, 1934.

Utting, Daniel J., and Nigel Atkinson. "Proglacial Lakes and the Retreat Pattern of the Southwest Laurentide Ice Sheet across Alberta, Canada." *Quaternary Science Reviews* 225, no. 1 (2019): 106034. https://doi.org/10.1016/j.quascirev.2019.106034.

Verner, Coolie. "The Arrowsmith Firm and the Cartography of Canada." In *Explorations in the History of Canadian Mapping: A Collection of Essays*, edited by Barbara Farrell and Aileen Desbarats, 47–54. Ottawa: Association of Canadian Map Libraries and Archives, 1988.

Vickers, J. Rod, and Trevor Peck. "Identifying the Prehistoric Blackfoot: Approaches to Nitsitapii (Blackfoot) Culture History." In *Painting the Past with a Broad Brush*, edited by David L. Keenlyside and Jean-Luc Pilon, 473–97. Ottawa: University of Ottawa Press, 2009.

Voget, Fred W. "Crow." In DeMallie, *Plains*, 695–717.

Wade, William D. "Temporal and Biological Dimensions of the Gray Site Population." *Canadian Journal of Archaeology*, no. 5 (1981): 119–30. https://www.jstor.org/stable/41058606.

Walde, Dale. "Mortlach and One-Gun: Phase to Phase." In *Archaeology on the Edge: New Perspectives from the Northern Plains*, edited by Jane Kelley and Brian Kooyman, 39–51. Calgary: University of Calgary Press, 2004.

Waller, David A. "An Assessment of Individual Differences in Spatial Knowledge of Real and Virtual Environments." PHD diss., University of Washington, 1999.

Warhus, Mark. *Another America: Native American Maps and the History of Our Land*. New York: St. Martin's Press, 1997.

Waselkov, Gregory A. "Indian Maps of the Colonial Southeast." In *Powhatan's Mantle: Indians in the Colonial Southeast*, edited by Peter H. Wood, Gregory A. Waselkov, and M. Thomas Hatley, 292–346. Lincoln: University of Nebraska Press, 1989.

Wilson, Michael C. *Archaeological Studies in the Longview-Pekisko Area of Southern Alberta*. Edmonton: Archaeological Survey of Alberta, 1977.

Wood, Denis. *The Power of Maps*. New York: Guilford Press, 1992.

Wood, R. Raymond. "The Earliest Map of the Mandan Heartland: Notes on the Jarvis and Mackay 1791 Map." *Plains Anthropologist* 55, no. 216 (2010): 155–76. https://www.jstor.org/stable/23057064.

Wood, W. Raymond, and Alan Downer. "Notes on the Crow-Hidatsa Schism." *Plains Anthropologist* 22, no. 8 (1977): 83–100. https://www.jstor.org/stable/25667426.

Wood, W. Raymond, and Thomas D. Thiessen, eds. *Early Fur Trade on the Northern Plains: Canadian Traders among the Mandan and Hidatsa Indians, 1738–1818*. Norman: University of Oklahoma Press, 1985.

Zedeño, María N., Evelyn Pickering, and François Lanoë. "Oral Tradition as Emplacement: Ancestral Blackfoot Memories of the Rocky Mountain Front." *Journal of Social Archaeology* 21, no. 3 (2021): 306–23. https://doi.org/10.1177/14696053211019837.

Index

Note: Page numbers with an *f* attached refers to figures, an *m* refers to maps, an *n* refers to endnotes, a *ph* refers to photographs, and a *t* refers to tables

Ac ko mok ki (Siksika Chief), 51–52, 162*n*10, 176*n*37, 177*n*54
Ac ko mok ki map (1801), 65–76
    introduction, 65
    Arrowsmith's interpretation of, 65, 75, 158–59
        authors' translation of, 6*m*
        circles, to indicate Indigenous communities, 135–36
        Fidler's redrafted version, 4–5*m*, 58, 65, 75–76, 156–57, 158
        Gros Ventre map, comparison to, 96–97
        Indigenous Peoples depicted, 96, 97, 129, 132, 133–35, 137, 138–41, 142*t*
        Ki oo cus map, comparison to, 99, 109, 115
        mountains depicted, 70–73
        naming conventions and, 57
        Old North Trail depicted, 120–21
        original map, 2–3*m*, 65
        plains features depicted, 73–75
        Rocky Mountains and, 55, 125
        scholarship on, 162*n*9
        streams (rivers) depicted, 65–69
        war track depicted, 119–20, 121, 124
Ac ko mok ki map (1802), 77–86
    introduction, 77
    authors' translation of, 8*m*
    Blackfoot cartographic conventions and, 84–85
    distances, estimated, 85
    Fidler's impressions of, 83–84
    long viewscapes, 85–86
    mountains depicted, 83
    naming conventions and, 56–57
    numbered features depicted, 77–78, 80–82
    Old North Trail depicted, 120–21
    original map, 7*m*
    other features depicted, 83
    redrafted version, 7*m*
Adams, Gary, 116
Ak ko wee ak, 51
Ak ko wee ak map (1802), 86–95
    introduction, 86, 88–89
    Ac ko mok ki maps, comparison to, 86
    authors' translation of, 10*m*
    bison jumps depicted, 86–87, 88, 90–91
    Gros Ventre attack (1801) depicted, 88
    original map, 9*m*
    other features depicted, 94–95
    redrafted version, 9*m*
    rivers depicted, 89–93
Amundsen-Meyer, Lindsay, 93, 166*n*60
Antler Hill, 126, 174*n*28
Apache. *See* Jicarilla Apache; Plains Apache
Arapaho
    Ac ko mok ki map (1801), depiction on, 97, 142*t*
    on Arikara, 182*n*121
    autonym, 180*n*95
    on Bitterroot Salish, 179*n*88
    Chesterfield House and, 96
    on Cheyenne, 180*n*96
    on Comanche, 180*n*104
    on Crow, 179*n*91
    on Europeans, 181*n*120
    Gros Ventre, relations with, 95–96, 137, 138, 144, 170*n*69, 180*n*95
    Gros Ventre map and, 95–96, 136–37, 143*t*
    on Hidatsa and Mandan, 181*n*114
    on Jicarilla Apache, 180*n*107
    on Kiowa, 180*n*98
    Nawathinehena and, 143*t*, 180*n*108
    on North Platte and South Platte Rivers, 132
    on Omaha and Ponca, 181*n*118
    on Plains Apache, 181*n*111

on Sioux, 181n119
as Tattooed People, 178n62
on Ute, 180n103
archaeological sites
Blackfoot ancestors, 174n3
Bodo Sand Hills, 112
Boss Hill, Buffalo Lake, 106
Chesterfield House, 75
Chin Coulee and Forty Mile Coulee, 117
earthlodge villages, 139
Gopher Head Hill, 104–05
Hunting Hill, 110
Ki oo cus map and, 61
Leithead Hill, 103–04
Manitou Lake, 113–14
Misty Hills, 111
Nose Hill, 113
Old North Trail, 109, 125, 126
One Gun culture, 174n3, 177n49
Pekisko Valley, 90
Porcupine Hills, 86
Red Deer and South Saskatchewan Rivers, confluence, 62–63, 166n60
Red Deer River, 116
Shoshone and, 174n3
Sounding Creek, 111
Women's Buffalo Jump, 93
Writing-on-Stone, 123
Archer, Gabriel, 157
Arikara, 132, 138–39, 142t, 144t, 175n4, 182n121
Arkansas River, 132, 137
Arrow Creek, 68, 97
Arrowsmith, Aaron
Ac ko mok ki map (1801), interpretation of, 158–59
Fidler's regional maps and, 156, 163n22
HBC and, 152, 158, 183n35
Indigenous mapping and, 150
North America map (1802), 28–29m, 65, 75, 85, 158–59
Arrowsmith, John, 152
Assiniboine
Blackfoot (Siksika), relations with, 51, 117
Gros Ventre, relations with, 51, 88, 95, 137
Gros Ventre map, possible depiction on, 143t
Gros Ventre names for, 176n32, 181n119
as map informants, 149
Nose Hill and, 113
not depicted on maps, 135
Assiniboine River, 62
Awaxawi, 143t, 181n113

Bad River. *See* Bow River; South Saskatchewan River
Banks, Joseph, 148, 158
Bannock, 142t, 143t, 178n77, 180n103
Battle River, 62, 101, 102, 103
beads-on-a-string cartographic style, 25m, 86, 183n22
Bears Paw Mountains
on Ac ko mok ki map (1801), 74, 76, 84
on Ac ko mok ki map (1802), 82
on Gros Ventre map, 96
on Ki oo cus map (1802), 102, 109, 122
Sweetgrass Hills and, 60, 85
Beartooth Mountain
about, 33ph
on Ac ko mok ki map (1801), 71, 84
on Ac ko mok ki map (1802), 83, 84
on Blackfoot maps, 53
Blackfoot war track and, 119, 121
on Gros Ventre map, 96
on Ki oo cus map (1802), 109
name, 58, 102
travel times to, 121
as wayfinder, 59, 60, 86
Beattie, Judith, 162n9
Beaulieu, Terry, 110
Beechey, F.W., 154
Belly Buttes, 40ph, 66, 83, 94, 107
Belly River
on Ac ko mok ki map (1801), 66
on Ak ko wee ak map, 91, 93, 95
on Ki oo cus map, 107, 115
naming conventions and, 57
See also Oldman River
Belt Butte
about, 33ph
on Ac ko mok ki map (1801), 71, 84
on Ac ko mok ki map (1802), 80–81, 84
Rocky Mountains, distance to, 85
routes and, 121, 124
as wayfinder, 60, 86
Belt Creek, 68
Belt Mountains, 43ph. *See also* Big Belt Mountains; Little Belt Mountains
Belyea, Barbara, 46, 162n9
Besawunena, 143t, 181n112
Big Belt Mountains, 41ph, 55, 71, 120, 124. *See also* Little Belt Mountains
Big Blackfoot River, 70
Big Hill Creek, 89
Bighorn Mountains, 55, 74–75, 97, 130
Bighorn River, 55, 69, 97, 121, 167n29
Big Sandy Creek, 122

Big Snowy Mountains, 41*ph*, 43*ph*, 55, 72, 74, 81, 84, 123, 167*n*40. *See also* Little Snowy Mountains; Snowy Mountains
Big Thompson River, 97
bison jumps and pounds
    on Ak ko wee ak map, 86–88, 89–91, 92, 93
    Head-Smashed-In Buffalo Jump, 92
    on Ki oo cus map, 111
    Milk River Ridge and, 73
    Red Deer and South Saskatchewan Rivers, confluence, and, 62
    Two Medicine River and, 67
    Ulm Pishkun (Buffalo Jump), 74
    Women's Buffalo Jump, 93
Bitterroot Salish, 51, 133–34, 137, 142*t*, 143*t*, 179*n*78, 179*n*88. *See also* Flathead
Blackfeet Reservation (MT), 70
Blackfoot
    archaeological evidence, 174*n*3
    on Arikara, Mandan, and Hidatsa, 138
    in Blackfoot and Gros Ventre maps, 137
    Bougainville on, 132
    on Crow, 177*n*57
    Great Sand Hills and, 173*n*7
    Gros Ventre and, 47, 66, 137, 177*n*54
    on *mistakis* ("Rocky Mountains"), 55
    naming conventions, 56–58
    non-navigational maps, 45–46
    Nose Hill and, 113
    plant resources and, 101
    relations with other Indigenous Peoples, 51, 130, 135
    rivers (streams) term, 65
    sacred landmarks, 61–62
    scholarship on, 163*n*28
    Sounding Lake and, 114
    war track (1801), 119–20, 121, 124
    Writing-on-Stone and, 123
    See also Kainai; Piikani; Siksika
Blackfoot Crossing, 107, 126
Blackfoot (Siksika) maps
    introduction, 45–48, 64, 146
    Blackfoot ways of thinking reflected in, 45–46, 60–62
    composition and uniqueness of, 48–49, 163*n*17
    distance, temporal, 124–25
    Fidler and, 48, 51–52
    historical context, 50–51
    on *mistakis* ("Rocky Mountains") and rivers, 55–56
    naming conventions, 56–58
    navigational role, 58–60
    oral information and, 45, 48–49, 53, 67, 75, 84, 101, 135–36, 157
    route knowledge and configural knowledge, 127
    scholarship on, 162*n*9
    straight-line cartographic style, 52–56, 61, 75, 86
    See also Ac ko mok ki map (1801); Ac ko mok ki map (1802); Ak ko wee ak map (1802); Ki oo cus map (1802)
Blackfoot River, 69, 97
Blackleaf, unnamed hills north of, 109
Blood, 137. *See also* Kainai
Bodo Sand Hills, 112
boreal forest, 100
Boss Hill, 36*ph*, 57, 106
Bougainville, Louis-Antoine, Comte de, 129–32, 133–34, 180*n*100
Bow River
    Ak ko wee ak map, tributaries depicted, 89–90, 91
    Devil's Head Mountain and, 70
    on Gros Ventre map, 96
    names, 80, 116
    routes and, 123
    Thompsons maps and, 91, 152
    Wildcat Hills and, 89
    See also South Saskatchewan River
Box Elder Butte, 82
Bozeman Pass, 120
Bozeman Trail, 120
Bradley, James H., 68
Bridger Mountains, 120
Bridger Trail, 120
Brings-Down-the-Sun (Piikani), 53, 67, 120, 125
Brink, Jack W.
    Imagining Head-Smashed-In, 169*n*47
Broadcast Hill, 94
Brochet, 131, 132
Brown, Annora, 59
Buache, Philippe, 148, 182*n*13
buffalo. *See* bison jumps and pounds
Buffalo Lake, 36*ph*, 57, 90–91, 100–01, 102, 106, 116, 127, 170*n*7
Buffalo Nose. *See* Canyon Mountain; Nose Hill
Buffalo Tail Creek. *See* Tail Creek
Bull Mountains, 72–73
Bull's Forehead, 110

Calgary, 53, 94
camp circles, 135–36
Canyon Mountain, 34*ph*, 72–73
cardinal directions, 53
Carrier (Dakelh), 153
Cartier, Jacques, 147

cartography
    Arrowsmith's North America map (1802), 28–29m, 65, 75, 85, 158–59
    beads-on-a-string style, 25m, 86, 183n22
    camp circles, 135–36
    as culturally bound, 46–47, 63–64, 162n7
    Fidler and, 145–46, 151–53, 158, 159–60
    Fidler's Indigenous map collection, 50, 146, 150, 151, 155–56, 157–58, 163n22, 184n56
    flat earth misunderstanding, 161n5
    HBC and, 146–47, 148–50, 155
    Indigenous contributions, 146, 147–50, 153–55, 156
    Indigenous maps, 46–47, 53–54, 150–51, 157
    selectivity and, 53
    straight-line style, 52–56, 61, 75, 86
    Thompson and, 152–53
    See also Ac ko mok ki map (1801); Ac ko mok ki map (1802); Ak ko wee ak map (1802); Blackfoot maps; Gros Ventre map (1802); Ki oo cus map (1802)
Cascade Butte, 74
Castle River, 93
Cavelier, Robert, 147
Centennial Mountain, 82
Champlain, Samuel de, 147, 157
Chesterfield House
    abandonment, 139
    on Ac ko mok ki map (1801), 75
    on Ac ko mok ki map (1802), 83
    on Ak ko wee ak map (1802), 95
    Arapaho and, 96
    Blackfoot (Siksika) and, 51–52, 62, 119, 164n29
    day's marches to, 115
    Fidler and, 50
    Gros Ventre and, 95
    location, 50, 62–63
    route from Nose Hill to Judith Mountains via, 122
Cheyenne
    Ac ko mok ki map (1801) and, 140, 142t, 178nn59–60
    Arapaho and Gros Ventre and, 137, 180n96
    Blackfoot on, 178n60
    Bougainville and, 133, 175n15
    correlation with maps and, 137
    Gros Ventre map and, 143t
    historical context, 134
    on North Platte and South Platte Rivers, 132
    on Omaha and Ponca, 181n118
    Truteau on, 133
    See also Hevhaitaneo Cheyenne; Northern Cheyenne
Chief Mountain
    about, 31ph
    on Ac ko mok ki map (1801), 70
    on Ac ko mok ki map (1802), 83
    on Ak ko wee ak map, 94
    on Blackfoot maps, 53
    Blackfoot significance, 61, 165n56, 166n60
    on Ki oo cus map (1802), 109
    name, 58
    travel time to Beartooth Mountain, 121
    as wayfinder, 59, 85
Chin Coulee, 115, 117, 123
Chin Lake, 115, 117
Chipewyan, 49, 50, 54, 148, 149, 155
Christopher, William, 149
circles, camp, 135–36
Clark, William, 70, 133, 147, 150–51, 159
Clark Fork River, 69
Cluny (AB), 139, 177n49
Coburn Mountain, 71
Cochrane Ranche Historic Site, 89
Coffin Butte, 34ph, 72
Colorado River, 132
Columbia River, 69, 159
Columbus, Christopher, 147
Comanche, 130, 133, 137, 140–41, 143t, 176n28, 178n73, 180n104. *See also* Jupe Comanche; Yamparika Comanche
configural knowledge, 127
Cormack, Lesley, 161n5
Cowell, Andrew, 174n1
Crazy Mountains, 34ph, 55, 72, 124, 168n52
Cree
    on Arikara, Mandan, and Hidatsa, 138
    Blackfoot maps and, 135
    cartographic style, 54–55, 86, 149
    on Garter People, 133
    on Hand Hills, 104
    HBC maps and, 149
    Indigenous maps collected by Fidler and, 155
    naming conventions, 57
    on Nose Hill, 113
    relations with Blackfoot and Gros Ventre, 51, 137
    Sounding Lake and, 114
Crone, Gerald Roe, 54
Crow
    Blackfoot and, 51, 72, 177n57
    Bougainville on, 132
    correlation with maps and, 137
    Gros Ventre and, 179n91
    Gros Ventre map and, 143t
    Hidatsa, dispute with, 139, 178n61
    historical context, 134
    on South Platte River, 132

on Yamparika Comanche, 178n73
on Yellowstone River, 58, 115
See also Mountain Crow
Crowsnest River, 80, 93
Cumberland House, 50, 156, 157
Cutbank Creek, 109
Cypress Hills
    on Ac ko mok ki map (1801), 74
    on Ac ko mok ki map (1802), 83
    on Ak ko wee ak map, 94
    Blackfoot significance, 61
    day's marches to Chesterfield House, 115
    on Gros Ventre map, 96
    on Ki oo cus map, 102
    name, 173n8
    route between Nose Hill and Judith Mountains via, 122
    Seven Persons Creek/Peigan Creek and, 114, 117
    Sweetgrass Hills and, 60, 85
    Swift Current Creek and, 114, 116–17
    war track (1801) and, 119–20

Dakota, 143t, 182n123. *See also* Sioux
Dalrymple, Alexander, 148, 158
Dane-zaa, 54
Davidson, George, 154
Dawson, George Mercer, 60, 61–62, 73, 80, 108, 115
day's marches, 115, 121
Dearborn River, 67, 70, 71, 77, 93, 95, 96, 168n50
Deep Creek, 65, 67
DeMallie, Raymond J., 133
Dempsey, Hugh A., 163n28, 177n54
Devil's Head Mountain (Swan's Bill), 30ph, 58, 70, 94, 166n60
distance, temporal, 124–25, 173n17
Doty, James
    on Belly River, 66
    on Blackfoot, 46, 119
    on Blackfoot term for river, 65
    Kainai and Piikani terms, transcription of, 64
    on Marias River, 78
    on Old Man's Bowling Green, 80
    on Pakowki Lake, 108
    on Sweetgrass Hills, 60
    on Writing-on-Stone, 123
Dragon Lake, 112
Drifting Sand Hills, 107
Drywood Creek, 95
Dupuyer Creek, 109

earthlodge villagers, 138–39
Ebbits (Tongass Tlingit), 154

Edmonton House, 113
Elbow River, 57, 90, 91
Esther (AB), 111
Etzikom Coulee, 108, 123
Europeans, 143t, 181n120. *See also* cartography; Spanish settlements
Ewers, John C., 163n28
Eyebrow Hills, 57
Eyehill Creek, 62, 101, 102–03

Fidler, Peter
    Ac ko mok ki map (1801) and, 65, 119, 120
    Ac ko mok ki map (1801), redrafted, 4–5m, 58, 65, 75–76, 156–57, 158
    Ac ko mok ki map (1802) and, 83–84
    Ak ko wee ak map and, 86
    annual district reports and maps, 145–46
    on Arapaho, 96, 138
    background, 49–50
    on bison jumps, 87–88
    Blackfoot maps and, 48, 51–52, 129
    on Blackfoot River, 69
    Buffalo Tail Creek and Buffalo Lake, 116
    cartographic contributions, 151–53, 159–60
    on Cypress Hills, 74
    on day's journey, 165n45
    on Devil's Head Mountain, 70
    on Gopher Head Hill, 104
    on Gros Ventre, 88, 138
    Gros Ventre map and, 95
    Gros Ventre woman and, 95
    Gros Ventre words and phrases, compilation of, 134, 137, 140, 175n19
    on Hand Hills, 104
    on Haystack Butte, 70
    on Highwood Mountains, 81
    on Highwood River, 89
    Indigenous map collection, 50, 146, 150, 151, 155–56, 157–58, 163n22, 184n56
    Ki oo cus map and, 99
    on Lone Pine, 106
    on Manitou Lake, 113
    map in account book (1800-01), 27m, 157–58
    on "Mud Houses," 139
    on navigation by Indigenous Peoples, 60
    on Oldman Gap, 78, 80
    on Old Man's Bowling Green, 78–80, 79f
    on parkland forests, 100
    Red River District map (1819), 17m, 145
    on "Rocky Mountains" (*mistakis*), 55

"A Sketch a la Savage of the Manetoba District 1820,"
    18–19*m*, 145–46
  on South Saskatchewan River, 66
  on streams (rivers), 65–66
  on Sun River, 67
  on Tongue Creek (possibly Pekisko Creek), 89–90
Flannery, Regina, 163*n*28
Flathead, 69, 179*nn*87–88. *See also* Bitterroot Salish
Flesher Pass, 69
Foothills Erratic Train, 126
Forster, John Reinhold, 148, 150
Fort Macleod, 107, 126
Fort Shaw, 119
Fort Simpson, 154
Fort Whoop-Up, 107
Fort William, 152
Forty Mile Coulee, 117, 123
Fowler, Loretta, 163*n*28
Fox Indians (To-che-wah-Coo), 133
Fraser, Simon, 154
Freeman, Randolph, 90, 93, 162*n*9
Fromhold, Joachim, 108

Gallatin River, 57, 120
Garden, James F., 101
Garter People (Gens de la Jarretière, Kiskipisounouinini), 132, 133, 142*t*, 178*n*64
Gates of the Mountains, 68
Gens de Chevaux, 133
Gens de l'Arc, 132, 133
Gens du Plat Côté (Ospekakaerenousques), 131–32, 133–34
Ghost River, 70
Gibson, Jim, 180*n*100
Gigantic Warm Springs, 42*ph*, 81–82
God's Lake (Manitou Lake), 44*ph*, 58, 101–02, 103, 113–14, 123
Gold Butte, 40*ph*
Gopher Head Hill, 36*ph*, 37*ph*, 104–05
Graham, Andrew, 150
  "A Plan of Part of Hudson's-Bay, & River, Communicating with York Fort & Severn," 22–23*m*, 149
Grand Canyon, 97
Grand Valley Creek, 89
Gray Site, 173*n*7
Great Sand Hills, 122, 173*n*7
Great Slave Lake, 49
Grinnell, George Bird, 64, 68, 69, 125–26
Gros Ventre
  Arapaho and, 95–96, 137, 138, 144, 170*n*69, 180*n*95
  on Assiniboine, 181*n*119
  attacks on (1801), 88

  autonym, 170*n*69
  on Bannock, 180*n*103
  on Bitterroot Salish (Flatheads), 179*n*88
  Blackfoot (Siksika) and, 47, 66, 117, 137, 140, 177*n*54
  on Cheyenne, 180*n*96
  on Crow, 179*n*91
  on English and French, 181*n*120
  fur traders and, 95
  geographic extent, 136–37
  on Hidatsa and Mandan, 181*n*114
  on Interior Salish, 179*n*89
  on Jicarilla Apache, 180*n*107
  on Kootenai, 179*n*86
  Nose Hill and, 113
  on Piikani, 176*n*22
  relations with other Indigenous Peoples, 51, 117, 130
  scholarship on, 163*n*28
  on Sioux, 181*n*119
  words and phrases compiled by Fidler, 134, 137, 140, 175*n*19
Gros Ventre map, unidentified cartographer (1802), 95–98
  authors' translation of, 16*m*
  camp circles, 135–36
  cartographic style, 96
  Indigenous Peoples depicted, 97–98, 129, 134–35, 138, 143–44*t*, 144
  original map, 14–15*m*
  rivers depicted, 96–97
  unidentified cartographer, 95

Hagen Site, 139
Hall, Charles Francis, 154
Hall, Ryan, 163*n*28
Hanahawunena, 143*t*, 180*n*101
Hand Hills, 37*ph*, 57, 104
Harley, J.B., 60, 146, 150
Hayden, Ferdinand V., 179*n*88, 179*n*91, 180*n*98, 180*n*104
Hayes River, 57
Haystack Butte, 32*ph*, 70–71, 83, 109, 121, 168*n*22
Head-Smashed-In Buffalo Jump, 92
Hearne, Samuel, 149
Heart (unidentified landform), 72, 83, 84, 167*n*39
Heart Butte, 32*ph*, 70, 83, 121
Heart Mountain, 167*n*39
Hevhaitaneo Cheyenne, 142*t*, 178*n*65
Hidatsa, 138–39, 142*t*, 143*t*, 178*n*61, 181*n*114
High River (AB), 89, 107
Highwood Mountains, 41*ph*, 43*ph*, 74, 81, 86, 97, 109, 123–24
Highwood River, 89–90, 91, 92, 107, 115, 165*n*46
Hill Spring (AB), 95
Hodgson, John, 183*n*20

202   Index

Hogback Mountain, 71
Holmgren, Eric, 104, 105
Holmgren, Patricia, 104, 105
horses, 51, 121, 130, 140
Hudson's Bay Company (HBC)
    Ac ko mok ki and, 162n10
    annual district reports and maps, 145–46
    on Arapaho and Gros Ventre, 138
    Arrowsmith and, 152, 158, 183n35
    bison pounds and, 87
    exploration and mapping, 146–47
    Fidler's background in, 49–50
    Fidler's cartographic contributions, 145–46, 151–53, 158
    Hayes River and, 57
    Indigenous contributions to mapping and, 148–50, 155
    Ki oo cus map and, 99–100
    North and South Saskatchewan Rivers and, 116
    See also Chesterfield House; Fidler, Peter
Hunting Hill, 110
Hutchins, Thomas, 149, 150

Idotlyazee (Chipewyan), 149
Indigenous Peoples
    Ac ko mok ki map (1801), depicted on, 96, 97, 129, 132, 133–35, 137, 138–41, 142t
    "band" vs. "tribe," 140–41
    beads-on-a-string cartographic style, 25m, 86, 183n22
    Bougainville on, 129–32
    cartographic contributions, 146, 147–51, 153–55, 156
    correlation between maps and contemporary nations, 137–38
    Fidler's map collection, 50, 146, 150, 151, 155–56, 157–58, 163n22, 184n56
    Gros Ventre map, depicted on, 97–98, 129, 134–35, 138, 143–44t, 144
    HBC and, 148–50, 155
    La Vérendrye and, 130, 132, 133
    maps by, 46–47, 53–54, 150–51, 157
    straight-line cartographic style, 52–56, 61, 75, 86
    See also Blackfoot maps; Gros Ventre map (1802); *specific Indigenous Peoples*
Interior Salish, 142t, 143t, 179n87, 179n89
Inuit, 50, 154, 155, 184n56
Iroquois, 58, 147

Jarvis, Edward, 24m, 149, 183n20
Jefferson, Thomas, 159
Jefferson River, 57
Jicarilla Apache, 143t, 180n107
Jolliet, Louis, 82
Judith Basin, 42ph, 43ph, 59, 84, 122

Judith Gap, 33ph, 60, 81, 84, 123
Judith Mountains
    on Ac ko mok ki map (1801), 74, 168n50
    Gigantic Warm Springs and, 82
    on Gros Ventre map, 96
    Judith Basin and, 43ph
    on Ki oo cus map, 110
    route to Bad River, 123–24
    route to Nose Hill, 122–23
    Warm Spring Creek and, 81
Judith River
    about, 43ph
    on Ac ko mok ki map (1801), 68
    on Ac ko mok ki map (1802), 81, 82, 84
    earthlodge villages and, 139
    on Gros Ventre map, 96–97
    Heart (unidentified landform) and, 72
    mistakis ("Rocky Mountains") and, 55
    travel routes and, 122, 123
Jupe Comanche, 142t, 178n74

Kainai, 64, 103, 107, 113, 137, 140, 177n54
Kalispel, 142t, 179n82
Kaye, Barry
    on Ac ko mok ki map (1801), 139, 162n9
    on Beartooth Mountain, 71
    on Belt Butte/Belt Mountains, 71
    on Belt Creek, 68
    on Bighorn/Little Missouri River, 69, 167n29
    on Big Snowy Mountains, 72, 167n40
    on Blackfoot River, 69
    on Bull Mountains/Canyon Mountain, 72
    on Cheyenne, possibly depicted on Ac ko mok ki map (1801), 178n59
    Crazy Mountains/Coffin Butte and, 72
    on Cypress Hills, 74
    on Deep Creek, 67
    on Haystack Butte/Teton Peak, 70, 167n35
    on Heart (unidentified landform), 72, 167n39
    on Highwood Mountains, 74, 168n51
    on Judith River, 68
    on Kootenay/Columbia River, 69
    on Little Snowy/Judith/Crazy Mountains, 74, 168n52
    on Marias River/Two Medicine Creek, 67, 166n9
    on Milk River Ridge, 73
    on Owl Creek Mountains, 73
    on Square/Shaw/Cascade Buttes/Judith Mountains, 74, 168n50
    on Wolf Butte/Rattlesnake Mountain, 72, 167n38
Kehoe, Alice B., 162n9
Kennedy, Margaret, 63, 110, 166n60

Ki oo cus, 51, 52
Ki oo cus map (1802), 99–117
    introduction, 99
    archaeological sites and, 61
    authors' translation of, 13*m*
    Chin Coulee, 117
    distance, temporal, 124–25
    geographic range covered, 99–100, 170*n*1
    Manitou Lake and, 101–02
    naming conventions, 102
    numbered features depicted, 103–14
    original map, 11*m*
    other features depicted, 55, 114–15
    plant resources depicted, 101
    redrafted version, 12*m*
    rivers depicted, 56, 102–03, 116–17
    Rocky Mountains depicted, 55
    routes through plains, 121–24
    scholarship on, 162*n*9
    straight-line cartographic style, 52–53
    woods edge, 100–01, 114, 125, 170*n*1
Kiowa, 132, 137, 143*t*, 180*n*98
Kiowa Apache. *See* Plains Apache
Kiskipisounouinini (Garter People, Gens de la Jarretière), 132, 133, 142*t*, 178*n*64
Klotz, Otto J., 59, 108
Knee Hills, 57
Knight, James, 148–49
Kohklux (Tlingit), 154
Kootenai, 142*t*, 179*n*86
Kootenay River, 69, 115
Kroeber, A.L., 138, 144, 176*n*22, 176*n*29, 179*n*88, 179*n*91, 180*n*95, 181*nn*119–20

Lafitau, Joseph François, 148, 182*n*15
Lahontan, Baron de, 147–48, 182*n*15
Lake Minnewanka, 70
Lakota, 132. *See also* Sioux
LaPier, Rosalyn R., 45, 46
Larocque, François-Antoine, 139
La Salle, Sieur de, 147
La Vérendrye, Pierre Gaultier de Varennes de, 130, 131–32, 132–33
Lawson, John, 147, 157
Le Clercq, Chrestien, 147
Leithead Hill, 103–04
Lemhi Shoshone, 142*t*, 178*n*72
Lethbridge (AB), 59, 66, 88
Levy, Jerrold E., 180*n*98
Lewis, Malcolm, 150
Lewis, Meriwether, 70, 133, 147, 150–51, 159

Lewis and Clark Expedition, 85
Lewis Range (Summit Mountain Ridge), 31*ph*, 165*n*43
Leyden, Jeremy J., 166*n*60
L'Heureux, Jean
    on Antler Hill, 174*n*28
    on Battle River, 103
    on Bears Paw Mountains, 82
    on Buffalo Lake, 106
    on Bull's Forehead, 110
    on Elbow River, 91
    on Gopher Head Hill, 104
    on Hand Hills, 104
    Indigenous place names and, 60, 64
    on Little Bow River, 92
    on Marias River, 78
    on Milk River, 78
    on Pine Lake, hills near, 105
    on Porcupine Hills, 94
    on Red Deer River, 66
    on Sheep River, 91
    on South Saskatchewan/Bow River, 66
    on Wintering Hills, 105
Little Belt Mountains, 33*ph*, 41*ph*, 55, 71, 72, 81, 83, 97. *See also* Big Belt Mountains
Little Bow River, 92
Little Missouri River, 133, 167*n*29
Little Rocky Mountains, 82
Little Snowy Mountains, 74, 167*n*40. *See also* Big Snowy Mountains; Snowy Mountains
Lone Pine, 105–06
Long, John, 148, 183*n*22
Lower Kootenai, 142*t*
Lower Oldman River, 90, 93

MacGregor, James, 90, 104
Mackenzie, Alexander, 147, 152, 153–54
Madison River, 57
Magrath, C.A., 106
Mandan, 132, 138–39, 181*n*114
Manitou Lake (God's Lake), 44*ph*, 58, 101–02, 103, 113–14, 123
Many Island Lake, 122, 173*n*6
maps. *See* cartography
Marias River
    on Ac ko mok ki map (1801), 67, 166*n*9
    on Ac ko mok ki map (1802), 56–57, 77–78, 85
    on Ak ko wee ak map, 93
    on Gros Ventre map, 96
    on Ki oo cus map, 109, 115
    naming conventions and, 56–57
    route from Judith Mountains to Bad River via, 123–24
    See also Two Medicine River

Marquette, Jacques, 82
Matonabbee (Chipewyan), 149
Maximilian, Prince Alexander Philipp of Wied-Neuwied, 140
McClintock, Walter, 93
McConnell, Richard G., 80, 105
McFarlane, John Steward, 113
McGillivray, Simon, Jr., 154
McKay (Mackay), Donald, 24*m*, 149, 183*n*20
McLeod, John M., 26*m*, 154
Métis, 105, 106
Mi'kmaq, 147
Milk River
    on Ac ko mok ki map (1801), 66
    on Ak ko wee ak map, 93
    creation of, 62
    Gros Ventre map and, 96
    on Ki oo cus map, 103
    Schultz on, 165*n*46
    Sweetgrass Hills and, 41*ph*
    travel routes and, 122, 123
Milk River Ridge, 73, 108, 166*n*60
Missouri Breaks, 122
Missouri River
    about, 33*ph*
    on Ac ko mok ki map (1801), 57, 68, 75
    on Ac ko mok ki map (1802), 82, 84
    on Gros Ventre map, 96, 97
    "headwaters," 57
    on Ki oo cus map, 56, 103
    name, 115
    travel routes and, 121, 122, 123–24
    war track (1801) and, 119
Misty Hills, 39*ph*, 61, 111
Monmonier, Mark, 53, 162*n*7
Moocoowan Ridge, 94
Moodie, D.W.
    on Ac ko mok ki map (1801), 139, 156, 162*n*9
    on Beartooth Mountain, 71
    on Belt Butte/Belt Mountains, 71
    on Belt Creek, 68
    on Bighorn/Little Missouri River, 69, 167*n*29
    on Big Snowy Mountains, 72, 167*n*40
    on Blackfoot and Gros Ventre maps, 48
    on Blackfoot River, 69
    on Bull Mountains/Canyon Mountain, 72
    on Cheyenne, possibly depicted on Ac ko mok ki map (1801), 178*n*59
    on Crazy Mountains, 168*n*52
    Crazy Mountains/Coffin Butte and, 72
    on Cypress Hills, 74
    on Deep Creek, 67
    on Haystack Butte/Teton Peak, 70, 167*n*35
    on Heart (unidentified landform), 72, 167*n*39
    on Highwood Mountains, 74, 168*n*51
    on Judith River, 68
    on Kootenay/Columbia River, 69
    on Marias River/Two Medicine Creek, 67, 166*n*9
    on Milk River Ridge, 73
    on Owl Creek Mountains, 73
    on Square/Shaw/Cascade Buttes/Judith Mountains, 74, 168*n*50
    on Wolf Butte/Rattlesnake Mountain, 72, 167*n*38
Mountain Crow, 96–97, 177*n*57, 179*n*91, 180*n*100
Mount Brown, 40*ph*
Mud Buttes, 38*ph*, 61, 110, 111
Murray Lake, 114
Musselshell Plains, 59
Musselshell River, 34*ph*, 55, 68, 72, 97, 121

naming conventions, 56–58, 102
Napi (Old Man)
    about, 46
    Old Man's Bowling Green and, 78–80, 79*f*
    Red Rock Coulee and, 124
    stone effigies, 173*n*19, 174*n*28
    Tongue Creek and, 90
    Whoop-Up Trail and, 125–26
    Writing-on-Stone and, 123
Navajo, 143*t*, 180*n*106
Nawathinehena, 143*t*, 180*n*108
Nelson, J.C.
    on Antler Hill, 174*n*28
    on Battle River, 103
    on Bears Paw Mountains, 82
    on Belly Buttes, 107
    on Belly River, hills by, 107
    on Big Hill Creek, 89
    on Buffalo Lake, 106
    on Bull's Forehead, 110
    on Calgary, SW plateau, 94
    on Chin Coulee, 115
    on Cypress Hills, 122, 173*n*8
    on Drifting Sand Hills, 107
    on Elbow River, 91
    on Etzikom Coulee, 123, 173*n*15
    on Fort Whoop-Up, 107
    on Forty Mile Coulee, 123, 173*n*16
    on Great Sand Hills, 173*n*7
    on Hand Hills, 104
    on Head-Smashed-In Buffalo Jump, 92
    on Hunting Hill, 110

    Indigenous place names and, 60
    on the Knees, 126, 173n20
    on Little Bow River, 92
    on Little Rocky Mountains, 82
    on Lone Pine, 105
    on Many Island Lake, 122, 173n6
    on Marias River, 77–78
    on Milk River, 78
    on *mistakis* ("Rocky Mountains"), 165n43
    on Neutral Hills, 101, 111
    on North Butte, 174n29
    on North Saskatchewan River, 68
    on Nose Hill, 94
    on Oldman River, 78
    on Pakowki Lake, 108
    on Porcupine Hills, 94
    on Seven Persons Creek, 114
    on Shaganappi Point, 91
    on Sheep River, 91
    on Sounding Lake, 114
    on St. Mary River, 80, 93
    on Sundial Hill, 62
    on Tongue Creek, 90
    on Wildcat Hills, 89
    on Willow Creek, 92
    on Wintering Hills, 105
Neutral Hills, 35*ph*, 101, 110, 111, 112, 113, 115. *See also* Nose Hill
Nez Perce, 70, 142*t*, 179n79
Nicholson, Francis, 150
North Butte, 174n29
Northern Cheyenne, 75, 142*t*, 178n69
Northern Shoshone, 143*t*, 179n90, 179n93
North Moccasin Mountains, 81–82, 122
North Platte River, 132
North Saskatchewan River, 68, 99–100, 115, 170n1
North West Company (NWC), 95, 152, 162n10, 176n37
North-West Mounted Police, 123
Northwest Passage, 148–49
Norton, Moses, 20*m*, 149
Nose Hill (Buffalo Nose, the Nose), 35*ph*, 57, 61, 94, 102, 111–12, 113, 122–23

Oevemana band (Northern Cheyenne), 178n69
Ojibwe, 50, 155
Oldman Gap, 78
Oldman River
    on Ac ko mok ki map (1801), 66
    on Ac ko mok ki map (1802), 78, 80
    on Ak ko wee ak map, 91, 92, 93, 94
    Blackfoot and, 58

    on Gros Ventre map, 96
    on Ki oo cus map, 115, 123
    naming conventions and, 57
    See also Belly River
Old Man's Bowling Green, 78–80, 79*f*, 94
Old North Trail, 53, 86, 94, 109, 120–21, 125–26
Omaha, 143*t*, 175n4, 181n118
O mok api (Siksika), 140, 177n54
One Gun culture, 174n3, 177n49
oral information, 45, 48–49, 53–54, 67, 75, 84, 101, 135–36, 157
Ospekakaeɪenousques (Gens du Plat Côté), 131–32, 133–34
Owl Creek Mountains, 73
Owl's Head, 73

Paint Pots, 69
Paint River House, 113
Pakowki Lake, 83, 108, 123, 124, 173n15
Palliser, John, 70, 170n7
parkland forests, 100
Parks, Douglas R., 132, 133
Parry, William E., 154
Pawnee, 132, 143*t*, 175n4
Pawnee-Loups (Skiri, Wolf Pawnee), 140, 142*t*, 178n70
Peace Hills, 127
Peigan, 137. *See also* Piikani
Peigan Creek, 117
Pekisko Creek, 89–90
Pend d'Oreilles, 142*t*, 179n82
Pentland, David, 54–55, 63
Petits Renards, 132–33, 142*t*, 178n63
Piikani
    bison jumps and, 87, 88, 90
    Dearborn River and, 67
    Fidler with Sakatow's band, 50, 60, 100
    Gopher Head Hill and, 104
    Gros Ventre on, 137, 176n22, 177n54
    Highwood River and, 89
    Lone Pine and, 106
    on Old Man's Bowling Green, 78, 80
    Porcupine Hills and, 94
    rattles, 81
    woods edge and, 100
Pike, Warburton, 54
Pincher Creek, 93
Pine Lake, 105
Plains Apache, 133, 143*t*, 181n111
Ponca, 143*t*, 181n118
Pope, Frank L., 154–55
Porcupine Hills, 59, 86, 94, 107, 126, 177n49
portages, 173n17

Pryor Mountains, 55, 73

Qu'Appelle River and Valley, 62

Rattlesnake Hill, 74
Rattlesnake Mountain, 72, 167n38
Rayburn, Alan, 66
Red Deer River
    on Ac ko mok ki map (1801), 66
    on Ac ko mok ki map (1802), 80
    on Ak ko wee ak map, 89
    archaeological sites, 116
    Bull's Forehead and, 110
    confluence with South Saskatchewan River, 39ph, 62–63
    on Ki oo cus map, 103, 115–16
    name, 115
    woods edge and, 100
Red River District map (1819), 17m, 145
Red Rock Coulee, 124
Reeves, Brian, 62–63, 109, 110, 125, 166n60
Rib People, 133–34, 180n100
ribstones, 61, 103–04, 105
Rio Grande, 132
Riplinger Trail, 125
rivers, 55–57, 65
Robertson, William, 182n15
Rock Slide Mountain, 71
Rocky Mountain National Park, 97
"Rocky Mountains" (*mistakis*)
    on Ac ko mok ki map (1801), 75, 84, 125
    on Ac ko mok ki map (1802), 83, 84, 85
    on Arrowsmith's map, 158–59
    Blackfoot approach to, 53, 55–56, 57–58, 61, 165n43
    on Ki oo cus map, 99
Rocky Spring Ridge, 109
Rodríguez Miró, Esteban, 132–33
Rogers Pass, 68, 69
Ronda, James P., 151
Ross, Malcolm, 49, 183n35
Ross Fork Creek, 81, 84
Round Butte, 43ph, 73, 81
route knowledge, 127
Ruggles, Richard, 150, 151, 152, 155, 156

Sakatow (Piikani), 50, 60, 100, 163n22
Salish. *See* Bitterroot Salish; Interior Salish
Salmon River, 69
Salt Lake, 112
Santa Fe Trail, 137
Sarcee, 180n94. *See also* Tsuut'ina
Schultz, James Willard
    on Arrow Creek, 68
    on Bears Paw Mountains, 82
    on Belt Butte and Mountains, 71
    on Bighorn River, 69
    on Big Sandy Creek, 122, 173n9
    on Bull Mountains, 72–73
    on Crazy Mountains, 72
    on Dearborn River, 67, 77
    on Deep Creek, 65, 67
    on Heart Butte, 70
    on Highwood Mountains, 81
    Indigenous place names and, 60, 64
    on Judith Gap, 123, 173n10
    on Judith Mountains, 110
    on Judith River, 82
    on the Knees, 126, 173n20
    on Lewis Range (Summit Mountain Ridge), 165n43
    on Little Rocky Mountains, 82
    on Marias River, 77
    on Milk River, 78, 165n46
    on Musselshell River, 68
    on Rocky Spring Ridge, 109
    on Round Butte, 73
    on Square Butte, 81
    on St. Mary River, 80, 93
    on Swift Current Creek, 114
    on Teton River, 67
    on Wolf Creek, 67–68
    on Yellowstone River, 69
selectivity, 53
Seven Persons Creek, 114, 117, 124
Shaganappi Point, 91
Shaw Butte, 42ph, 71, 74, 83, 86, 119
Sheep Mountain, 71
Sheep River, 90, 91
Shew dithe da (Chipewyan), 149, 183n23
Shield River, 58. *See also* Dearborn River
Shields River, 73, 120
Shonkin Creek, 124
Shoshone
    Ac ko mok ki map (1801) and, 140, 142t, 178n75
    archaeological evidence, 174n3
    Bougainville on, 133
    Gros Ventre map and, 143t, 179n93, 180n104
    historical context, 134
    relations with other Indigenous Peoples, 51, 130, 137
    Salmon River and, 69
    on Yamparika Comanche, 178n73
    See also Lemhi Shoshone; Northern Shoshone
Shuswap, 142t, 179n83
Signal Hill, 94

Siksika
- Ac ko mok ki's band, 51–52
- Cree/Assiniboine and, 51
- Gros Ventre and, 117, 177n54
- Manitou Lake (God's Lake) and, 101
- North Saskatchewan River and, 170n1
- Nose Hill and, 113
- parkland forests and, 100
- Rocky Mountains and, 125
- travel times, 121

Siksika maps. *See* Blackfoot maps
Simpson, George, 154, 163n17
Siouan people, 144t, 182n123
Sioux, 181n119. *See also* Dakota; Lakota
Sixteenmile Creek, 120
Skiri (Wolf Pawnee, Pawnee-Loups), 140, 142t, 178n70
Sleeping Giant, 59
Smith, John, 147
Smith River and Valley, 55, 97, 120
Snake River, 69. *See also* Sounding Creek
Snare Indians, 142t, 179n83
Snowy Mountains, 82, 83, 96. *See also* Big Snowy Mountains; Little Snowy Mountains
Sounding Creek, 62, 101, 102–03, 110, 111, 112, 124–25
Sounding Lake, 103, 114
South Moccasin Mountains, 81–82
South Platte River, 132
South Saskatchewan River
- on Ac ko mok ki map (1801), 66
- on Ac ko mok ki map (1802), 80
- on Ak ko wee ak map, 89
- Bull's Forehead and, 110
- confluence with Red Deer River, 39ph, 62–63
- on Ki oo cus map, 103, 116–17
- name, 57, 116
- routes from, 123
- *See also* Bow River

Spanish settlements, 137, 143t, 180n105
spatial acuity, 52
Square Butte (Cascade County), 42ph, 71, 74, 83, 86, 95, 119
Square Butte (Chouteau County), 43ph, 81, 109, 123
Stettler (AB), 103–04
St. Mary Lake, 80
St. Mary River, 80, 90, 93
stone effigies, 37ph, 61, 105, 115, 173n19
stone tools, 61
Stoney, 113, 180n94
straight-line cartographic style, 52–56, 61, 75, 86
Summit Mountain Ridge (Lewis Range), 165n43
Sundial Hill, 62

Sun River
- on Ac ko mok ki map (1801), 67
- on Ac ko mok ki map (1802), 77
- on Ak ko wee ak map, 93
- on Gros Ventre map, 96
- Haystack Butte and, 70, 109, 168n22
- on Ki oo cus map, 115
- war track (1801) and, 119

Swain, James, Sr., 25m, 154
Swan's Bill (Devil's Head Mountain), 30ph, 58, 70, 102, 166n60
Sweetgrass Hills
- about, 40ph, 41ph
- on Ac ko mok ki map (1801), 74
- on Ac ko mok ki map (1802), 83
- Dawson on, 61
- distance to Rocky Mountains, 85
- on Gros Ventre map, 96
- on Ki oo cus map, 102, 108
- travel routes and, 120, 123, 124
- as wayfinder, 59–60

Swift Current Creek, 114, 116–17

Tail Creek, 57, 101, 102, 107, 116
Taylor, George, Jr., 151
Tenewill (Babine (Natoot'en) Chief), 154
Teton Peak, 167n35
Teton River
- on Ac ko mok ki map (1801), 67, 85, 166n12
- on Ac ko mok ki map (1802), 56–57, 77, 85
- on Ak ko wee ak map, 93
- on Gros Ventre map, 96
- on Ki oo cus map, 109, 115
- route from Seven Persons Creek to Highwood Mountains and, 124

Thigh Hills, 57
T-Hill, 73
Thompson, David, 90, 91, 93, 106, 152–53, 156
Thooh (Chipewyan), 49
Thwaites, Reuben Gold, 175n4
Tilander-Mack, Barb, 92, 165n46
Tomison, William, 50, 175n19
Tongue Creek (Tongue Flag Creek), 89–90
Truteau, Jean-Baptiste, 133
Tsuut'ina, 113, 135, 137, 178n58. *See also* Sarcee
Tsuut'ina Reserve, 94
Turnor, Philip, 49, 149, 151, 183n23, 183n35
Twin Butte, 95
Twin Sisters, 72, 81, 83
Twodot Butte, 72

Two Medicine River, 57, 67, 93, 93, 115, 166n9. *See also* Marias River

Ulm Pishkun (Buffalo Jump), 74
Upper Kootenai, 142t
Ute, 142t, 143t, 178n77, 180nn103–05

Vézina, Robert, 133

Walker, William, 96
Warm Spring Creek, 42ph, 81, 84–85
war track (1801), 119–20, 121, 124
Wegg, Samuel, 148
West Butte, 40ph, 41ph, 119
Whiskey Gap, 108
Whoop-Up Trail, 109, 125–27
Wildcat Hills, 89, 174n29
Willow Creek, 92, 123
Willow Pound, 90–91
Wind River Canyon, 35ph, 73, 97
Wintering Hills, 105, 120
Wolf Butte, 33ph, 60, 72, 84, 121

Wolf Creek, 67–68, 71
Wolf Hill Ribstone site, 105
Wolf Mountains, 75
Wolf Pawnee (Skiri, Pawnee-Loups), 140, 142t, 178n70
Women's Buffalo Jump, 93
Wood, Denis, 53
woods edge, 100–01, 114, 125, 170n1
"woods enemy," 143t, 180n94
Writing-on-Stone, 83, 123

Yamparika Comanche, 142t, 178nn73–74
Yellowstone River
    on Ac ko mok ki map (1801), 69
    Ac ko mok ki's tour of the Old North Trail and, 121
    Canyon Mountain and, 73
    earthlodge villages and, 139
    on Gros Ventre map, 97
    on Ki oo cus map, 114
    mistakis ("Rocky Mountains") and, 55, 56
    names, 58, 115
    route from Highwood Mountains to, 124
Yukon, 154